JOHN MAJOR

JOHN MAJOR

NESTA WYN ELLIS

Futura

A *Futura* Book

First published in Great Britain in 1991 by
Macdonald & Co (Publishers) Ltd
London & Sydney
This edition published in 1991
by Futura Publications

A CIP catalogue record for this book is available from the
British Library

ISBN 0 7088 5378 1

Typeset by Selectmove Ltd, London
Printed and bound in Great Britain by
BPCC Hazell Books
Aylesbury, Bucks, England
Member of BPCC Ltd.
Futura Publications
A Division of
Macdonald & Co (Publishers) Ltd
165 Great Dover Street
London SE1 4YA

A member of Maxwell Macmillan Publishing Corporation

CONTENTS

To
Edward

ACKNOWLEDGEMENTS

S O MANY PEOPLE HAVE HELPED in so many ways with this book. It could not have been written without the exceptional contribution of John Major, whose valuable insights and honest reflections on his life, his thoughts and feelings, his dreams and disappointments, his struggles and triumphs, make this, his story, one of poignance, romance and a kind of heroism.

I am grateful to Norma Major for her time and solicitude, and her delightful contributions and honesty. I wish to thank both John and Norma for allowing me into the privacy of their home and their quarters at Number 10 for our several wide-ranging conversations; for letting me meet their children, Elizabeth and James; and for recommending me to their friends and associates. I am also very grateful to Terry Major-Ball, for his extensive and very pertinent reflections on his family's past.

I thank John Major's Cabinet colleagues, friends, and long-time associates for their willing help and valuable contributions to the telling of John's story. In particular I would like to thank Jeffrey Archer, David Mellor, John Wakeham, Cecil Parkinson, Lord Pym, Lord Renton, Clive Jones, Jean Lucas, Lawrence and Aine Kennedy, William Waldegrave, Norman Lamont, Douglas Hurd, Councillor Greenwood, Councillor Hugh Chambers, Robert Atkins, Peter Golds, Ken Livingstone, Andrew Thomson, Peter Brown, Baroness Blatch, Margaret Jay, Ian Cameron Black, Peter Seager, Stan Hurn, Sir Sonny Ramphal,

Lord Barber, Will Manser, David Rogers, Brian Haynes and Bob Gregory, all of whom were generous in giving me their time and their insights into various aspects of the Prime Minister's life, work, and character.

I am indebted to Deirdre Vine and Christie Hickman of *Woman's Journal* for first sending me to interview John Major in September 1989 when he was Foreign Secretary, enabling me to conceive the idea of a book of his life well in advance of him becoming Prime Minister.

I am grateful to my friends and neighbours for their encouragement and support throughout the duration of this demanding task, and to those various members of the squad of secretaries and researchers without whose efforts I could not have completed the work in time. I would especially like to thank Dr Joan Freeman, Godfrey Barker, Patricia Sohl, and Sally Angel for timely help; and Alun Fon Jones, June Walker, Victor Olliver, Yoshinari Yamamoto, Tony Engleman, Caroline Shaw, Gudrun Jonsson, and Paulette Vieux for their enthusiasm, interest, and friendship.

I would like to thank my research assistant Stewart Lawley, his colleague Karen Steyn, and my friend Thea McNeish who contributed to the research effort. Also, my friend Nancy Retchin, my secretary Catherine Moy, Jill Beck, Lucy Gibbons, and Angela Robertson, who together spent over one hundred hours transcribing taped interviews.

I thank my Washington-based husband Edward Moss whose research and observations in the USA provided valuable confirmation of the American contribution to John Major's life and beliefs.

I am grateful to my publicist Melanie Cantor for

her astute, timely and lively input; to my publisher Alan Samson and his colleagues, and to my agent Jane Judd for their solid efforts in bringing this project to fruition. I want to thank Gus O'Donnell, John Major's Press Secretary, and Barbara Wallis, his Constituency Secretary at Number 10, who were tireless in helping me with appointments and other details.

I should thank all those taxi drivers of London who sped me to and from my many appointments through snow and freezing cold.

Finally I must register my gratitude for the companionship of the Montagu Square blackbirds who sang steadily outside my window throughout the long hard nights of early spring during which this book was written.

PROLOGUE

WHEN YOU WALK INTO 10 Downing Street you enter the mythology of a nation. Here resides the power that once was thought of as the Divine Right of Kings. No monarch has this power in Britain today. The focus has shifted from inherited to elected leadership, and power – no longer purely divine, and far from anyone's right – is conferred as much, it seems, from below as from above: the electorate attains the leadership it deserves by electing the leader who most accurately reflects and responds to the majority's aspirations.

If divine power plays a role in nations' destinies, it is through their leaders' thoughts, words and deeds. The forces of governance, whether divine or collective, work through the man or woman who is the nation's first minister. It may be that the leader only changes when there has been a shift in the majority's aspirations. However, caught in the crossfire between divine and the electorate's will, as they may be, Prime Ministers can only do the job their own way. While Mrs Thatcher was well known for doing it her way, there is no doubt that John Major is equally definitely doing it his.

Call it personal style, call it a reflection of social change, a mirror of the electorate's mood, or even a manifestation of divine will, it is impossible as soon as you enter Number 10 not to register this change of atmosphere from one Prime Minister to the next.

The very texture of time and space seem dramatically changed. Pass through the black-painted door with its brass numerals into the large square hallway with red silk-covered walls, and the sense of invested power here is as awesome and serene as in an ancient cathedral; eternal, yet subject to some altered flow. With every step across the black-and-white-tiled hall you feel history forming, even as a tulip forms, deep underground. Somehow here, in this hall, there is a feeling of a special moment, as if time itself were more strongly focused, perhaps pivoted. There is a sense of being in slow motion, as if every syllable and every breath hang and are recorded. You pass into its density, receiving the past's presence, and beyond, into the splitting moment of time's frontier where the spotlight falls on to the figure with the outstretched hand and the completely unaffected smile of welcome who walks towards you.

Some moments are frozen in time. In this one, on this day so soon after his election, a cold dark day, John Major seems like the sun at midnight, present though not yet shedding his light on the world. He is dapper, dark-suited, a little – but only a fraction – more formal than the private self one has seen lounging at home in sweaters. Or is this the product of apprehension, tension stemming from finding himself the focus of all this history, and of all eyes? One is made aware in this intense focus of energy, in the power of this moment, that the force of destiny is with him. Many are appointed but destiny elects only the brave. And how brave one must be to carry, and so lightly, the enormous task of governance. But, of course, this is no ordinary person. No one who fills this office could be ordinary. And once filling it, no one can remain what they once were.

This is not just John Major, whoever or whatever he has been before. This is the Prime Minister, and as such he is no longer entirely himself. As with the President of the United States who is, unlike the British Prime Minister, also head of state, monarch and chief executive in one, it is the office of Prime Minister which *is* power. The man or woman who fills the office is more than merely themself. The person becomes the office. But as the office changes the person, so too their personality alters the office. The atmosphere and the action are different. With each leader there is this change, referred to as style. But style is only the superficial manifestation of what is really essence, which is also a reflection of the mood and needs of the community being served.

John Major became leader of the Conservative Party and thereby instantly Prime Minister by the will, not of the entire enfranchised nation, but by that of a somewhat select constituency, the Conservative Parliamentary Party. Of course these MPs had taken soundings in their local parties, though ultimately they voted according to their own inclination. However, opinion polls, that transitory measure of spontaneous will, revealed that John Major could equal, indeed surpass, Michael Heseltine as a vote-grabbing leader for the Tories. The polls may have influenced the MPs' voting to a degree. In the event, the result was that at 6.28 p.m. on November 27 1990 John Major became

the first new Conservative Party leader for almost
fifteen years.

There was an instant change of tempo; a huge
outlet of joy and relief that at last the terrible
bloodletting was over. It seemed everyone shared
the feeling. Even Labour MPs cheered the new
Tory leader when he entered the lobby of the
House after that vote, an unprecedented incident.
Suddenly, in place of grimness, anger, tension and
rivalry, there was euphoria, even ecstasy. Then, it
seemed as if time, turning over like a sleeping
beast, wakened to a new day, a new leader, a
new channel for the force of history. Everything
suddenly changed. Something had passed: not only
the remarkable Margaret Thatcher, but an entire era.
Number 10, like Old Father Thames, a few hundred
yards across Whitehall and the Embankment, seemed
the same and yet subtly different. As the old river's
sluggard stream rolls through barely changing banks
of mud, so Prime Ministers pass through 10 Downing
Street. For the moment – and in history years are but
moments – the colour of the water seemed changed:
its brilliance muted, its shade and quality less clear,
its flow gentler and its cargoes subtly different.

Of Mrs Thatcher, there remained no ghostly
presence. Number 10 Downing Street seemed
more innocent of her passage than the nation
or world in which she effected so many sweeping
changes. Not a petal of that avalanche of flowers
that attended her resignation remained. Like the
river's banks, Number 10 seemed unmarked by her
eleven-and-a-half-year occupation. While there she
could not have been a more vivid presence: there
was so much action, so much intensity of burning

ideas and intentions, so much conflict, so much
bustle and energy, so much exhilarating change,
so much progress, and such speed and unerring
effectiveness.

From here she radiated the intention of dispelling
the suffocating bunker mentality of socialism, reviving
the liberal economics of the free market – and with
them the spirit of freedom and democracy with
which they are indelibly linked. The intensity of
her personal vision infected the wider world. Such
was the force with which she pursued her passion
for libertarian politics that her determination spread
as if carried on the air: all over the world dictators
began tumbling.

When she went and the turmoil subsided, after
the joy of welcoming such a clean-cut and youthful
new leader, there was a sudden deafening silence. So
much so that when John Major first became Prime
Minister people could have been forgiven for asking
if there was anyone there at all. After the tornado
of Mrs Thatcher's years and the final hurricane of
her departure, Major's presence was so low-key as
to fool the casual onlooker. After that initial flurry
of excitement, he almost disappeared. But those were
early days and the pattern of silence was characteristic
of the man who makes no move until he is absolutely
sure of his position. John Major is not one for sound
and fury. In public, at least.

But there is a fire and guts in this superficially
prosaic-looking man which showed itself in his
election campaign. And there is an impeccable
sense of timing. Here, it seemed, was a man who
had known for years that this day would come.
His antennae were tuned to the distant signals

of fortune. He held himself in readiness, and as
the signals grew stronger, acted with energy and
swiftness. A gambler? Perhaps, but one who only
bets on certainties, who works out the system and
plays it smart. Then breaks the bank at Monte
Carlo.

1
A DREAM COME TRUE

'I was thinking about what I had to do next.'

O N SATURDAY, NOVEMBER 24 1990, JEFFREY ARCHER and his wife Mary travelled from their cottage on the outskirts of nearby Cambridge to have lunch with the Majors in their Great Stukeley house in John's Huntingdon constituency. Friends of long standing, the two couples sat around the highly polished reproduction table that almost fills the small dining room and on which Norma sometimes lays out her dressmaking patterns. Grey November light passed through the leafless trees in the large grassy garden. John, at the head of the table, his back to the window, faced his wife sitting at the other end. She had just cleared away the home-made moussaka which Jeffrey Archer remembers was the delicious main course, and was serving pudding. Breaking in on their talk of the coming election, she said, a little alarmed, 'Do you realise you're talking about being Prime Minister next week?'

As she handed John the glass dish of wobbling red jelly, his favourite, he simply said, 'Why do I only get jelly when my teeth hurt?'

Norma replied with her customary mildness, 'You have jelly all the time.' So John announced, with mock triumph, 'Certainly when I'm Prime Minister, I shall have jelly all the time.'

The group broke into laughter. This was, Jeffrey Archer says, 'a good illustration of John's sense of humour,' and of how he is also adept at turning a joke against himself. It is also a good illustration of how, in dodging the real question Norma was asking, he often avoids confrontation.

John's toothache was an important part of the story that brought him a few days later to Number 10. But, on that pre-election Saturday, there was no certainty that he would win the three-horse race scheduled for the following Tuesday November 27, and become the Tory Party's new leader. Yet, at 10.30 a.m. on the following morning he drove to Buckingham Palace where the Queen received him as the new leader of what was also to be in effect an almost completely new government.

As the Prime Minister's official black car carrying John and Norma drove up The Mall and through Buckingham Palace's main gates, past the saluting guardsmen in their black busbys and red jackets, Norma felt, she says, quite unreal. Is this really happening to me, to us? was the question rapidly emerging through the bewilderment and shock she felt at the speed with which their lives had changed.

The morning was grey and cold. A slight fog cast its dirty net among St James's Park's bare-branched trees, and the cherubs adorning the great fountain before the palace gates seemed frozen, as if holding their breath. Norma was wearing the familiar blue suit she had worn two days before. John was silent. Was he thinking of the extraordinary suddenness with which this change had come about? Did he think of the distance he had travelled since the day almost thirty-four years before when, as a spellbound thirteen-year-old schoolboy, he had sat in the Strangers' Gallery of the House of Commons and heard his first debate; and of how he had known then, with that absolute certainty with which he has known many things in his life, that being there, in that place, was what he wanted? Wanted so badly that afterwards he was afraid to return too often to see debates because of the greater fear that he might never be able to achieve his ambition.

As he drove that royal route, writers and broadcasters were feverishly commenting on his sudden elevation, at the unusually early age of 47, to Britain's premier political office. John Major's reflections would probably have been in sharp contrast, for some of his thoughts surely drifted over what only he knew of the slow purposefulness, the steely determination and the resolute persistence, that had brought him to this day.

He has often compared his progress to that of the tortoise, rather than the hare. To others, his extraordinarily rapid progress through a series of junior ministerial offices to several senior Cabinet posts, and now to Prime Minister, seems very much the lightning success of the hare. Had not all this happened in just over ten years, since he was first elected in 1979 as MP for Huntingdon, one of the country's safest Conservative seats?

But whatever they were saying about him, John Major knew how long it had taken him, and how his will had prevailed when the road was much less easy.

His election as Conservative Party leader was seen as a triumph for Thatcherite values, a working example of the meritocratic freedom to rise in which he himself so passionately believes, for here was a man who had started from nothing and risen by his own efforts to the pinnacle of public office.

To John Major himself, however, his rise was just that little bit more than an example of Thatcherism. It was an example of what he wants for everyone: the chance to rise from any background or origin whatsoever, without encountering the artificial barriers of real or perceived class.

Mrs Thatcher herself was a supreme meritocrat: grocer's daughter, Oxford scholar who won a First in Chemistry, barrister, MP, and first woman Prime Minister. But John Major's story is one in which the rags to riches element is stronger, for his early years were harder and his chosen path rougher than his predecessor's. This is a story of struggle, and of disadvantage overcome with energy, determination, persistence and passion for his mission. Without the backup of academic credentials due to his fudged schooldays, he knew he had limited options. Many bright and ambitious youngsters starting from a similar position become traders, street-sharp entrepreneurs,

Rolls-Royce Corniche-driving millionaires. A few turn to crime. For John Major, there had only ever been one aim, one love, one drive, one thing worth whatever pain or sacrifice: politics.

As the car slowed to a halt outside the Palace he must have thought briefly of the immediate task ahead, of his conversation with the Monarch, of receiving the historic seals of office, and of the burden this would place upon his shoulders if the job were to be well done. But, also, his thoughts were working on another level. He has the ability of the extremely intelligent, to think about more than one thing at a time. When asked later what he was thinking when he took the seal of office, and on the short drives to and from the Palace, he said: 'I was thinking of what I had to do next. I had my mind pitched forward rather than necessarily thinking about what would happen at the time. The other thing I had on my mind was what I would say on the way back, in Downing Street, outside Number 10. And a good deal of the morning I was thinking of the Cabinet changes to come.'

While John planned, Norma saw the crowds lining the railings outside Buckingham Palace. Are they really there for us, she wondered, or is there something else going on? The Changing of the Guard had already taken place, surely? Was this the overspill or were these people really waiting to catch one of those eternally tantalising glimpses of the new man at the heart of a historic moment? After all, the Changing of the Guard at Downing Street doesn't happen very often. Mrs Thatcher's achievements and duration in office had made this a much more important occasion than

simply the change from one Prime Minister to another.
And then there was the immense public curiosity about
the new young leader with the romantic family history
whom a waggish columnist dubbed, 'Our Unknown
Prime Minister'.

Norma Major, shy and nervous, did not go with her
husband to see the Queen. She says, 'I was taken into
a room where I had been once before and I was looked
after by the Duchess of Grafton, I must say, very
beautifully.' Norma doesn't remember how long she
waited or a great deal about how she felt because, she
says, 'I was so numb. I really couldn't believe what was
happening. I don't know how long we were there for –
perhaps twenty minutes. I remember the Duchess and
I talked about clothes, about having to have so many
different outfits for all the different occasions.'

When they left and drove silently down The Mall
again, Norma felt inhibited from talking by the driver's
presence. Then at last she decided she would have to
get used to talking to her husband in front of other
people or else there would be very few occasions when
she would be able to talk to him at all. But John did not
want to talk. There was that speech to make . . .

As the fingers of Big Ben pointed to just a few
minutes past eleven, their car swept them through
the mid-morning traffic jam of Parliament Square
and around the corner into Parliament Street towards
Whitehall. The crowd outside Downing Street's huge
black-and-gilt wrought iron gates was dense and deep
and cheering. Excitement and curiosity were running
high. Outside Number 10, John and Norma faced the
press together, he with his arm around her waist. Now,

since his visit to the Palace, he was indeed the Prime Minister, not merely the elected Conservative Party leader, and as such he made his statement of intent: to build a meritocratic, classless society in which everyone would participate.

Referring to a small piece of paper on which were the jotted notes he had made in the car, he said, in that rather harsh voice that is his public but not his private one: 'I want to see us build a country that is at ease with itself, a country that is confident, and a country that is prepared and willing to make the changes necessary to provide a better quality of life for all our citizens. I don't promise you that it will be easy, and I don't promise you that it will be quick, but I believe it is an immensely worthwhile job. Now, if you will forgive me, because it will be neither easy nor quick, I will go into Number 10 straight away and make a start right now.'

Norma smiled shyly by his side, then as he hugged her to him he also grinned with the open delight of a man who has achieved his long-time ambition, and raised his right arm in a bold salute. Perhaps this picture of John and Norma will forever remain in our minds: their freshness, their seeming innocence, their unaffectedness. Their obvious happiness and comparative youth made them seem both vulnerable and a symbol of something new. Another generation had come to power and, it seemed, a new class-transient breed of Briton was proving his own meritocratic creed. A new spirit seemed already abroad in the land. Time had moved on in one of those sharp jolts with which it opens history's new chapters.

At a high-powered Reform Club cocktail party someone joked that taking over from Mrs Thatcher was like coming on after Maria Callas. No one was more aware of the contrast than John Major as he turned away from the cameras and insistent calls from the press and led Norma through the black door into Number 10, like Alice into Wonderland. His gums and jaws were sore, still not fully healed after the wisdom tooth surgery of the previous Tuesday. Yet so much had happened in that week since the day when Mrs Thatcher, still in Paris for the Conference on Security and Cooperation in Europe, had failed to win an absolute majority in the first ballot of the election brought by Michael Heseltine's challenge. So much in such a short time . . .

The forces leading to this culmination had been forming and gathering for years, at least as far back as the general election of June 1987. Mrs Thatcher, a tired figure at the campaign's outset, had somehow gained a second wind during the June election and turned the opinion polls around. Despite the glamorous 'red rose' packaging of the Gould–Kinnock Designer Socialism campaign, the Tories won a third term, with Margaret Thatcher as Prime Minister. There was no doubt as to her popularity with the majority of her own party, especially among constit- uency workers. If doubt was felt, it was by those Ministers and ex-Ministers who had, over years of withstanding barbed – if possibly justified – comments from the Prime Ministerial tongue, retired into their corners to brood on revenge.

After the June 11 election, John Major was promoted from his job as Minister of State for Social Security to the Cabinet as its most junior, yet one of its most powerful members. As Chief Secretary to the Treasury he would be in charge of controlling public expenditure by all government departments. Mrs Thatcher, by this time concerned like Elizabeth I with the succession, began to make it known among her confidants that she considered John Major a very promising young man, to whom she wanted to make available as much experience as possible of different departments of government.

The Chief Secretary's job was perfect for this as it is the one post which enables its holder to come into direct contact with all departments of state, while examining their budgets. Through the holding of this office John Major was to gain an insight into and overview of government expenditures which stood him in good stead as Chancellor, but which is now invaluable to him as Prime Minister.

John Major thus became number two to Nigel Lawson, who had been Chancellor since 1983. All was still sweetness and light between Mrs Thatcher and Nigel Lawson, as much as it ever could be between two individuals with such different instincts and objectives in economic management: he boldly optimistic and expansionist; she cautious and concerned with strict market disciplines.

It was at this point that things began to change, and not only between Mrs Thatcher and her Chancellor. The third-term strategy was to build on the achievements of the first and second. Socialism was in retreat while the market economy was at full throttle. Lawson was able to claim that the British economy was as strong as that of West Germany with a growth rate higher than most of its rivals. Meanwhile, the thrust of reform had moved beyond the economic sectors where the fires lit by the first- and second-term economic policies were now burning nicely, and on into the entrenched sectors of professional monopoly.

During the third term, the long established cosy practices of lawyers and estate agents, and the bounds of competition between building societies and banks, were to be reformed; the health services and education were to be given an unceremonious kick into the future; and poll tax was to be introduced to replace the antiquated rating system of local government finance. Of course, by threatening the comfortable structures of the professions the government was bound to make itself less popular, and this rapidly became apparent. It was soon slipping badly in the opinion polls and voices were raised loudly against its reforms.

However, a closer look at opinion surveys from MORI (Market Opinion Research International) in the period 1987–9 shows that these particular issues were significant only for short periods while they were in the headlines. Whereas the one clear correlation in charts drawn from the polls is that dissatisfaction with the government, and with Mrs Thatcher as Prime Minister, increased in line with the upswing in interest rates and the rise in public concern over inflation and the cost of living. So it was economic conditions and the way they affected individuals' spending power and financial well-being which had the most impact on the government's, and Mrs Thatcher's, popularity.

At 7%, interest rates had reached their lowest point for two decades before the 1987 election. Soon after, they were put up following adverse trade figures, and then again to 9%. At this point, the Wall Street-led Crash of 1987 changed the immediate picture. Following the collapse of share values and of investor confidence around the world, the Group of 7 finance ministers agreed to measures which would encourage economic growth to ward off a 1929-type Depression. Interest rates in Britain were forced down again. Confidence was restored and the boom continued.

Meanwhile the hurricane which had preceded the crash by a few days swept away hundreds of thousands of acres of woodland, symbolic of the dead wood that was to be hacked away from the undergrowth of British society by the equally strong wind of Thatcherite reform, and as disruptive in its effects on the quiet rhythms of British life.

Nigel Lawson has since admitted that he overreacted to the Crash of '87, and that he failed to anticipate the enormous growth in credit that was already underway, fuelled by the rapid drop in interest rates which he instigated during 1987 and the first half of 1988. John Major says, 'I did not dissent from anything Nigel Lawson was doing at the time. What went wrong was that we misjudged the implications of financial deregulation, and secondly the statistics didn't tell us what was happening. They were too poor to guide us. If we had realised what was happening to monetary growth, we would have taken action earlier.

That's why I improved the method of gathering the statistics.'

But this was not the only problem. Lawson also came increasingly into conflict with the Prime Minister over two key economic policies. One was that very same rapid bank rate fall during the first part of 1987, the other the policy of shadowing the Deutschmark as a prelude to joining the Exchange Rate Mechanism (ERM) of the European Monetary System (EMS). Both policies ran counter to Mrs Thatcher's instincts and beliefs. Many of those who did not accept that she was right at the time have done so with hindsight. Nigel Lawson's principal economic strategies during the crucial years of 1987, 1988 and early 1989 are now seen by many economic observers to have damaged the fabulous business success of mid-Eighties Britain.

These policies became the cause of battle after battle in Downing Street. As the communicating door between Numbers 10 and 11 slammed more often, and stories of the rows leaked into the press, relations between the Prime Minister and her Chancellor deteriorated. Meanwhile Mrs Thatcher's own economic advisor, Sir Alan Walters, became a public thorn in Nigel Lawson's side, advocating a rise in interest rates and the freeing of sterling from its artificial links with the Deutschmark. Mrs Thatcher voiced her disavowal of the twin policies with the phrase, 'You can't buck the market.'

The row persisted throughout 1988 and into 1989. Meanwhile the economy went steadily downhill. As inflation heated up, the Chancellor was forced to raise interest rates in an attempt to curb the flow of money.

Mortgage rates rose and rose, businesses faced heavier interest charges on their loans. Gradually the ebullience was squeezed out of the economy. Businessmen, especially small entrepreneurs, felt betrayed, and as their disaffection was added to that of other groups up in arms over the government's reforms, its popularity plummeted. Add to this in 1990 the advent of the poll tax and the hiked business rate, and government unpopularity was compounded. It was at this point that Mrs Thatcher's much vaunted fourth term was holed and began to sink under the rising waters of electoral disapproval. The government seemed unable to do anything right and almost every sector of the community, from teachers to doctors to businessmen to poll tax payers, were at its throat. The Conservative Party's own community of the professions and small businessfolk was the worst affected. But, as the opinion survey data clearly shows, if the economy had been doing well, the other issues would not have had the power to drive Mrs Thatcher from office.

Was Mrs Thatcher herself to blame for the forces which finally sank her premiership? Perhaps so, in that by leading the onslaught on entrenched customs, from local government finance to the school curriculum, she contributed to the process of disaffection. The programme for the third term was radical, audacious, and brutal in its speed of implementation and apparent lack of consultation with the groups affected. To move Britain forward into the Nineties, reform was necessary, but somehow when combined with rising interest rates and unprecedentedly extreme meteorological conditions, the impetus was just too much for a people who, if not at football matches, seem to prefer a quiet life. The British are a conservative nation. Too much change, too fast, especially when it did not seem to put more cash in their pockets, began to provoke resistance. Thus an over-zealous reforming instinct and a bad economic strategy combined to weaken the Prime Minister's power base. As Machiavelli advised in *The Prince*, 'A man who is made prince by the favour of the people should work to retain their friendship.' He also advised that the leader who owed his power to 'the favour of the nobles' should, before anything else, try to 'win the people over'.

This latter was the situation of John Major in November 1990 when he was elected as first among equals by his peers. Only by winning a general election can a new leader prove his appeal to the people directly. John's difficulties with the party during the spring of 1991 were owing to the fact that he had no electoral mandate. This despite his popularity in opinion polls.

When Michael Heseltine made his bid for the leadership in November 1990, he had considerable support from the opinion polls and a groundswell among MPs who wanted to remove Mrs Thatcher, or at least cause her enough unease to make her more responsive to their pleas for caution. Many tried to stop him standing in the second ballot, however. There was a strong feeling that enough was enough and that Mrs Thatcher was already well enough warned that she should be more responsive to the many voices calling for a slowing of the pace of reform and a more considered approach. Poll tax was now perceived as the major problem, but Europe had been the trigger. Yet Heseltine refused to withdraw.

As one Tory MP confided at the time, 'Michael's got a rush of blood to the head. He believes he's got the whole country behind him.' But Heseltine had assiduously courted public opinion for several years without similarly gaining the majority support of his fellow MPs. The received wisdom among them was, 'Michael is unclubbable.' Had there been a general election he could have swept his party to victory, but this was an election by the 'nobles', the Tory MPs.

Mrs Thatcher, while still ardently endorsed by most party members and Westminster insiders, no longer had the support of the majority of the electorate. By November 15–19 1990, the week of the leadership election's first ballot, only 25% of the electorate was, according to MORI, satisfied with her leadership. A thumping 71% were dissatisfied. Only 22% were satisfied with the government while 73% were not. By the time John Major was elected a week later, 31% said they were satisfied with the government as against 62% against, while 37% were already satisfied with the hours-old new PM, John Major, and only 22% expressed dissatisfaction.

So much for opinion pulse-taking and its effects, for clearly, as Tory MPs began to panic about signs of a rout in the forthcoming election, due before July 1992, Mrs Thatcher was vulnerable to their manoeuvres to save their own skins. The murmurs against her had been growing for some years, but were checked from gathering any damaging momentum by her popularity in the polls and her success in elections. A large number of Tory MPs were aware that they owed their presence in the House to Mrs Thatcher's policies, her success in generating an enterprise culture on the rubble of socialism, and her resounding electoral successes since 1979. From June 1987, unease among MPs and party members grew as canvassers' reports from the nation's doorsteps revealed growing anger among the electorate about the latest reforms, especially the economy and eventually the poll tax. Not only this but the lady appeared to be running out of Cabinet Ministers as, one after another over a decade, she sacked and replaced, or otherwise lost, her original inner circle of close friends.

The plotting to remove her had begun in earnest during the summer of 1988. While the groundswell of electoral unpopularity had not yet gathered, there were other forces at work. One was the petty-minded bitterness of thwarted Cabinet and ex-Cabinet colleagues. Mrs Thatcher was tough and abrasive with an attacking style of arguing her case, cutting strong men down to size and proving their wimpishness when they failed to stand up to her, and thus had made some permanent enemies among them. Not only Michael Heseltine and other ex-Cabinet Ministers had reason to hold grudges against her; some of those closest to her were the most active dissenters. They were to play a key role in her ultimate removal.

Geoffrey Howe and Nigel Lawson were both Cabinet Members of long standing in their jobs of Foreign Secretary and Chancellor, and both were pitted against Mrs Thatcher's very adversarial European stance. Despite the fact that this same style had, for Ronald Reagan, won enormous dividends in the INF arms negotiations with the USSR, Lawson and Howe were among many Tory MPs and ex-Ministers to denounce this method of argument in relation to the Europeans. Yet Mrs Thatcher's gladiatorial approach stemmed partly from the fact that so many of Europe's governments were socialist. What she reacted against most strongly was the idea that Britain might jeopardise its hard-won victory against socialism at home, and succumb to a more insidious version creeping in through the European doorway. To Mrs Thatcher, the plans for a European superstate, and many of the proposals put forward by Jacques Delors, were unacceptably socialist. To a British Labour Party so recently converted to Europeanism, no doubt by this very same fact, Mrs Thatcher was the exemplar of backward-looking British nationalism, while at the same time critics in the ranks of her own party were using her European attitudes as a convenient stick with which to beat her.

Among these, Lawson and Howe were preparing their own case to hasten Britain's entry into the ERM. Both wanted Britain to be committed to joining early. Mrs Thatcher made entry conditional on Britain's inflation rate coming down closer to the average of European nations' inflation, and stipulated it would be after other Community nations matched Britain's exchange control freedoms, especially for capital investment in other Community countries. The Prime Minister grew angrier as her opponents' disaffection became increasingly overt. As stories appeared in the press about their joint plots against her, she was openly and frequently fighting with both.

In the mid Eighties, Nigel Lawson had already begun his campaign to persuade Mrs Thatcher to take sterling into the ERM. He managed the economy entirely himself. Mrs Thatcher, the only person he was obliged to consult over his plans and who believed in his ability, allowed him a free hand. After the Crash of 1987, however, Lawson's policies over exchange and interest rates brought him into increasing conflict with the Prime Minister, and also with the Bank of England. Newspaper columns carried frequent stories on the struggle between the Prime Minister and the strong-minded colleague she called, 'My brilliant Chancellor'. Many of these stories were leaks whose origin, reporters say, was the Chancellor's office, though Lawson denies this. (Leaking is a fairly standard method of political manipulation.) However, the presence of Sir Alan Walters, Mrs Thatcher's personal economic advisor and an expert at getting his arguments across in the newspapers, acted as a catalyst to an already explosive mixture. Lawson and Walters were at loggerheads over the exchange and bank rates. The Governor of the Bank of England was also critical of Lawson's policies in this area, especially because of the huge cost to the reserves of trying to shadow the Deutschmark, a game Lawson later called 'living in sin with ERM'.

In 1987 the Chancellor was still riding high in public and peer group estimation and spoken of as a future Prime Minister. By 1988, headlines told of plots by

Howe and Lawson to unseat Mrs Thatcher and replace her with Lawson. Press reports of their disagreements forced the PM to enter into public debate over the press allegations.

The public rowing in the press throughout late 1987 and 1988 about the management of the economy did little to help the Prime Minister retain her hold on public opinion. Especially when alongside these headlines were others reporting increasing economic problems, among them those two old favourites, rising inflation and negative trade balances. In May 1988, the Iron Lady who had told the Chancellor, 'You can't buck the market,' now bowed to the chorus of voices raised against her in the press and all around and affirmed that the Chancellor had a free hand with the exchange rate, a moment of weakness she must have regretted often since.

But besides all that, the picture projected by the press was of a Chancellor who was fattening the rich by massively reducing their tax burden. In his controversial budget of March 1988, Lawson had benefited higher tax payers by cuts which seemed unnecessary and inexplicable given the economic signals. The rich were generally astounded. Some higher paid executives were interviewed on TV saying they didn't need the money and were embarrassed by the tax cuts which sloshed more cash through their pockets while the lower paid remained on the breadline. This did the government and Mrs Thatcher a grave disservice.

By the summer of 1989, while interest rates had been rising steadily but not fast enough to counter still rising inflation, Europe became the headline issue. At the Madrid summit, Geoffrey Howe and Nigel Lawson claimed they had persuaded the Prime Minister to commit Britain to join the ERM as soon as British inflation was low enough and certain other conditions were met by Community countries. When the trio returned from Madrid, stories to this effect appeared in the press.

Mrs Thatcher must have felt, at this point, that Geoffrey Howe had become too persistent an opponent and so decided to move him sideways. This was the point at which John Major became Foreign Secretary. It was also the point at which the chorus of disgruntlement rose deafeningly. It was led by Geoffrey Howe's evident pain at losing not only his top job of six years' tenure but his grace and favour country residence of Chevening. Perhaps it is no coincidence that rumours now grew that a stalking horse would challenge Mrs Thatcher in that coming November's annual leadership re-election. Various backbench names were murmured. The intention, it was said, was not so much to replace Mrs Thatcher as to show her how much opposition there was among Conservative MPs to her policies. Or was it to her leadership style?

Margaret Thatcher's biggest problem in the end was one which she had always said was never an issue during her rise: she was a woman. The fact that the Conservative MPs had chosen a woman to lead them seemed extraordinary at the time, but the Seventies was a better time for gender equality than the late Eighties by which time a backlash had gathered momentum. But, when they elected Margaret Thatcher, Tory MPs certainly had no idea of the real nature of the person they had made their leader.

She had always been very feminine, and was admired by her male peers as an attractive and intelligent colleague. Men found her alluring and usually clustered around her. She played her game adroitly and with subtle seductiveness. She was once seen at a *Punch* cartoonists' lunch being approached by an adoring young man, one of many asking for her autograph. He was treated to the husky murmur of the words as she wrote them: 'To David, From Margaret, with love.' The paper was handed back to the dazzled fellow with a smoking glance from La Thatcher's ice-blue eyes.

Once she was ensconced as leader she discovered, as every woman in a powerful position before and since, that getting men to deliver the goods as subordinates may require more brutal methods than winsome wiles. Certainly more brutal methods than any man would have needed to use. One woman newspaper editor told me, 'You ask once, nicely. You ask the second time a bit more firmly. And when they still haven't done what you've asked, you have to start shouting.' Now Mrs Thatcher, after eleven years of managing her male colleagues more with her gloves off than on, had insulted so many male egos that she had created a huge groundswell of revolt which began at least to wet her ankles. And she had to spend a lot of time shouting, in and out of the House of Commons.

Matters were made worse when Nigel Lawson, in confrontation with the Prime Minister once more over the same economic issues, decided he would resign. There are many versions of what actually happened and as many questions about what Lawson really intended. There had been constant stories in the newspapers for two years that he would leave politics for a top City job. What was the source of these rumours? There is no clear answer. Lawson wanted his own way with the economy. He believed Mrs Thatcher depended on him, and that he was highly regarded by the City, MPs, the party as a whole. Had he not just saved the day with the most brilliant conference speech after speculation that he was sulking and might not even turn up? Was he not her 'brilliant Chancellor'? And did she not say, afterwards, or even at the time to his face, that his position was 'unassailable'?

Whatever the truth, in November 1989 Mrs Thatcher seems to have had no choice but to accept his resignation. She made John Major Chancellor. The stalking horse manifested itself as Sir Anthony Meyer, MP for Clwyd North-West. Everyone knew this was not a serious challenge, but it was an opportunity for disgruntled MPs to abstain and register their disapproval.

The Tory tabloids immediately went to work, digging for dirt about Meyer in order to damage his chances. They found a beautiful black woman called Simone Washington who for twenty-five years had, with the knowledge of his wife, been favouring Sir Anthony with beatings. Meyer had even paid for her to be properly trained in this art in Amsterdam.

Now the *News of the World*, owned by Rupert Murdoch's News International, was among several newspapers offering her six figure sums to reveal all. Miss Washington confides that one night before the first ballot, Rupert Murdoch was dining with Mrs Thatcher. A message was brought to him saying the story had been secured by the paper and that Miss Washington was standing by with her bags packed, waiting to be spirited to a safe house somewhere on the Riviera, away from the attentions of other newspapers who would come baying after her for follow-ups to the revelations.

According to reports Miss Washington received from *News of the World* political staff, Mrs Thatcher told Murdoch, 'I want to win on my own merit.' And not only did she win, but Meyer's constituency deselected him. Mrs Thatcher seemed firmly back in the saddle.

But events were now conspiring towards that fatal election of 1990. After its introduction in April 1990, poll tax was wreaking havoc with Tory support in the constituencies. Marginal MPs realised they would lose their seats if an election were called. Canvassers, even in safe constituencies, were tired of arguing against criticism of the tax. They felt they had nothing reasonable to say in its defence. Opinion polls showed Labour yomping into the lead while Tory spirits sank further. The economy was in a mess and the terse comments of the new Chancellor, John Major, and his grim expression whilst revealing problems which were only the tip of an iceberg, did nothing to reassure either business or the markets.

As one ex-MP, now a peer, told me: 'John looked so serious when he was Chancellor because he inherited such an awful mess. The economy was in a terrible state and he was very worried at the time.'

The nation was not told the true extent of the economic horrors that had followed so swiftly on Nigel Lawson's years of growth, but it was apparent that there were serious problems. The blame fell on the administration, and ultimately the Prime Minister. As interest rates rose further and mortgages were hit again, the voters turned against Mrs Thatcher in droves. But, in the end, it was not to be the electors' votes which counted, for it was at this point that Geoffrey Howe and Nigel Lawson resurfaced. The dagger was in Howe's hand, and the moment of his speech condemning Mrs Thatcher's European remarks to the House was like a scene from *Murder in the Cathedral*.

Shots on the Commons' cameras of Mrs Thatcher's face showed that she immediately recognised the true import of this moment. An hour or two later, Sir Robin Day walked into the Garrick Club and told fellow members he had just witnessed the most extraordinary moment of his entire career as a political journalist. Many observers said that it was like a medieval act of betrayal. What was unexpected was that this was so passionate a speech from the mild Sir Geoffrey. It widely shocked many, and some said they felt physically nauseated after it, and by what followed. Many observers commented privately about the poor relations that had existed between Lady Howe and Mrs Thatcher, and about the way in which this may have influenced her husband's relationship with the Prime Minister whom he had served in the two most senior offices of state, Chancellor and Foreign Secretary. So long standing, and so widely known, was Elspeth Howe's dislike of Mrs Thatcher that one MP told me, 'It took her ladyship, his wife, ten minutes to write it and him ten years to deliver it.'

Howe denied personal vengefulness and insisted that his attack was an honourable act on behalf of the nation. His bitterness was plainly visible on his face and in his voice, let alone in the words he uttered.

Now, Lawson made his position clear. He spoke for only the third time since his resignation a year before as Chancellor and announced his intention of retiring from Parliament at the next election. He also claimed that he had tried for five years to persuade the Prime Minister to join the EMS, and that if this had been done in 1985, the economy would not now be in such bad shape.

Was this timing also intended as a knife blow at the Prime Minister? Newspapers reported that there was a plot by Howe and Lawson to remove her in 1988 and 1989. Westminster rumours fed the speculation that indeed there was. One story concerns Nicholas Ridley, one of the last of Mrs Thatcher's close allies and friends in the Cabinet of 1990. He was obliged to resign earlier in the year from his position as Trade and Industry Secretary after a row following an unfortunate gaffe over Europe reported in an interview in *The Spectator* magazine, edited by Nigel Lawson's son Dominic. Ridley had been caught offguard and been quoted when he thought he was off the record, and protested as such. There was a clear difference of opinion about this.

Ridley seems to have been removed by accident. Or was it the deft use of an unforeseen opportunity to embarrass the PM? Ridley's downfall left her isolated. He was almost the last old friend to leave the government. Even if the Ridley incident was not part of a more far-reaching strategy, there are many who believe there was a plot to remove Mrs Thatcher from office. Sir Alan Walters is one of these and has, since November 1990, added his own theories to the rumours.

On December 5 1990 *The Times* published an article by him headlined, 'Get Thatcher, and they did'. In this article, Sir Alan cited several instances in which he had been used by the 'get-rid-of-Thatcher-gang', for which, he wrote, 'I was a splendid target. Because of my position, I could not publish what I knew to be true or point out the implausibility of . . .' And here he quotes a story, in *The Independent* of June 15 1989, which he claims was just one of several attempts to 'get Thatcher'. This particular story referred to boardroom lunches in the City where, it was claimed, Sir Alan 'rubbished the Chancellor's policy – with the clear implication that he had the Prime Minister's approval.' Sir Alan commented, 'I could only recall two City lunches, at both of which I made clear that I would not discuss current policy, the hosts agreed, and there was no such talk.' Among other newspaper stories which Sir Alan alleges were written after deliberate leaks from high sources was an article in the *Financial Times* by its political editor

Phillip Stephens on November 14 1990, and one in the *Economist* on November 24.

Sir Alan wrote that the articles 'told how, on the eve of the Madrid conference in June 1989, after a tremendous row, Sir Geoffrey Howe and Nigel Lawson persuaded her to accept the so-called Madrid conditions for entering the Exchange Rate Mechanism. Mr Stephens said both Mr Lawson and Sir Geoffrey threatened to resign unless she accepted them.' Sir Alan continued: 'I find this odd. It was at least three days before the meeting that I put into final form a memorandum setting out the so-called Madrid conditions.'

After summarising the conditions Sir Alan continued, 'I am certain that before putting forward my memorandum, I had discussed the condition with officials both at Number 10 and the Treasury. It seemed to me that those enthusiastic about entering the ERM forthwith (Sir Geoffrey and Mr Lawson inter alia) and those who were reluctant (Mrs Thatcher and other prominent Conservatives) could agree to settle on these conditions. I believed Mrs Thatcher could present these as the basis of a consensus and that she accepted them as such.' Sir Alan believed it was important to go to Madrid with proposals that could be fully supported by both Howe and Lawson. He wrote, 'I do know that the compromise of the Madrid conditions came from Mrs Thatcher and not after threats of resignation "imposed" upon her by the Howe–Lawson axis.

'Indeed my impression was exactly the opposite. The anxiety of Sir Geoffrey and Mr Lawson to claim credit for Madrid was undoubtedly due to the widespread perception that it was a great success for the

Prime Minister. But even at the time, the Howe camp briefings let it be known that the Prime Minister had caved in to pressure from Sir Geoffrey and Mr Lawson (see, for example, *The Independent* of June 27 1989). Phillip Stephens went much further with his detailed description in the article of November 14 1990.

'I do not know where he got his story from, but he is clearly a journalist who would rely only on a highly reputable source – which, in the circumstances, must surely mean Sir Geoffrey and/or Mr Lawson.'

Nigel Lawson certainly denies that he ever leaked information to the press. He has done so through his lawyers in a suit against *The People* newspaper whose magazine carried an article in February 1991 criticising his economic policy, reporting the many other criticisms of it by, among others, the Governor of the Bank of England, Robin Leigh-Pemberton, and Lawson's own admission of three major errors. It further proposed the thesis that the Lawson management of the economy was causal in creating the conditions for Mrs Thatcher's demise.

Sir Alan quotes a number of other occasions on which he was used as an intermediate target. He writes that, 'Perhaps the first step on the slippery slope of Mrs Thatcher's decline was associated with my return to Number 10 in May 1989. I was a tempting target who could never hit back. But my views on the Chancellor's monetary policy from 1987–8 were well known from previous newspaper articles and radio and television interviews.

'The second fatal move leading to Mrs Thatcher's overthrow was the transfer of Sir Geoffrey Howe from the Foreign Office to Deputy Prime Minister and Leader of the House. His violation of the confidential discussion with the Prime Minister, when he let it be known that he had been offered Douglas Hurd's job, was clearly designed to detach Mr Hurd from Mrs Thatcher and sow dissent in the party.'

The most probable explanation for Mrs Thatcher's offer of Douglas Hurd's job of Home Secretary to Howe is that she intended to move John Major to another post while offering the Foreign Office to Hurd. This was the only job Hurd had ever really desired and Mrs Thatcher clearly knew he would not be unhappy to give up the Home Office to do it. This would have put John Major out of the picture for the moment and there is no whisper of where he would have been placed had Sir Geoffrey accepted the possibility of going to the Home Office. There are many who think this offer was, under the circumstances, extremely generous.

The press are not innocent of participation in Mrs Thatcher's downfall, as the newspaper coverage of the events of the week leading to the first ballot shows. Long before this harsh criticism, often unjustified, was being levelled at the Prime Minister. Sir Alan refers to 'the media being full of tales of her being overweening, out of touch, opposed to Europe and its consensus and a liability'. Clearly there were plenty of people willing to collaborate, given any opportunity to remove her from office.

There are many who will never forget the disgust which accompanied those treacherous days of November 1990. What was being done was often shameful and much of it completely irrational. Tory MPs ran around like headless chickens motivated by the polls of the moment, those transitory readings of spontaneous, often ill-informed opinion that are taken so seriously but which have little long-term value unless taken over a period and covering a large number of detailed questions of policy areas, where information and arguments are readily available to the respondents.

Did this emotional and confused response reveal the existence of an underlying plot or plots? Apart from the Howe/ Lawson axis, there was certainly plenty of theoretical plotting and it had been going on for at least two years. But there is a difference between discussion of strategies on a 'what if?' basis and the deliberate pursuit of a campaign to destroy the Prime Minister. Among Westminster insiders, strategies for the succession were being discussed, as they will always be discussed after a certain length of office-holding. Mrs Thatcher had been in occupation of Number 10 for an unusually long time and she herself had for many years chosen and groomed a number of potential successors.

Throughout the decade of her premiership a succession of men of the moment tripped across the stage like auditioning starlets. There was John Moore, there was Cecil Parkinson, who who both peaked long before the moment; there was Kenneth Baker (still a contender); and Michael Heseltine was always the understudy waiting in the wings to be the star of the show. Nigel Lawson, during his height of perceived genius as Chancellor in 1987, was the name most often spoken as a successor when the time came. Even Geoffrey Howe was once thought of as a possibility, though unlikely to have been Mrs Thatcher's choice.

One of the more recently formulated strategies was that Mrs Thatcher would retire (with a little encouragement from the party elders and her husband) and Geoffrey Howe would take over as a sort of benign Chief Steward to see the party through the next General Election. After this there would be a leadership election in which a number of bright young names would feature, including, it was thought, that of John Major. Indeed there was much outlining of possible strategies by various groups which included those around John Major. But many of these so-called plots were merely plans held in readiness, and which only sprang to life when a remarkable combination of conditions occurred.

Sir Geoffrey Howe had evidently been awaiting his opportunity. Mrs Thatcher's dramatic 'No, No, No' de Gaulle-style speech over British sovereignty, in the House of Commons in October 1990, was the cue for him to make his move. Michael Heseltine took the next decisive step. Was he in cahoots with Sir Geoffrey? It seems that the opportunity was the trigger rather than a pre-set plan. Heseltine wrote his open letter on Europe, fell into the midst of controversy with his own constituency party and with the party in Parliament and nationwide. He had put himself in a position from which he was unable to back down.

That letter's timing was a characteristic error of judgment, the triumph of desire over common sense. Poor Heseltine had been waiting and grooming his image for five years since the Westland fiasco, planning and dreaming of his entry to Number 10 since his Oxford undergraduate days or before. In the end (though it may not be the end entirely), it was that fatal flaw in his make up, the vulnerability to rushes of blood to the head, to the blurring effect of emotional biochemistry on an otherwise excellent brain, that cost him his chance of the premiership.

Without the Heseltine open letter, there would have been no serious challenge to Mrs Thatcher in

November 1990. More than one stalking horse may
have bucked and shied in mimic intent to throw Mrs
Thatcher into the pages of history, but there was still
no majority among MPs seriously seeking her removal.
Most still sought to make her listen and bend towards
a more consensus view on policies such as the poll tax
that were an electoral liability, to amend her style
and approach to Europe, rather than dispense with
this towering leader.

Alas, poor Michael. He was to take the blame,
perhaps more than Geoffrey Howe for the way events
accelerated out of control. Plots? By now there were
many. The soundest strategy conceived by party elders
to deal with the outcome of any such plots was prepared
well in advance. In that week before the first ballot,
when Mrs Thatcher's campaign was in the hands of
others while she attended to affairs of state in Paris,
the scenario was this: on the first ballot, Heseltine
was expected to win between 120 and 130 votes,
while the Prime Minister would obtain a majority,
but one which was clearly flawed by the large vote
for her opponent. Abstentions were also expected.
It was thus planned that Lord Whitelaw and Lord
Carrington would go to Mrs Thatcher and tell her
that as she had lost the support of one-third of her
Parliamentary Party, she had no choice but to stand
down. It was said that if she refused to listen to the
two peers, Douglas Hurd and John Major would also
go in and tell her the game was up. This accomplished,
new candidates would come forward to stand in a fresh
election, John Major among them.

In the event Mrs Thatcher, true to her fighting
character, gave advance notice from Paris that she
would stand in the second ballot. The elder statesmen

had not even had the chance to press their point. But when she returned from Paris, voices were raised about the fact that she had typically decided to go on fighting without consulting her colleagues. The process of persuading the Prime Minister to give up the fight for the second ballot now began. Lord Whitelaw and a stream of Cabinet Ministers went to see her. It is still not known for sure who advised her which way though there are many rumours and hints.

If Mrs Thatcher were running true to the character in which she had been cast by innumerable newspaper stories and Parliamentary gossip, she would have seen off each and every one of the men who advised her to give up. Even the tiny handful who still had her true respect would have found her hard to persuade. Margaret Thatcher give up? Unthinkable. Apart from Denis Thatcher's husbandly concern for her feelings and her dignity, only one factor prevented the brave lady from a fight to the finish with Heseltine. It was the evidence, brought to her by a number of her colleagues, that her vote was slipping and too many MPs were changing sides.

Rumours have since been put about that this evidence may not have been true, that the story of MPs changing sides was deliberately concocted to convince her to stand down in order to allow her favourite, John Major, to stand and prevent a Heseltine leadership. Norman Lamont, who later volunteered as John Major's campaign manager, is one of those it is whispered by journalists and others who, on the basis of the information about vote changing, helped to persuade Mrs Thatcher to give up. He has convincingly denied this, however.

Whatever the truth, to be revealed perhaps in the lady's memoirs, or those of other retiring Ministers, she did stand down and an era ended. Perhaps it had ended already and her going was merely the symbol of its passing. John Major allowed his name to go forward and emerged at the end of a momentous week as Britain's first new Prime Minister for eleven and a half years.

The universal comment was that Mr Major's style was in stark contrast to Mrs Thatcher's; that he was a healer where she was incurably combative. No one mentioned the fact that Mrs Thatcher had been forced into combat from the time her name went forward for the leadership election of 1975. The party divided between herself and Heath, a split that would surely have been repeated if Heseltine had succeeded her. A few noted that, of course, Mrs Thatcher was leader in opposition for four years and that this inevitably contributed to her attacking style.

Most people seemed to have forgotten that Margaret Thatcher's great achievement was to destroy the emphysema of socialism and restore Britain to the fast track as a nation able to compete in the world and have pride in itself. At the start of her career few gave credence to her economic doctrines. Newspaper columnists were among those slowest to surrender the received ideas on political consensus and stateism, while socialists could never forgive her. Mrs Thatcher had a hard fight to lay waste the socialist state and replace its paralysis with a dynamism based on individual response to free market forces. But she did it, and she had to fight to do so, never allowed to rest by those opposed to her. She had not quite completed her task when she was removed.

A substantial vestige of old unreconstructed state-ism remains. Perhaps a truce has now been called in that fight so that John Major can begin to build a new, more overtly compassionate, free market democracy on the old socialist-dominated mixed economy's still smoking ruins.

Compared to Mrs Thatcher's last bloody struggle, John Major's arrival in power was akin to that of birth by Caesarean section. For after the fight to remove Mrs Thatcher, in which he played little part thanks to a well-timed indisposition, he emerged as leader as sweetly as Venus riding on the waves. Can anything be that easy?

What really lies behind John Major's achievement of the premiership, and for how long had he dreamed of being Prime Minister? Different friends make different estimates of the duration of his ambition. The first task was clearly to get elected to the House. If he dreamed of anything else, it would not have been practical to plan it without first becoming an MP.

Constituency parties in the Seventies, after all, were looking for good constituency MPs rather than inspiring front bench material, though in the Sixties there had been a slightly different emphasis within the local parties. Robert William Elliott, now Lord Elliott, who in 1971 was Vice-chairman of the Conservative Party in charge of candidate selection, told me that then he tried to persuade constituency executives to look beyond the qualities needed for a good MP and to the qualities needed for the Cabinet. By the mid Seventies, when John Major was hunting for a winnable constituency, priorities had shifted more towards community politics, so Jean

Lucas, the Conservative Party Agent he met through South London politics who was a powerful mentor and influence on him, advised him that his first task was to become an MP and not think of what might follow. She is one of many who say, however, that they had no doubt that he would go to the top once he entered Parliament. None of these friends realised how quickly or how satisfyingly their judgment would be proved good.

Many of those close to him believe that, for John, becoming an MP was the limit of his ambition at first. An old friend, David Rogers, speechwriter to Iain Macleod in the Sixties and a neighbour of John's in Beckenham during the Seventies, remembers that: 'At dinner parties and social gatherings he would never talk about his private political ambitions. Only about ideas.' Jeffrey Archer, however, thinks the idea of being Prime Minister may have been in John's mind as far back as his days as a councillor in Lambeth in the late 1960s.

Robert Atkins, MP, who knew him during the Sixties, initially through Greater London Young Conservatives activities, and who is still a close friend and cricket buddy, and now Minister for Sport, does not think they ever spoke about it in those days, except perhaps in jest. Atkins is a tall, balding, athletic-looking figure with a direct no-nonsense style and a frank way of speaking. He says the first time the matter came up for real was in August 1987 soon after John had been made Chief Secretary to the Treasury and the most junior member of the Cabinet. The Conservatives, following their victory in the election of June 1987, were getting ready to launch their vigorous third-term reforms. There were five clear years to the next election, years in which an ambitious young politician with talent might start laying down a strategy for attaining the leadership. Atkins takes up the story: 'We were on the back of a narrow boat on holiday in the Midlands, listening to cricket, and our wives were in the front, and he said to me, "This is unreal. Here I am now a Cabinet Minister, and you are a PPS. I really do think it's extraordinary that we've got to that level if you think back to our YC days." And I said, "Yes, and there's no reason, is there, why you shouldn't go all the way, if you wanted to?"

'He said, "Well, I have my family pressures, but there's no doubt in my mind, sitting around the Cabinet table, that I could do the job."

'Now, at that stage, you don't plot. What we thought about further, particularly when he was Foreign Secretary, was to make sure his position was such that he wasn't pigeon-holed as representing a certain strand of the party. That meant that he had a PPS who was quite right-wing and anti-Europe, and there were certain avenues he could talk to, like the No Turning Back Group on the one hand, and Nick's Diner on the other extreme. But the key was that he wasn't to be pigeon-holed.

'His politics are the same as mine, essentially liberal, in the Macleod tradition. Predominantly right-wing or dry on economic issues, but on the social issues, on things like racism and poverty, very liberal. He became quite dry on economics – the traditional approach, "You can't spend more than you've got" – but his instincts are very much of the liberal disposition. So the skill, if you like, only it's not even plotting, was just thinking about how we could make sure that he was set in the right place for when the lady went.'

Rumours have circulated since the leadership change that certain leading members of John Major's campaign group had been involved in plotting Mrs Thatcher's removal so that their candidate could stand. The plot seems to hinge on the advice Mrs Thatcher was given on the crucial Wednesday, November 20, after the first ballot of the preceding day.

It seems inconceivable that Mrs Thatcher, though surely tired after her round of Paris meetings and out of touch with the campaign which had been managed in her absence by George Younger, would not have been offered accurate knowledge of the voting intentions of MPs for the second ballot. Her campaign managers should have had their finger on the pulse, even if, as they were accused later by other of her supporters, they had not fought vigorously enough on her behalf. The implication of the rumours is that more than one person she trusted to give her a correct impression, may have given her an exaggerated picture of Michael Heseltine's chances of winning on the second ballot. But, his friends insist, it was not John Major.

One of his closest allies and longstanding friends, a member of his campaign group, says, 'I can tell you that John is actually quite *Boy's Own*-paperish in his attitude to things. I do not believe that he would have said anything to her that would, in any sense, have been capable of appearing self-seeking. He would certainly have gone on and supported her loyally had she decided to stand again.'

John Major confirmed this convincingly. 'I may stay silent because (to say) something at that moment might be hurtful, but I will never, never dissemble. Politicians are often thought of as giving the view they want people to hear rather than what they truly think.

I'll never do that. And I never do what other people want me to. I only do what I think is right.'

John Major's old-fashioned sense of honour would certainly have prevented him from doing anything to tip the scales in his own favour. After all, he must have calculated that the moment was not the most auspicious one for taking over the leadership, knowing as he did the full scale of the economic problems of which he was in command as Chancellor. To a man of 47, with time and popularity on his side, there was no reason to rush things. To let Mrs Thatcher go on until after the next election and come in afterwards with five clear years ahead of him might have been a more appealing prospect. But it would not be in his character to plot and manoeuvre for his own advantage or to alter his advice to her in line with whatever interest he perceived as his own. That does not mean, however, that others might not plot on his behalf and without his concurrence.

Robert Atkins adamantly states and restates the fact that there was no plot, as such, to replace Mrs Thatcher with John Major. Predictably, he declared at the outset of a conversation on the subject, 'There was absolutely no plotting to make John leader, and therefore PM, at any point.' Later he returned to the subject: 'In terms of the leadership itself, I didn't talk to Lamont or Ryder who were the other key members of the campaign until the day of nominations. I only spoke to David Mellor on a couple of occasions as a joint mutual chum. There was no plotting as such, although quite a lot of movement of dispositions about how he should do it.'

In the autumn of 1989, while a stalking horse was being rumoured for the leadership challenge that

November, an informed source close to Conservative elder statesmen told me that John Major was considered a serious candidate for the leadership when Mrs Thatcher finally went, either by choice or *Putsch*. And there were always rumours of *Putsch* because of the smouldering dissatisfactions and punctured egos in Conservative Party circles. Atkins confirms, 'There's no doubt that there were a large number of people who thought John ought to be doing the job.'

Mrs Thatcher was foremost among the group who wanted John Major as the next Prime Minister. It is said that she spotted his potential as far back as the early Eighties. There is the story of the famous row at the Whips' dinner when he challenged the Prime Minister and came to her attention. Later she told colleagues that she thought him very promising. Certainly by 1987 when John, now Chief Secretary to the Treasury, was given his own table of guests to manage at a Chequers lunch, it seemed as though Mrs Thatcher was grooming him, perhaps also testing his less obvious social skills. By 1989, when he became Foreign Secretary, she was making it much clearer that she believed the next Tory leader should come from the younger generation rather than from the ranks of the established senior figures like Lawson and Howe. Other prospective candidates for the inheritance having fallen out, she was also making it clear that she believed John Major was the one who should succeed her at an appropriate time.

In the summer of 1989, Lord Carrington, the pre-Falklands Foreign Secretary, now chairman of Christie's the auction house, was asked by a business colleague what kind of a Foreign Secretary he thought the newly appointed John Major would make. Lord

Carrington confided, 'I don't know him, but I'm sure he'll be very good. But what I do know is that Margaret has told me several times that he is her heir apparent.' Lord Carrington went on in his jocular way, 'If that's so, I'm really sorry for him, because I can't think of a worse cross to bear than being Margaret's heir apparent.'

Lord Carrington has a wonderful sense of humour and admits to being entertainingly indiscreet on occasion. His words were spoken with the kindly and affectionate humour for which he is well known. He had been a long-time friend and confidant of Mrs Thatcher's, and in his role of Buckinghamshire farmer, a weekend neighbour of hers who often popped in for Saturday lunch at Chequers.

In November 1989, a section of the Parliamentary Party wanted to send a signal to the Prime Minister that they were growing restless and would use their power if she did not heed their concern. But there had already, for some months, been serious discussion that she might be persuaded to stand down in good time before the next general election, in order that a new leader might build support in the country. Some of these smokeroom strategists suggested that she might go in the autumn of 1990 in time for the party to prepare for an election during the autumn of 1991. In the event, that is what happened. Plots and plans aside, a greater force seemed to manifest itself, one which dwarfed the roles of the individual movers and players.

The accumulation of tendencies and events, of MPs' fears for the electoral future and of manoeuvrings of the fallen mighty, were gathering into a tide. Mrs Thatcher obdurately faced it, her posture often likened in newspaper columns and cartoons to that of Canute, the Danish King of England who tried, on the shores of the Thames near the present Palace of Westminster, to hold back the rising waters.

John Major's vigour and his dazzling smile were brought to the country's notice on the Thursday after Mrs Thatcher announced she would not continue. He bristled with energy and confidence. There was a freshness and born-again innocence to his demeanour and a youthful zip to his campaign that made Michael Heseltine, the champion victorious though not the technical victor of the first ballot, look somehow worn and defeated. John Major looked like a winner from the start of that second campaign. But up to that point he had been reluctant.

On the Tuesday of the first ballot he had been out of action, recuperating from dental surgery he had had the previous Saturday. Had he chosen the date deliberately? It seemed inappropriate that one of the leading contenders for the Tory leadership, should Mrs Thatcher fall, was having his wisdom teeth removed then. The surgery had been scheduled weeks before.

Jeffrey Archer, a close friend and cricket buddy of John's since 1979, tells the story: 'He was full of admiration for Mrs Thatcher and backed her loyally. I was of course involved in taking down the nomination sheet for him to back her. John was recovering from having his teeth out and asked me to spend the day with him, and of course we talked about it. We talked about nothing else. People were asking him to stand. Several people phoned that day but he wouldn't take the calls. He said it was disloyal to Margaret. And there were other friends who begged him not to go into hospital and have his teeth out and he refused to do that too. He said that would be like a vulture waiting over the bones.

'He said, "I shall go to hospital. I shall back the Prime Minister and I hope she wins." And that was the end of the discussion: which is typical of the man's character. The moment that the Prime Minister decided she wasn't going to stand, he then of course quite rightly considered himself a serious contestant and discussed with his friends whether he should stand.

'What he actually wanted to do was to get the Chief Whip or the Whips' Office to go round and find out whether he or Douglas Hurd had a better chance of beating Michael and not bother with all three of them standing. But of course it was not possible because they all had six hours to make up their minds, and so, quite rightly, they both stood – and that, in my view, was the correct thing to do.

'John is always for the more dignified way of doing something, and so he felt that if his colleagues thought it should be him or Douglas that he would go along with that, he wouldn't even argue with it. It's typical of his modesty and honesty that whatever the Chief Whip had told him, he would have accepted.'

This acceptance of whatever happens, good or ill, is part of John Major's philosophical approach to life. Once, he confided, 'If it all ended tomorrow, I wouldn't be upset. I could do something else. Life wouldn't come to an end.' And he often says, 'There's a life after politics.'

Robert Atkins says, 'The amazing thing is he's done this, he's got this job, without having to lust after it.'

Of course, he wanted the job. No question. But there is that same feeling of fatalism among John's friends about both the events and the man. It is as though John Major simply fell into place as Prime Minister, by appointment. And as he told me, 'Even when I was on Lambeth Council, I wasn't doing it because that was the way to get experience to be a Parliamentary candidate. I don't do a job to get on, because of where it would or could lead. I do it because I want to do the job.'

And of course, he *did* want to do the job. He reveals that without saying so, in so many ways: gestures, looks, even blushes in response to questions. But he is not the kind of fatalist who leaves everything to chance. Rather he seems to believe that you have to work for everything you want. However, his life has been too shaped by odd turns of fate for him to take a completely self-determinist position.

Once, he said gravely: 'I don't think that you can just leave things to work out on their own. There is so much going on. Things are changing all the time. What seems possible one year is out of the question the next. You simply don't know what will happen.'

Major is the real politician, the practical artist of the possible with an unerring sense of timing. Perhaps this is why Lord Pym, a former Foreign Secretary and MP of a neighbouring constituency, feels that the reason John Major became leader of the Conservative Party was that he was the right man in the right place at the right time. 'He was the right age,' Lord Pym says. 'There was a feeling that the party wanted someone younger, and they wanted someone who would unify the party. Douglas Hurd was much older, and Heseltine was not considered as unifying.' Lord

Pym believes luck is the essence of Major's arrival at the right place at the right time.

If luck were the sole reason for his sudden success, though, why is it that no other younger and potentially unifying candidate came forward? To say that his face simply fitted a mood of the moment is to ignore the talents which John Major's colleagues well recognised, and the efforts which had for years brought him step by step into position. Had this election taken place two or three years later, he would still have been the right man for the job because he is eminently qualified and fitted by his nature, skills and experience to lead Britain at this particular period in world history.

To John Major, the man who equates his progress with that of the tortoise rather than the hare, the idea of happenstance is laughable. Of course timing is all, and being prepared for opportunity, and being fitted to the opportunity – as well as having had such an opportunity in mind for a long time. Luck is too random a concept in a causal universe. John Major became Prime Minister because his whole life prepared him for that moment.

Robert Atkins describes how he and John first realised that the moment of opportunity might have dawned. 'We were sitting in his office after an evening debate, a day or so after the lady made her statement to the House on Europe, and we both said: "Our thumbs are prickling. There's something happening, something going on." And I said, I'm not a great believer in fate but when Tony Favell, his PPS, resigned I was the person who said to him, your new PPS, it's got to be Graham Bright, who is an old mutual friend of ours who does the job excellently.

'But then he told me he was going to have this operation. I knew he had been having trouble with his tooth, and I said to him, "You go away, you do the operation because the lady's let you off Cabinet and you don't come near the place." He said "I'm coming back on Tuesday (the day of the first ballot)." "You will not," I said and I told him that if he did, I would try and get the doorman to lock the doors and keep him out. "You are not to come near the place because that way you are going to be looked upon as a party to all the plotting if there is any."

'And I knew then that it all fitted in. Everything was falling into place, but it was fate if you like, in that sense . . . but I think he decided, certainly he said to me, I suppose, about three months before, while he was Chancellor, "I really have decided that sitting around this Cabinet table, I'm as good as any of them, if not better." And he's not an immodest man. Quite the reverse. When I say he is not immodest, he has this delightful way of dealing with people but underneath it he is a very determined individual, and once he makes his mind up he'll do it and he's very conscious of his own abilities and his own virtues and weaknesses. He just made a straightforward assessment that he was perfectly capable of doing the job, and therefore it was only a matter of time.'

Robert Atkins admits the whole thing seemed fated but says, 'He would be the last man to call himself a man of destiny. He would look askance at anyone who says (that) because he doesn't believe in that sort of thing. He is essentially a pragmatist, but certainly he took the decision that he was going to run for it and it was only a matter of time.' And opportunity. Again, that was a matter of John's innate sense of timing, his sense of political rhythm. Atkins says, 'That comes from sport and politics. You are no good at either of those two things unless you are conscious of timing and he is a consummate master of it.'

So the moment came and, minus his wisdom teeth, John Major came back to London to face his fate. As the insiders tell the story of how his supporters came together and ran his winning campaign, it seems simply to have developed in moments like a flash growth of desert flowers after rain. One minute there was just the nomination and the next there were fifty people working for him. Norman Lamont came forward immediately to propose himself as the campaign organiser. The other close chums, Robert Atkins, David Mellor, Richard Ryder and scores of Majorettes, as they became known, just piled into the borrowed terrace house in Gayfere Street and started rallying support. But their problem quite soon, it is said, was not getting pledges but trying to prevent an ever growing bunch of supporters from over zealous canvassing of Tory MPs for their support.

It quickly became broadcast that John was Mrs Thatcher's preferred candidate and had been all along. Other Cabinet Ministers such as Kenneth Baker, John Wakeham, Peter Lilley and Chris Patten, revealed themselves to be on the Major team. Notably, Geoffrey Howe and Nigel Lawson waited until the pre-poll weekend to slip it to the Sunday papers that they were putting their joint weight behind Michael Heseltine. If it made a difference it may have been to accelerate the already buoyant impetus of the vigorous younger generation campaign behind John Major. The Heseltine campaign already looked tired and jaded and the presence of the Howe/Lawson names behind the ticket did not add glamour, honour or prestige. The surprise was John himself, suddenly smiling and waving to the cameras. He came to life as if a great wind was blowing him effortlessly towards success. After a year of keeping his head down while dealing with the economy, he seemed a fresh spirit with dash and sparkle. He, of the three candidates, looked like a winner.

David Mellor says, 'I thought all along John would win because it was quite obvious that there was this spontaneous wave from across the party of people who wanted him. He would manage by his personal characteristics to find loyalty in those who felt loyal to Mrs Thatcher, but he was not restricted to her part of the party. There were plenty of other people who knew full well that John Major's personal qualities and outlook transcended any narrow Thatcherite label, and that is why he won.' A vote for John Major in November 1990 was a vote for continuity with the achievements of the preceding decade but it was also a vote for change in the things that had been causing discontent.

So, when the votes were counted, John Major had 185, Michael Heseltine 131, and Douglas Hurd 56. There was unprecedented applause in the lobby of the House when the news came through that Heseltine had waived his right to a second ballot. Observers told of the great sense of relief among Conservative MPs that at last the terrible rending of their unity was over. But there was more than this. Even opposition MPs joined in the demonstration of pleasure at John Major's election and he made a little speech of acknowledgement, again an unprecedented event. Here, it was felt, was a leader who not only united his own party but had qualities that could unite the nation.

Is that confidence likely to be justified? Much has been made of his approval of and claim that he was inspired in his youth by the ideas of Iain Macleod, summed up in his 'One Nation' address to the Conservative Political Centre. But to look back at the words of those days is to look back at another age. The sentiments survive the decades but the speeches also convey the stale odour of the 40 years of unimaginative consensus that saw Britain slide further and further towards stateism, third world economic standards and loss of national pride and influence. John Major's ideas are no more a carbon copy of Iain Macleod's than they are of Margaret Thatcher's. Like the times to which he is so appropriate, Major moves on, constantly adapting. What Major is and what Major will do is to translate his beliefs into the needs of the now. The causal connection between his character and experience and his plans for Britain will slowly unfold.

But for the moment, we flash back to November 27. Michael Heseltine has appeared before the waiting press corps on the doorstep of his Belgravia home, his wife beside him unable to hide her disappointment. He, brave but weary in defeat, has renounced the title for which he has so long worked and striven. (Not indefinitely, for Heseltine is still young enough to make a comeback within the decade.) For John Major, though, the youngest Prime Minister since William Pitt, this is the moment of triumph. In the lobby, he stops his friend and Parliamentary pair Dafydd Wigley, Plaid Cymru MP for Caernarvon and says, 'Come over for a whisky.'

Wigley had often been to Number 11 while John was Chancellor. He and his wife had dined with the Majors often. So Wigley went over to what was to become the victory party.

Baroness Blatch, Under Secretary of State for Environment and a former chairman of Cambridgeshire County Council, who has known John since he was selected for Huntingdon, had already been invited by Norma Major to come for a drink that evening, whatever the result of the ballot. She describes the euphoria and almost giddy sense of joy of those first hours after the result.

'I was in the House of Lords that Tuesday evening, waiting for the vote on the second reading of a bill I was putting through. The first thing that happened was my bill finished at about 6 pm and I rushed to the Whips' Office to watch the screen and see what had happened and when the results came through went absolutely crazy. I couldn't believe it because it all happened so quickly. Out came Heseltine and out came Douglas, so the whole thing was over within the minute. Then, because they had the cameras at Huntingdon, there were all my friends and my husband and children on the screen.

'So I decided to go over to Number 11. Norma and John, by the time I got there, were away in a bedroom where they had gone to be quiet together for a moment or two. There were lots of people saying "hello" to each other and a terrific atmosphere. Mark Thatcher came into the room while I was there and so did Mrs Thatcher at one stage. I didn't go up and speak to her because there was a sort of nervousness about what to say. Norma told me she desperately wanted to put her arms around her . . . well, Norma did eventually but in another place . . .

'Eventually John and Norma came out and there were great hugs all round and I thought it was marvellous. He wanted to speak to his local people first. He'd already called home and spoken to the children. The phone was ringing constantly, then one call was answered by one of the campaign secretaries who said, "The White House is on the line." In fact, the President was ringing from Air Force One. John took his call. There was a kind of bedlam and excitement and a huge feeling of euphoria. There was a marvellous Britishness about it all. It was a relief the fight was over.

'The irony of it was that Mrs Thatcher ended up with more votes than any of them, and lost.'

It was significant also, Lady Blatch observes, that John Major did not win outright in that first ballot. He failed by two votes to get the fifty percent of the vote required to win without a further ballot. She says, 'If he had won by two votes, the kind of speeches the other two candidates would have made would have been quite different. I'm sure they would have been gracious and wished him luck, but the fact that they conceded that way meant that John was able to come back and thank them, and it set the tone for the new era.' This tone, Lady Blatch feels, is one of unity and cooperation. But she adds the warning that: 'Politics is fickle and he's not without his enemies. Fewer than most, but I would hesitate to say he's got none.'

John Major stepped from the haze of victory straight into a whirl of international travel. During the first week of December 1990 he went to Rome for the EEC summit, and a few days later flew to the US to meet President Bush. He was still riding high in the opinion polls but the House of Commons emptied as he gave his dry and sometimes evasive answers in the first Prime Minister's Question Time after Rome. Had Mrs Thatcher been behind the despatch box both sides of the House would have been packed, conflict would have raged, voices would have been raised to drown her out, the cabaret would have kept them on the edges of their seats until the Speaker called a halt. In John Major's hands Question Time was merely routine. But he was not yet sure enough of himself to ad lib. His curt and unrevealing statements, delivered in a monotone, drove MPs out to finish their Christmas cards. He asked friends, 'How was it?' and they said, 'Very good.' He was unhappy and replied, 'It could have been better.'

After the lull of Christmas, spent by the log fires amid green views of Chequers, he began his fiery baptism as war leader. He read himself into his job as usual, and his body language and off the cuff comments became more assured in content and in tone. His broadcast to the nation at the Gulf War's onset on January 16 1991, showed him in a new light: resolute, strong, calm, considered, compassionate. His stock climbed once more in the opinion polls. But the economic news was still black and observers still wondered if the new Prime Minister's shoulders would be broad enough for the burdens he would have to carry.

Slowly, however, the man from nowhere began to fill the great office of Prime Minister with his own firm presence. Who would have thought that exactly one hundred days after he reached the highest office, he would have been standing on a captured Iraqi tank in the Saudi desert, addressing Her Majesty's troops after their part in the successful Allied campaign, and doing so with the confidence of a natural leader? After a surprise detour of 1700 miles from his Moscow summit with Mikhail Gorbachev, and clad in khaki pants and an army sweater, he thanked them for their magnificent efforts and was mobbed in return.

As he returned home to face the real business of governing Britain and of meeting his economic deadline for a fast approaching election, he could not avoid reflecting on the fact that now the nation would begin to discover who John Major really was.

2

A LIFE OF SURPRISES

'But events are unpredictable and can take a nasty turn. You ought not to take too much for granted.'

THE EVENTS WHICH MADE JOHN MAJOR Prime Minister were sudden and overwhelming. They seemed to have a logic of their own despite the turmoil of their genesis. But then, things often happen to him suddenly and unexpectedly. Not randomly, not accidentally, but as a life pattern. The course of his entire life so far has been defined by sudden changes and impulsive decisions, both of his own and in the way events seem to operate around him. He aims, he plans, more carefully than most – but no one knows better than he how plans can be upset. For, as he said while discussing the future two years ago, 'Anything can happen and things are changing all the time.'

John Major, in a sense the reluctant Prime Minister, might like a quiet life, might like a routine that would allow more time with his family, a bit of cricket, evenings with friends. But his life is about something else and events in it have steered him, often brutally, along a course that seems predestined; events have opened doors to fulfilment of some other self, one that is driven, workaholic, ambitious. Are those events entirely external or are they triggered by unconscious processes within him, his inner will?

To those closest to John, his rapid progress from his election as MP for Huntingdon in 1979 to the moment he returned from Buckingham Palace as the newly accredited Prime Minister, seemed fated. Certainly in November 1990, as at any time during the preceding 47 years, John Major will say he had little choice at each stage of his career. And when there were alternatives, when there were moments when he might have taken some other path, external events often prevented him or else promoted his political destiny. To look back over John Major's life is clearly to see the powerful hand of fate at work.

His story, like all good ones, is full of conflict and complication, moments of despair and grief, joy and triumph. The hero suffers and at times falters in his purpose; he receives fresh inspiration, help, a new opportunity, or through his own grit and refusal to be defeated, overcomes. John Major has overcome. He has also languished. But his early fear of defeat has evolved into an indelible will to win. Outrageous fortune has given his life the cachet of a fictional hero's. Rags to riches? Not quite. But the journey from unskilled early school leaver living in Brixton to Conservative Prime Minister seems at times to have the fairy tale magic of a frog's metamorphosis into a prince. And, like all romantic heroes, John has been strengthened by the tribulations he has faced rather than by his successes. The intervention of sudden turns of fate in his life, often to his disadvantage, has been seminal in shaping his career. There have been accidents and near misses which have not changed the course of his life but may have altered his perspective, while other traumatic events have had a direct impact on the choices available to him and on his ultimate destination.

The circumstances surrounding his birth, for instance. 'I was a mistake,' he says, with a hint of apology. At the time he was born John's mother was 38, his father 64. Not so extraordinary today for such a couple to conceive a late baby, in 1943 it was much less likely.

Tom and Gwen Major had had three children before John: 'Thomas who died as a baby, Pat and Terry. The closest to John in age, Terry is eleven years older. He doesn't remember much of John as a child. 'The gap was too great,' he says. But he does remember something of his brother's difficult birth on March 29 1943.

Their parents were former circus and vaudeville performers, at that time running a garden ornament business and living in Worcester Park, Surrey, a London suburb in a cosy bungalow at 260 Longfellow Road. John was born in a nearby hospital, the St Helier in Carshalton, and as his mother was very ill at the time, the birth was a difficult one.

Terry recalls what happened. 'I remember my mother going into hospital to have John. She had double pneumonia and pleurisy, and I remember John coming home as a baby. Father said Mother was largely kept alive on bread and milk and brandy. John was perfectly healthy when he was born but became ill because he contracted something in the hospital. I remember his little ankles had marks all over them.

'My mother said, "Don't worry, that's where they gave him the blood transfusions." They gave him quite a few. It was a germ he'd picked up from a maternity nurse at the hospital that she didn't know she was carrying. She was distraught that she had given him this infection.'

John says, 'I still have scars on my ankles.' And when he continues, 'I nearly died,' there is a look about him, an intonation to the voice, that suggests he is keenly aware that he owes his survival and the whole extraordinary success story of the rest of his life to the intervention of fate in his earliest hours.

Now, as Prime Minister, he is a target for terrorism. But he once told me he would accept whatever comes, even death. One thing is clear: John Major survives, has survived, all the nasty corners of his life. Having survived his birth, and one or two serious accidents, he demonstrated his cool familiarity with deadly surprises when the IRA dropped a mortar in Number 10's garden. 'I think we had better continue in another place, gentlemen,' he said as they all gathered their papers and left the Cabinet Room whose windows had been fractured by the bomb.

This was not in fact the first time he had been close to an explosion. When he was a baby and still in the cradle, a German V2 rocket landed somewhere near the family home, scattering glass from a broken window on to the crocheted blanket that covered him. He remembers nothing of this – or at least, not consciously. Yet perhaps it is not too fanciful to suggest that his sang-froid under the mortar attack was based on subliminal memories of this earlier incident.

Once, he told me, on a Parliamentary visit to the
Middle East, he was almost killed by a rock thrown
by a Palestinian. 'I went there with a number of
Parliamentarians, Richard Needham and others. We
were in Israel and we got caught between some stone-
throwing Arabs and some rifle-shooting Israelis. I was
standing next to Ken Weetch and a huge rock was
thrown which came smashing into the side of the car
right between Ken and I. It would undoubtedly have
killed us. Then the Israelis fired back and we dived
under the car.' A bad experience? He says quietly, with
a slight shudder of distaste, 'It wasn't very great.'

There is regret still for the bad car accident in Nigeria
which deprived him of the enjoyment of playing a game
of cricket. 'It was never true that I would have been of
County Cricket standard, but I would have been a
good club player.'

Some friends think differently. Ian Cameron Black,
a friend since John's days at Standard Chartered Bank
and godfather to his son James, says: 'He has this
amazing ability. When he catches a ball he seems just
to stroke it out of the air.'

Jeffrey Archer comments, 'I bowled to him once,
and the way his body moved you could see the boy
knew how to do it properly.'

The accident happened in 1967, while John was in
Nigeria as a manager for Standard Chartered in the
city of Jos. He was driving with a friend when their
car went off the road. African roads are often tricky,
especially the local gravel on dirt variety. Cars can go
into uncontrolled slides on bends on the loose stones.
What precisely happened John does not remember,
only that, 'I'd been to the Jos clubhouse where they
showed films. Richard had been in the clubhouse

drinking Coca Cola. He was the other boy in the bank who shared the flat with me. He drove us home. The next thing I remember is lying on the verge, absolutely unable to move, with a fair amount of blood about and my clothes just torn to pieces. I realised I couldn't move at all. Richard was sitting beside me with his head in his hands, looking pretty white and shaken.

'I can remember lying there thinking very plainly, Oh God, I've done it this time. I was trying to move my hands and then I realised I could lean up slightly and that the main damage was to my legs.'

He had multiple fractures of the left leg. 'For quite some time I thought I'd lose it.' He came home, had several operations and spent about a year in bed or on crutches, lying around reading. He claims to have read all of Agatha Christie's works and to have become an expert at solving her crimes. The bank continued to pay his salary, for which he is grateful.

To this day he is never free from discomfort and often in considerable pain with his left leg. 'See how flat my knee is,' he said, holding it up for inspection. He admitted that the pain travels up his back and into his neck. As a result he is unable to play cricket or any other sport and is even prevented from enjoying a country walk, though he does enjoy going out at weekends. Jeffrey Archer says, 'About an hour is the limit. We went for a walk once in the forest and got lost and it took us about an hour and a half to get back and he was in quite a lot of pain then. He refused to ask anyone the way out of the forest because he said, "Look, I am the Chancellor of the Exchequer and this is my constituency. I can't admit I don't know my way around my own constituency." '

Less time playing cricket and more playing politics may have been a crucial factor in the progress of John's career during the late Sixties when he became a council candidate for the unlikely-sounding ward of Ferndale in the heart of the Brixton area of the Borough of Lambeth – the same place where, as a local resident (his family's first Brixton address was in Coldharbour Lane) and young Conservative in his teens, he had stood on a soap box and preached Conservative policies. 'We would be lynched now,' his friends say laughingly.

He had not expected to be elected for this tradition-ally Labour ward, but there was a Tory landslide in that year's local elections. Even the most solid Labour wards of the solidly Labour Brixton turned Tory. In the next two years John was to gain invaluable experi-ence in local government there, especially in the field of housing of which committee he became Chairman in 1970. Would continuing to have played cricket have interfered with this crucial step on the path to power?

The Nigerian accident was not in fact the first blow against his dreams of becoming a cricketer. This had been struck at about the same time as his first formative visit to the Houses of Parliament which awakened another, rather different dream. The period around 1956, when he was thirteen and a lacklustre pupil at Rutlish School, seems to have been of key importance in the turns of fate that were eventually to direct him on the path to Downing Street.

He passed his eleven plus exams and remembers, 'I think you had three choices of where you went and Rutlish was my first so we were quite pleased to have got it. When I was about thirteen and very keen on cricket, I decided I would like to go to a school where they played good cricket and Charterhouse was where they played the best.

'So at the age of thirteen an option came to take a scholarship examination and get into Charterhouse. I was quite keen to do that but I must say they (Rutlish masters) were not encouraging about it, largely because I'd been idle. I thought they were actually rather obstructive about it. So I didn't take the exam.' He adds with customary modesty: 'Perhaps I was too stupid to have passed, but anyway I didn't take it and I remember thinking then that it's a mistake to judge people superficially – not a mistake I like making myself, these days. It didn't help at the time.'

John's unease with his grammar school was connected with another turn of fate. Between the time of taking the eleven plus and entering Rutlish School in Wimbledon, the Major family had suffered a reversal of fortune. Terry Major tells the story of how their father's business got into difficulties: 'In the latter years after retiring his act, my father ran four revues and had them on the road. The garden ornament business came later. That was going well but my father had borrowed a sum of money and this was absorbed into the business. My father always did business on a handshake and everything had been agreed, but then the other party wanted their capital back and the family decision was to repay the money. Had we gone to court, it would have been found in my father's favour, but he was ill.

'It has been reported that this was an injudicious business deal but the only injudicious thing about it was that Father trusted someone and perhaps he shouldn't have. Anyway, the family decided the

money should be repaid, and the people were repaid.
My father was not the sort of man who would have
gone bankrupt and paid someone a few shillings in the
pound.'

So the comfortable bungalow in Worcester Park was
sold to repay the business debts and the family moved
to rented accommodation in Brixton. Today this is
one of the toughest parts of the bedraggled Borough
of Lambeth, but in earlier days Brixton was an area
popular with showbusiness people because the trams
from the West End, which continued running after
the theatres closed, used to terminate there. It would
have been a natural choice for a showbusiness couple
like the Majors to search there for a low rent flat to tide
them over until they could improve their finances.

But in the early fifties, Brixton was undergoing a
transformation from the setting of the jolly 'Lambeth
Walk' to the area of choice for an immigrant community. As London Transport, unable to find drivers
for its tube trains and buses after World War II, had
advertised for staff in the West Indies, hundreds
of Caribbean families had come to live in the area
where the Northern line, trams and buses that served
Central London had their depots and termini. The
new vitality to the area would have been a bonus for
the Major family who had no bias on class or colour.
John remembers the move as being 'something of an
adventure for a ten-year-old boy'.

But now, instead of travelling to the very middle-
class Rutlish School from the respectable suburb of
Worcester Park, John took the train from Brixton.
He blushed with discomfort when he spoke of his
embarrassment of having to have a grant to help
pay for his second-hand school uniform. There is

consciousness of disadvantage here, and it must have affected his relationships with his peers who came from more comfortable middle-class backgrounds.

John says the move had a powerful effect on his parents. It is not unreasonable to suppose that his schoolwork would have been adversely affected by this traumatic change of circumstances. Today such trauma, if identified, might well be dealt with by school counselling or visits to an educational psychologist. In the Fifties however one just got on with life, traumas and all. In an interview with Norma Major, I commented to her: 'If John had been given any therapy, you might today be married to a well-adjusted bank manager.' She laughed and reminded me of Somerset Maugham's short story 'The Verger'.

The Verger was sacked from the church where he worked when the Vicar discovered he couldn't write. So he started a business which was very successful. After many years he went to his bank to verify some papers and the bank manager too discovered he couldn't write. 'But you're such a successful businessman,' said the manager. 'Just think, you might have been even more successful had you been able to write.' 'No,' replied the man, 'I would still be a verger.'

John laughs at this story. He agrees that education can sometimes be a barrier to success, stifling originality, shaping minds according to a pattern. He says, 'There are too many people around with too much learning and not enough knowledge.' He adds soberly however that he thinks there is sometimes a use for academic training. The improvement of the state education system is in fact one of the concerns closest to his heart.

He is, of course, largely self-educated, but how exactly did he slip through the net of formal education? One thing that seems to have prevented his succeeding at school is that, 'It was a fairly firm school of the 1950s and very regimented. I hate authority. I hate regimentation of any kind . . . and perhaps the rather silly way of not being pushed was simply not to do the work.'

But there was another problem that may have turned the boy bright enough to have passed his eleven plus and to have attained his first choice of grammar school into a lacklustre student whose reports often said, 'Could do better' and 'Doesn't try'. He says: 'Part of the problem was that for a considerable period of time, I really couldn't see what was going on all that well, I hadn't got any glasses, and it was some time before we realised that.' And that would also have been a problem for a cricketer. Fate was already determining that John Major would not be able to pursue his dream of a white flannel future.

It seems odd that he should in fact have turned to a career in such marked contrast to a life of physical prowess in the open air. Politics, the stuff of smoke-filled rooms and mental callisthenics, was not however a fallback. Perhaps it was always in him? Even so, its first conscious manifestation in his life also came out of the blue. And hardly a Tory blue because the Fairy Godmother who opened this particular enchanted palace was the then Labour MP for Brixton, Marcus Lipton.

Lipton was a colourful character: Jewish, a barrister, and a Lieutenant-Colonel who served in the British Army in World War II and was afterwards elected MP for the safe Labour constituency of

Brixton in the landslide Labour victory of 1945. Always a backbencher, Lipton once told me that when he first went to the House, 'I wanted to be Prime Minister, every MP does.' MPs, it seems, want to be Prime Minister the way small boys want to drive fire engines. How ironic then that he unwittingly introduced a future Conservative Prime Minister to politics.

John recalls, 'I met him in St James's Church in Knatchbull Road. The vicar was a lovely old boy called J. Franklin Cheyne. He was small and bald and used to visit my mother a lot when she was ill – an absolutely super man. I just went along to help occasionally at church fêtes when I had nothing else to do. Marcus Lipton was an extremely good constituency MP. He turned up at church fêtes and he talked to me about politics. I suppose he didn't think someone from the middle of Brixton like that would necessarily be a Conservative, though he didn't ever ask me. So he invited me to the House of Commons to have a look around, which I did. I must have been thirteen then.'

John sat in the Strangers' Gallery and watched a debate. The whole experience hit him with the force of a cannon-ball. 'I was pretty clear I wanted to go back to the House of Commons. Indeed, so clear was I that I wouldn't actually go back very often and listen to the debates because it was too frustrating to go there and not be a part of it. I feared I might never get there.'

John did nothing about joining a political party but stumbled on unhappily through his schooldays until another formative event in his life – his decision to be an early school leaver. His father was now very ill and his mother not so well either, due to smoking-related asthma and bronchitis. His brother and sister were out at work and contributing to their parents' upkeep, but the family needed another income.

'I decided on an impulse to leave school after my sixteenth birthday.' John can't remember exactly when he took his 'O' levels. He thinks he may have left at Easter after the mocks and then come back to take the official exams in the summer.

Glen Knight, though not a friend of John's, is an old boy of Rutlish School who remembers him. Knight, a Labour supporter whose sister is a Labour councillor in Merton, was a year ahead of John, and, as he lived at Tooting, travelled on the same train to Wimbledon. He says the school was heavily academic and concerned with maintaining its status as a quasi-public school by achieving a high rate of university entrances. 'If you weren't a high flyer and going to go to university, they weren't interested in you.' He says the school 'had very poor teachers on the whole', though there were exceptions, such as the history master.

John enjoyed history and English literature, and sometimes mathematics. His decision to leave school, however, was more the result of family pressures than his lack of academic success. He claims never to have regretted it, yet admits that his lack of academic background made his life harder than it need have been.

He became aware very soon after leaving school that most avenues to interesting jobs were closed to him. The law, medicine, the higher reaches of the Civil Service, were not open to people without academic qualifications, particularly with the attitudes that existed in the late Fifties and early Sixties.

There was, at this time, a crushing sense of the failure of his recent school career; a keen sense of having been misjudged and underestimated. He was, however, aware that his school career did not remotely reflect what he was, what he thought, or what he thought he could do. As the realities struck home he realised he would have to work extremely hard to make up for the fact that he had left school without any qualifications, that he had no hope of going to university and getting a foothold in any decent career. He would have to start from the outside.

Thus the first and dominating need was to get a job and bring money into the family. Not, he says, 'because I wanted to become wealthy, but because the family needed the money'. The inadequacy he must have felt, the painfulness of his position and his family's situation at that time, is evident as he looks back.

Speaking in a soft measured tone that conveys sadness, he recalls, 'I got a job with Price Forbes. I remember I was very nervous, very poorly dressed. I had a suit on that I'd got from . . .' and here he hesitated, swallowed and went on '. . . purchased for a very modest sum.' He continues, not trying at all to make light of that awkward youth and his discomfort both in the suit and the situation: 'It was the first suit I'd ever had. It wasn't a great fit and I wasn't very self-confident. I was in a strange element. I wasn't very sure what to do.' A sense of loneliness emanates from him. One can almost see again the shy boy exposed to an alien world in which he found no familiar landmark. Though he has a lively sense of humour and will often laugh and make jokes at his own expense, it seems John Major cannot laugh or even pretend to laugh at the expense of the boy he once was that boy's griefs are still too real, too alive in him, to be treated humorously.

He conveys too without self-pity what it was like to feel himself a misfit, at odds with a world in which he would now have to make his way without the weapons of class or money or qualifications that he knew others had. As someone cast out of a middle-class lifestyle, he was not even working-class, could not bond himself to that tough culture that is a protection against the harshness of being at the bottom and having no power other than the sheer spirit of survival.

Perhaps this was another reason for his joining a political party. One day in 1959, a young man knocked on the door of the housing estate in Burton Road, Lambeth, where the Majors were then living. John came to the door and was canvassed by the Conservative Party. He joined on the spot. This was not a turning point, more an event that had been long coming: but it is interesting that he had to be asked. He had not gone out and searched for the party. It had come to him. Just as the nominations and election to the party's leadership also came to him, after an even longer period of gestation.

After a year at Price Forbes, he changed jobs to help his brother make garden ornaments in the business which his father had once owned, but which had been sold and was now operated by someone else. 'I earned a lot more there, because I knew a fair amount about it, and it was while I was there that I started studying again. I realised I would have to take more school exams.' It was like a penance, a discipline which he set himself, perhaps to prove that he could do it, that he was really not the failure his school career's bad end had made him out to be.

He began studying for 'O' levels by correspondence course and eventually passed six: English language, English literature, history, mathematics, British constitution and economics. To achieve this, 'I started the habit of getting up at five o'clock in the morning.' This is a habit he has resorted to many times for long periods whenever he has wanted to achieve something. In that sense he has never simply waited for the prizes to come to him, without first working for them as hard as is humanly possible.

He was a consistently early riser while in the Cabinet, and now as Prime Minister. He cat naps in the car, and sometimes during the day sneaks a sleep, as for instance during the Gulf War when, night after night, his few hours of rest were disturbed by news from his commanders. But he has trained himself to manage on little sleep and in this rivals his predecessor. Mrs Thatcher used to manage on five hours nightly with a catch-up ten-hour night on Saturdays. During the period when he was seventeen and eighteen John Major was 'getting up at 5 o'clock in the morning because I was trying to combine three things: doing some studying, working quite long hours at my job because there was a lot to be done, and beginning to get a grounding in politics which was taking every evening. So they were long days, up at five and rarely in bed before midnight, in order to get those three things in at the same time.'

This, then, is where fate gave him his grounding in the style of work and effort needed to sustain him throughout the slow difficult days of getting his first foothold in politics, and then living through the extraordinary pressures of learning and carrying out the three most senior Cabinet posts – Foreign

Secretary, Chancellor and Prime Minister – in just over one year.

He says that this pattern of life went on for some time. Then he says quietly, again sadly, 'I drifted out of that job into a series of other jobs. At one stage I was unemployed for a while. It was because my parents were both rather ill and somebody had to look after them, and I was earning less than my brother and sister so it had to be me. After I'd been unemployed for a few weeks, people wondered why and then I couldn't get a job. I can't remember how long that went on for – not less than nine months, not more than fifteen, but that sort of period.'

His father died on March 27 1962, aged 82, when John was two days short of 19. His father had been ill for some time, but he had always been a powerful presence and John now had to pass through a period of grieving. The family continued to live together in a house on the Minet Estate on Burton Road, not far from the Oval, and now John had to find another job.

He says, 'It was the London Electricity Board that actually gave me the opportunity and took me back in, and I moved from there to the old District Bank and started taking the Banking Diploma. That was quite a mercenary decision. I realised that was a qualification I could get without being articled, that I could get whilst working and continuing politics, and that I could take in stages. By and large, I took the exams two at a time at six-monthly intervals. So I went back to my old habit of getting up at five in the morning – it was the best time to study – and politics in the evening. I got through the first time and it really was quite mercenary because I knew I needed a qualification.

I knew I needed a reasonable background. I needed a
reasonable job in case politics failed, and I also knew
that without that, the chances of getting into politics
were that much more difficult. So I suppose you could
say it was quite mercenary.'

He mentions the mercenariness of his motives so
often that it seems he has a sense of guilt about
them. On other occasions he has said repeatedly
that he does things because he is interested in
them not because of where they might lead him.
Was this 'mercenary' decision uncharacteristic then?
The answer will emerge in the next chapter. For the
moment it seems enough to say that all this hard work
was the result of an intense desire to make up for what
he had lost by leaving school without qualifications,
to substitute practicality and slog for dreams, and to
move himself forward into a position with greater
opportunities. Many finding themselves in the same
situation succumb to a drifter's life. Others, blaming
society for their ills, opt for crime. Not so John Major.
Because of his nature and upbringing, his response was
to take responsibility for his own fate and to work his
way out of the mess with a clear aim and strategy. This
was to be the way he handled situations at every stage
in his life when fate seemed to be against him.

His attitude in response to the difficult circumstances that had prevented him from succeeding
at school, and which had even brought about the
impulsive decision to leave before taking his 'O'
levels, was a remarkably calculated and determined
one. During the period between his sixteenth birthday on March 29 1959, when he decided to leave
school to help earn money for the family, and his
successfully achieving his banking qualifications in

his early twenties, John Major may have been down but he was never out. His spirit showed the true 'On Yer Bike' grit which is an essential ingredient of his character and whole philosophy of life.

Now the banking credentials he was acquiring at the rate of two exams per year gave him the scope to apply for a job he saw advertised in 1966. This was for qualified bankers interested in serving in the then Standard Bank's overseas branches.

He applied on impulse because he wanted to go abroad for a while. He was offered a post in Jos, Nigeria and went out there in December that year, nine months after the General Election in which Harold Wilson won a 97-seat majority. He says, 'I took the decison to go to Nigeria on impulse. I've never regretted it.' He had solid reasons. 'I was very conscious that I needed the experience of working abroad. Secondly I wanted to go to Africa – I wanted to see what it was like. And thirdly it was a possibility of earning some more money. We got paid a lot better there. I was saving £100 a month which was a lot of money then.'

But of course it was here – where he chose perhaps temporarily to escape his political destiny, immersing himself in that easeful limited world of white man's burden, drinks at the club and local cricket matches under the huge skies; where the silence which he loved enclosed him on this cool plateau far from the seething, joyful, raucous vitality of West Africa's steaming cities – here that he was interrupted from distraction by a violent event. The accident brought the brief African interlude to a close after only seven months. John's return to London enforced a period of reading and reflection and led to the opening of a new chapter in his political life.

In May 1968 John Roy Major was elected as one of three Tory councillors to represent Ferndale Ward in the heart of black urban Brixton. That year's election results reflected the turning tide of British public opinion away from Labour and back to the Tories. The Brixton result may also have been affected by racialist considerations, coming as it did during the period immediately following Enoch Powell's 'rivers of blood' speech. People who were afraid of the encroachment of other races on their home ground felt the Tories would help them change the picture. Later there were to be problems with local Tories who used the race issue as a political lever.

But for the moment there was unalloyed joy at the election of the 25-year-old John Major as one of 57 Conservative councillors out of 60, an event for which, despite the apparent hopelessness of their efforts, the local Tories had been striving for many years. They felt that hard work and organisation was the backbone of their surprising success, though it is possible, as on so many similar occasions of nationwide electoral swings, that the electoral force would have been with them even if they had done no work at all! What the victory did prove was that if you canvass between elections, attend to case work and organise to get your vote out, you can benefit from the swing even in wards like Ferndale, which they were frankly surprised to win.

John Major's close friend of those days, Clive Jones, who was elected at the same time for a ward in the Norwood constituency, thinks the reason John stood in Ferndale was that by the time he had recovered from the car accident, all the more easily winnable wards had selected their candidates. Only Ferndale was left.

So John, during daylight hours busy advancing his career with the Standard Bank and in the evenings slogging away at local politics, was elected almost by accident. Laughing, he describes the picture of Tory politics in Brixton as one which often looked quite hopeless. 'Brixton was always the end of the Borough that lost us Lambeth Council. They did magnificently well holding their seats in Norwood and Streatham but Brixton was a complete shambles. We were always contesting seats in Brixton but even getting on to the council seemed a million light years away.'

The exhilaration of winning sent him shinning up a lamp-post that night. A friend from those days, Peter Golds, describes what happened. 'We came out of the count and walked up Brixton Road in very high spirits. We wanted to tell this older lady who had done a lot of work for John in Ferndale Ward that John had won. We went up her street which was just off Coldharbour Lane. It was very late in the evening and we knew she would be in bed and wouldn't hear the doorbell. John shinned up a lamp-post and started to throw stones at her bedroom window, at which point two PCs came along, saying: "Now, now, what's going on 'ere?" And John had to explain that he was the new Conservative councillor.'

Hands-on experience of local politics in action following this unlikely election continued for three years. At first John was just one of 57 Conservative and three Labour councillors comprising the new Lambeth Council.

Ken Livingstone, the well-known Labour MP and former Lambeth councillor during the Seventies, remembers the sudden appearance of what he calls, without much originality, 'all these grey young Tories'. He does not remember distinguishing John Major from the others. 'They all looked alike.'

John's interest in housing took him on to the Housing Committee and in 1970 he became Chairman. This opportunity helped broaden his experience and gave him credentials which, at another time, would have been impossible to attain in Brixton for it is as unlikely to vote Tory as any other poor working-class inner city area. And yet that experience in a crumbling, deprived, inner city area turned out to be so much more valuable to a rising Conservative politician than a smooth ride in a middle-class suburb. It was this time as a local councillor in Brixton which eventually provided Great Britain, twenty years on, with a Conservative Prime Minister who understands urban deprivation as well as he understands the economic measures needed to tackle its causes.

In the spring of 1970, during the GLC elections, John met Norma Johnson. This was another fateful moment, and one which both appear to have recognised immediately for what it was. Both have told me that it was love at first sight and although there were some interesting courtship strategies (see Chapter 7) played out between them, in which Norma made much of the running, John says he made up his mind very quickly that he would marry her. They were engaged within three weeks of meeting and married in six months. John says, 'I took the decision to marry Norma within a few days of meeting her, and I think it was the best decision of my life.'

Every rising male politician needs the right wife. Norma was not a political woman but interested enough in politics to have been helping at the elections. The main thing was that she was Conservative and it may also have helped that she always saw herself as a homemaker rather than a career woman. She would obviously provide loyal and competent backup to the man who spent so much of his free time on politics that he barely even stopped to eat and had, at that stage, not even furnished his flat. Norma was to be the perfect helpmeet. Not only that, but they were in love with each other. What more could any ambitious politician want?

So now, as a rising young City banker and Tory councillor with the perfect wife, John Major was well placed to try for a Parliamentary seat, the thing for which he had been dreaming and planning and working since that day when, aged 13, he looked down at the Conservative Government benches from the Strangers' Gallery of the House of Commons. Fate seemed to be disposing things in his favour. But then, when everything seemed to be going so well, there were no sudden turns of fate in the next few years to help him on his way, but rather the opposite. John plodded with tortoise-like persistence through the wastelands of solidly Labour St Pancras North as their Conservative Prospective Parliamentary Candidate. He stood there in the two elections of 1974 and was said to be surprised that after all his work his vote was no more and no less than the national percentage for the Tories.

There were no miracle Tory landslides to unseat left-wing MP Jock Stallard. When, soon after, John began hunting for a more winnable seat, he seemed to get nowhere. The main reason, it appears, was that his CV containing details of his excellent experience as a councillor, Chairman of Housing and three-year slog in a Labour heartland, remained in Central Office's files while that of another John Major, similarly a councillor but otherwise lacking John's credentials, was being sent out instead. The mistake was discovered after two despondent years in which John appeared to be getting nowhere, by Jean Lucas, now agent for Putney.

At the time Putney was reselecting in readiness for a general election in the late Seventies and Jean, who had asked for John Major's particulars, had received those of his namesake. She rang John and said, 'Why don't you put all your council experience into your CV?' He replied, 'But I have,' and then discovered the error and put it right. After this he received many more invitations to interview and was shortlisted frequently. But could it be that fate had kept him on the back burner of selection processes in this curious way so that it could save him up for something much better?

Prime Ministers need very safe seats so that they don't have to keep worrying about their majorities while they run the country. They cannot afford to nurse their constituencies the way backbenchers can. A marginal or even a moderately safe seat would not have been a good basis for a Cabinet career, let alone for the future occupant of Number 10. Huntingdon, even before John became its member, was one of the nation's safest Conservative-held seats. Now, thanks to his popularity, it is safer still.

In the summer of 1976, the seat became available. John says, 'Norma thinks it was fate that I got Huntingdon. She was convinced I would.' Sir David Renton, the QC, Knight and Privy Councillor who had been Huntingdon's MP since 1945, was approaching his seventieth birthday and had decided not to stand

at the next election. John had been on the market as
a candidate for almost two years and had not as yet,
despite discovering the muddle over his namesake
and then enduring much toing and froing to selection
meetings, found a seat. Huntingdon (before the
boundary redrawing of the early Seventies known
as Huntingdonshire) was a typical shire constituency
with a comfortable Tory majority, usually around
10,000 votes. It had a rather more distinguished than
usual Knight of the Shires, an MP who had held junior
ministerial office in the Macmillan governments of
the late Fifties and early Sixties. Sir David Renton,
now Lord Renton, was the sort of MP with whom
old-style rural Tories, landowners, small businessmen
and others, were most familiar. He was married to the
daughter of an Irish peer, a glamorous blonde who
combined personality with social graces and was the
life and soul of constituency party activities.

This was the seat for which John may at first have
appeared an awkward choice. With his exclusively
inner city experience of life and politics, his CV
might suggest he was hardly appropriate for an East
Anglian rural constituency complete with squirearchy.
However, as it turned out he was truly tailor made for
the place, and this presumably is why he was selected
from an initial list of more than 270 applicants.
Andrew Thomson, then Agent for the constituency,
remembers the selection procedures were many and
exhaustive. They continued from the summer when
Sir David intimated his retirement to December
1976 when John was adopted as the new prospective
Parliamentary candidate.

Thomson, who remained with Huntingdon for five
and a half years after John's selection before going to

Finchley as agent for Mrs Thatcher, explains why John Major succeeded in getting Huntingdon against very stiff opposition from much more experienced and well-known candidates such as Alan Hazelhurst, the Marquis of Douro, Jock Bruce-Gardyne, Peter Brooke, Michael Howard and Chris Patten. Many were MPs who had lost their seats in the 1974 election; others were simply very high quality candidates with good experience, the front runners among whom are now MPs and Ministers. Andy Thomson says that it took some time to whittle the list down to a final shortlist of four, but at each step of the selection procedure, 'This chap Major kept appearing at each process and on each list. Looking back, one can see why.'

One reason was that the demography of the constituency was rapidly changing. London overspill was effectively drowning out the old rural population and bringing to the area new, mainly young, voters, largely London commuters with new values and aspirations. In 1966, the electorate of the old Huntingdonshire constituency was 53,745. By 1970 it had become 66,602. By 1974 it was 79,724, was then reduced by a boundary change, but by 1979 was back over 80,000 and still growing. Thomson says, 'Forty thousand overspill were now living with fifty thousand local people. Therefore in every walk of life there was the uneasy feeling: "They've taken over our badminton club, our drama group, our golf club." Some of it was agreements with the GLC, some of it was young people getting into the car and driving for an hour and finding they could buy a house for £8,000, some of it was local industries bringing in people. They were all young and had young families. The issue was, how do you make town and country talk, how do you make London get on with Huntingdon?'

Finally the list was down to four for consideration on December 3 1976: Jock Bruce-Gardyne, Alan Hazelhurst, Charles Douro and John Major. In his broad Glasgow accent, Thomson recalls, 'The final speech was drawn by lots and John was last. Alan Hazelhurst was third. Alan's speech was brilliant and I thought, "He's got it. The other two are not in the running." Then Major arrived and he just swept it on the first vote. I have been asked a dozen times why. Well, he was 33, had two young children and an attractive wife, was personal assistant to Anthony Barber who was Chairman of Standard Chartered Bank at the time, he'd been a councillor and had fought a constituency in a hard part of London, and he looked like an identikit candidate for the Seventies.

'But, let me tell you a story – it was a very emotional moment for John and Norma after the votes were counted. John stood up – enormous applause in the hall – and he rather shakily said, "It's a long way from the back streets of Brixton to the green fields of Huntingdon." Then a chap got up who lived in a very splendid house locally, a very well-known character, and he said, "It may be a long way from the streets of Brixton to the green fields of Huntingdon, but let me tell you, many of us here tonight have followed that route." There was absolute uproar and it only dawned on me then that what had happened during the last four or five years was that the constituency executive had come to reflect the new electorate. So that was one of the main factors.'

So John Major, skills and experience aside, was the face that fitted. He had demonstrated that uncanny knack of being the right person in the right place at the right time that was to manifest itself even more tellingly during the 14 years between his adoption meeting at Huntingdon and his election as leader of the Conservative Party.

Andy Thomson says that as soon as John was elected as MP for Huntingdon in May 1979: 'I told Norma, "That's the first step to the Cabinet." ' Norma, he says, 'looked surprised'.

But John did not surprise or disappoint his Agent. He began that slow climb up the ladder of ministerial appointments that was to accelerate into a rapid sprint to the top. The first appointment in the Whips' Office led to another significant turn of fate, an event that could, like others in his life, have gone as badly as it went well. John was present at a whips' dinner at Brooks's Club in the early Eighties. John Wakeham was Chief Whip at the time and he recalls: 'What happened was that the PM was banging on about tax exemptions, and John interjected with, "I do not think that we have persuaded the public or the electorate about the advantages of tax exemptions and reductions." Mrs Thatcher took this to mean he was against it. He actually said what he meant – that he supported the policy but believed that the message wasn't being received. She thought otherwise. They argued and he held his own. It wasn't what a whip would usually do.'

Afterwards Denis Thatcher came up to John and slapped him on the back, saying, 'Well done. That will have done the old girl a lot of good. She loves an argument.' John says that a few days later Mrs Thatcher rang up and was very friendly and not long after that he was promoted to Parliamentary

Under Secretary at the Department of Health and Social Security; his first, if very junior, ministerial job. However, immediately after the fateful dinner, he was worried and unhappy.

John Wakeham says, 'I talked to him afterwards and he thought he had ruined his political career. He said, "Oh God, I've buggered it now." I said, "Don't worry. I'll have a word with the Prime Minister," and I did.' He chuckles. 'A year or two later, in my retirement speech at the same club, I said how I remembered happy times at the club and dinners with the Prime Minister which were very happy events, with just the occasional sound of a whip committing suicide!'

But Mrs Thatcher had now noticed John Major and, as the friendly telephone call a few days later showed, bore him no ill-will. Rather, the reverse. John told me, 'She doesn't like wimps,' but it was later, according to Wakeham, that the Prime Minister really began to realise John's qualities. He says, 'I don't think she recognised him at that stage for being as good as he was. I think it came when he was a Junior Minister at the DHSS which is the most arduous job as you have to deal with hundreds of letters from Members of Parliament about pensions and hospitals and boring matters. It isn't the job men destined for greatness usually get. But he did extremely well and Norman Fowler was keen to have him promoted, and then he started to come to various Cabinet committees at which she was presiding and it was at those that she really saw his value because he was so well prepared, so clear in his arguments, that he could be seen by her to be someone of quality.'

Fate was working with good material. John Major never seems to have failed to make good use of an opportunity. He prepared himself, as his habit was and still is, by informing himself exhaustively of the factual background to every situation, all the time working and striving towards an objective that was never obvious. He never seemed overly ambitious, but always promising. Every position was attained because he was recognised by those around him to be so good. There seemed nothing unusual or fated about his steady progress and the growth of his reputation among those who saw the daily evidence of his hard work, accurate diagnoses and problem-solving techniques.

It was after the general election of 1987 that John Major came into the Cabinet in his own right. John Wakeham says: 'I had told the Prime Minister when I was retiring as Chief Whip, "This is the guy I want to be Chief Whip." She made no comment but decided he was better in the Treasury.'

By this time Mrs Thatcher had already decided John Major was so promising that he should be given a wide range of experience and the job of Chief Secretary was one to which his background and skills were ideally suited. This was a key job whose value to him as Prime Minister may well have been in Mrs Thatcher's mind even then. If fate was busy in his life at that point, it was in league with the Iron Lady.

But this was in no way a jumping-off point for his next appointment. No one could reasonably have anticipated what would happen in July 1989 after Mrs Thatcher, Geoffrey Howe and Nigel Lawson returned from the EEC summit in Madrid. The story has been told in Chapter 1, but the Prime Minister's reshuffle after the sacking of Geoffrey Howe posed her some difficult problems.

Press speculation was rife and John Major was unsure of what would happen to him. He was being tipped for Transport, Environment, even Trade and Industry.

Once the reshuffle was underway, Ministers nervously prepared themselves for changes. From early that morning, calls from Number 10 put some frazzled Ministerial nerves at rest. But not John Major's. On the day of the reshuffle he was lunching with Godfrey Barker, a member of the *Daily Telegraph*'s political staff and also an old friend of one of John's closest friends, Jeffrey Archer.

Barker says, 'I had spotted John as a high flyer some time before and sought him out. We had lunch together fairly often.' So the two were on easy terms and there was no strain between them of the sort there might have been on a day such as this between a Minister and a journalist less well known to him. Even so, by 1 pm, when the two men sat down at their table in The Ritz's lovely dining room overlooking Green Park, John was tense with anticipation. Finding themselves about to be seated at a table next to Norman Fowler, they asked to be moved and eventually settled in a corner near the window where they could chat discreetly without danger of being overheard. John had left word of his whereabouts in case there was a call from the Prime Minister, but throughout lunch the absence of any such call was clearly making him uneasy.

Barker recalls, 'We talked of nothing else but what job he would be offered. John's main position was that he thought the Prime Minister would leave him where he was as Chief Secretary. He had been there two years and was generally thought to be doing well in the job.

The only other job which we thought possible was Transport.'

This was the area where, in 1989, trouble was mounting. Road, rail and airport jams had been a feature of the summer of that year, to which the twice-weekly tube and bus strikes were an added pressure. The Clapham rail crash and the Zeebrugge ferry disaster were two other dramatic incidents which helped point the finger at the need for an imaginative reorganisation of transport policy and reallocation of expenditures. The latter was something for which John, as Treasury Secretary, had shown he had a talent.

'As the lunch wore on and still no call came, John, who had been making a very good case for being kept in his current job, then began making a case for the Prime Minister moving him to Transport,' Barker recalls. By the time lunch ended there had been no call. John went back to his office in the Treasury, a large, square, oak-pannelled room with windows overlooking Parliament Square and the House of Commons. He busied himself for about an hour. Then the Prime Minister rang and asked him to go over to Number 10. He walked up Parliament Street and into Downing Street in a state of contained tension. Outwardly calm as usual, there was nevertheless a slope to his shoulders that suggested uncertainty. When he was shown into the Prime Minister's flower-filled study and asked to sit down, he received the bombshell: he was offered the Foreign Office. Whatever was fate up to now?

It was extraordinary. No one, even those closest to the Prime Minister, could understand what motivated her to give John Major one of the two most senior offices of state. Two months after he had numbly accepted the last job on earth he ever expected, his expression and gestures in conversation revealed that the position he really coveted was the Chancellor's.

But that, despite constant newspaper rumours of his pending resignation to take up a top City job, was still occupied by Nigel Lawson. Howe's was the head on the block that day. He was the one who had, it seemed, been offered the Home Office and turned it down so that Douglas Hurd, the man who had long dreamed of becoming Foreign Secretary, could have been offered the Foreign Office. If Howe had accepted Hurd's job at the Home Office then John might well have remained as Chief Secretary until Nigel Lawson's resignation a few months later.

So this time his fate had probably hung on Geoffrey Howe's answer. When the Prime Minister told Howe it was curtains for him as Foreign Secretary, he had taken instead the option of becoming Deputy Prime Minister and Leader of the House. Was that because he considered becoming Mrs Thatcher's deputy made it more likely that he would inherit her throne should she fall under the hooves of some stalking horse come that or the following November? Only Geoffrey Howe, and perhaps his wife, know the answer to that one.

There had been more surprising appointments than John's as Foreign Secretary. When, a decade earlier, Jim Callaghan made the relatively junior David Owen Foreign Secretary aged 40, it caused as much of a stir. But the comments on John Major's appointment exaggerated the fact that this was not the most appropriate job he might have been offered. Friends think he was poleaxed by the appointment. Norma was distressed not only because of the amount of travelling he would now have to do, leaving her at home with the family, but at the security arrangements that were to be imposed on their privacy. In the event, John simply shrugged, accepted the hand of fate and started reading himself into the job.

Of course, that period in the Foreign Office gave him, with his intense capacity for swift absorption of facts and situations, a crash course in British diplomacy as it was managed by the mandarin breed of the FO that now stands him in good stead as Prime Minister, dealing with many crucial international issues. In fact, the emphasis of his premiership – with the reshaping of international power balances between East and West, and in the Middle East, and the accelerating development of political, economic and currency harmonies within the EEC – is probably more on foreign than domestic issues. This grounding was brief but of crucial value.

He is unhappy about the things that were written at the time, and later when he had moved on to his next job. For he was only Foreign Secretary for three and a half months before the next great turn of fate. Not knowing that, he had at least to seem grateful at being offered that great prize of statesmen, the Foreign Office, and to work himself into it. But did he enjoy this period?

In a discussion about the day he became Chancellor he said how much he regretted not being longer at the Foreign Office. There seemed to be genuine regret, irritation and frustration that he had not had time to work himself in there, to show that this too was a job he could master. He hates to be thought to have failed.

Robert Atkins enthuses: 'He's a man who briefs himself up to the eyeballs and has a very good memory. He reads all his papers. He has the skill

– essential in a Minister – of being able to spot the problems, or spot the political nuance, and act on that.'

That summer of 1989, Atkins says, 'Norma was wanting a break and my wife said to her, "Okay, we'll fix it." And we went to Spain to a friend's house, and he sat all day reading through boxes. Now I was required to sit alongside him, which in fact I did because I don't like the sun very much, and I was reading my Macmillan memoirs and every so often throwing things at him, and every so often he was throwing things at me which was a convivial way of spending the time. Our respective families sat in the shade and he just read his way through papers.'

When asked whether he felt at ease at the Foreign Office, John replied as if rising to a challenge, 'Well, let's talk about the Foreign Office. It was a great shock when I went there. I didn't expect to go to the Foreign Office at all, but I found nothing but friendliness when I was there. I knew very little about it. It was one job for which all the other things I'd done hadn't particularly prepared me, except I knew a good deal more about the world than people thought. I had worked for an international bank with interests all over the world and I had travelled a good deal more widely than was thought. The rather sneering comments that I hadn't got a passport and I didn't know where the Isle of Wight was were not wholly true. In fact, they weren't true at all! I'd spent a good deal of time abroad and I knew a good deal about the politics of all those countries and their business establishment, so that wasn't difficult.

'But I wasn't familiar with the intricacies of diplomacy, and so I went to Tristan Garel-Jones's house (in Spain) and sat there all through August. From seven o'clock in the morning until very late at night, I was just sitting there with piles and piles of papers, just reading myself into everything you possibly could read yourself into. Not just what the problem is but how the problem arose, who takes which particular view of it, how much is historical, how much to do with direct commercial interests, what are the options – all the very professional background that the Foreign Office provides with such skill. So I spent the whole of August doing nothing else but absorbing that, day after day.'

There was quiet anger behind his words as, speaking steadily and evenly, without pausing to rethink or alter a phrase, he continued, 'Then, September and October were very busy months, extremely busy months, and if you actually look at the press of the day nothing went wrong. Everything went right and the meetings were actually rather good, and I felt that it was coming along extremely well.'

It was true that the citizens of Hong Kong found him likeable and trustworthy and he was already offering to allow key passport holders the right to live in Britain. But the East was the focus of confusion after the upheavals on the Chinese mainland, particularly the massacre at Tiananmen Square the previous June. Already in July and early August, John had tough-talked the Chinese Government over Hong Kong following their crack down on the student democracy movement.

He had become involved with the problem of the Vietnamese boat people, more than 50,000 of whom were then crowded into hideous camps in Hong Kong and threatened with forcible repatriation because no other countries would take them. In September he had talks over them with US Secretary of State Baker in Paris. He visited the US to discuss a number of issues which included the boat people and the Cocaine Wars in Colombia in which the British SAS were involved. He had also welcomed the possible restoration of diplomatic relations with Argentina though he questioned the timetable for that event.

He impressed everyone he dealt with as courteous and considerate, even if not quite the old breed of mandarin stock favoured by the Foreign Office. He told me, 'I was a change at the Foreign Office, that is true. They weren't used to someone who moved out of the large room and into a small ante-room because it was nearer the private office and had a larger desk on which to spread papers out.' This was indeed odd. The Foreign Secretary's room is one of the grandest available to any Minister. A huge, high-ceilinged, football pitch of a room, perhaps fifty feet by forty, with rows of high sash windows on two sides, it is on the corner of the first floor of the massive Foreign and Commonwealth building, overlooking St James's Park and Horse Guards Parade. It is decorated with sage green wallpaper printed with large and small four-pointed gilt stars and furnished with heavy, leather-upholstered chairs and sofas and solid mahogany desks, tables and bookcases. It must be one of the least comfortable but most desirable rooms in government.

The fact that John Major spurned it says a great deal about his dislike of grandeur, his preference for practicality, and of the sort of disturbing effect he must have had on the Foreign Office, a ministry in which

the grand old way of doing things dies hard and one
in which the civil servants, more than in any other
ministry, expect their advice to the incoming Cabinet
Minister to prevail over any whims of his own. Even
his then Minister of State, William Waldegrave, had
reservations. 'William,' I was told by one observer,
'is an aristocrat, son of a viscount. He thought John
couldn't possibly understand diplomacy because he
didn't come from the right stock.'

No wonder that John Major surprised them. 'They
weren't used to having meetings in which we actually
discussed the issues and tossed ideas around before
deciding what would happen, and they were a bit
startled when I met ambassadors in shirt sleeves when
it was warm. But then the ambassadors were equally
happy to take their jackets off as well. And there
were a few people at the Foreign Office who were
very pleased with the organisational changes we were
just putting into place. It was only after I'd gone that,
for one reason or another, this drip feed of malevolent
publicity began. But I did enjoy the Foreign Office. I
wasn't fully at home there because I was there such a
short time and you aren't fully at home in any job for a
short while. My first three months as Chief Secretary
were the hardest I've ever known in my life. It takes a
while to work yourself in.'

By early September, after the great read-in at Tristan
Garel-Jones's house in Spain, he felt more confident.
He aroused interest by his comments on apartheid,
saying it was time to 'dismantle' the system and
adding, 'It does not deserve to survive and it must
not. Seventy per cent of white voters want change
and so do one hundred percent of those not permitted
to vote. That is a formidable mandate.' With that

statement going before him he was welcomed with interest by the Commonwealth Heads of Government in Kuala Lumpur in October.

The events there are part of the story of his wider viewpoint and preparation for the premiership told in Chapter 8. For the moment, John Major was beginning to find his feet as Foreign Secretary. He was imposing his own style inside the Foreign Office, playing it by the book as far as diplomacy went and yet with his own distinct moral edge. This created the strong impression that, in time, this particular Foreign Secretary would start to lead foreign policy according to his own world view. That is what is happening now that he is Prime Minister. Slowly, gradually, the Major view of world politics is emerging.

It was very soon time for the next twist of fate in John Major's extraordinary career. He was about to be switched away from foreign affairs in another of those marionette moves that have so often been a feature of his life of surprises. His period as Foreign Secretary was not long enough to show him in any distinctive light or to reveal much independent thought on his part to observers. Though that would have come: he was planning a speech to coincide with the thirty-year anniversary of Macmillan's 'Winds of Change' speech at Cape Town in March 1960.

So what in fact happened on the day Nigel Lawson resigned as Chancellor? 'We'd just come back from Kuala Lumpur. The Tuesday after, Mrs Thatcher was reporting to the House and I was sitting beside her. We went into her room afterwards and she told me then that Nigel had told her he was going to resign and that she had been trying to dissuade him but couldn't. So I said, "Look, I know Nigel very well.

Shall I go and see him?" She said she thought it was too late.'

Norman Lamont, currently Chancellor but in those days Financial Secretary, had been with Lawson for much of the day trying to dissuade him from resigning. When asked if he thought Mrs Thatcher was in any way relieved that Nigel Lawson was finally going after the two years or more of conflict over economic policy, John replied, 'No, she wasn't glad, she said she was very sorry, but if Nigel did go, it would definitely be now.' It would appear from this curious statement that the Chancellor and the Prime Minister had reached a final impasse and that she was unlikely to give way at this point or any other to Lawson's ultimatum on Sir Alan Walters.

John further recalls, 'She said she was very sorry but she didn't want to lose me from the Foreign Office back to the Treasury earlier than I had expected to do so. So I went back to the Foreign Office and waited for an hour or so to see what happened. Then she phoned me up and asked me to go across and see her.'

He was not, in the event, excited about the prospect of becoming Chancellor. 'It was a job I'd always wanted, but I wasn't excited because I knew that three and a half months at the Foreign Office were not enough to have settled in, and I knew instinctively that it would be misrepresented and misreported ever after because I'd only been there for such a short time. And so it has proved.'

John Major had leaped from the job of Chief Secretary, the most junior Cabinet position, which he had held for two years from the summer of 1987, into the job of his dreams, Chancellor of the Exchequer, and had done so with a seemingly extraordinary rush of good luck. Yet was it that? The job changes of those years dated from Mrs Thatcher's decision to make Major what Lord Carrington called 'her heir apparent'. She had, in that time, not entirely by her own management but rather by her response to events caused mainly by Howe and Lawson, been able to give her heir experience of three vital areas of governance. First, as Treasury Secretary in a Treasury-dominated government, he was witness, arbiter and ultimate controller of the way every department of state set its budgets; as Foreign Secretary he had, even in those three months, received an insight into foreign policy issues and the arts of diplomacy through the arcane workings of the Foreign Office.

Lastly, as Chancellor, he became the architect of economic policy. He was finally in the hottest seat in the land. The way he fared there would determine his future. For, as one close Cabinet colleague told me, 'Chancellor is the job in which you get blamed for everything and it's very hard to get to be Prime Minister from there. Much easier, in fact, from the Foreign Office.'

Perhaps John Major's best stroke of fortune was never to have been in any job long enough to be blamed for anything. Nevertheless it would be unfair to suggest that he was thriving on some kind of benign beginner's luck in his three most senior positions. Had he not demonstrated his skills, patience and determination, his logical pursuit of objectives, in all his earlier jobs? Besides, as Chancellor he took over an unenviable package of problems: inflation rising steeply under pressure of wage demands, and a growing negative trade balance brought about by the standard British tendency to suck in imports whenever there is a boom, thanks to the lack or uncompetitive nature of so many domestically produced products. This endemic configuration, set in motion during the latter years of Lawson's economic policy, was now reaping a hideous harvest. There was only one solution – for the Chancellor to up interest rates and keep his nerve while a chorus of agony went up all around him. The brief spell of apparent wizardry brought about by the decision to enter the EMS was cut short, before criticism could reach a crescendo, by the leadership crisis. The means by which John Major persuaded Mrs Thatcher into the EMS before all the conditions she set out at the Madrid summit had been met is another story (see Chapter 8).

Does his passage to power seem all too easy and too swift? His answer is characteristic. 'The thing you learn is people who make great quantum leaps only have backwards to go. People who crawl along gradually, picking up experience at every layer as they go along, have less far to fall when they look over their shoulders, and they fall down to the next layer as it were. In everything I've ever done I've always been edging along.'

The tortoise victorious? Perhaps. But in the world's casual assessment, John Major's progress seems more that of the hare. But then, people see only the results and not the dedicated years of learning and toiling, of hoping and yet not daring to hope, that have gone into the creation of a man who can see the opportunities when they come to him, and survive the test of doing the job where others failed before him. It was never merely a question of being a face that fitted, a man in the right time and the right place by happy accident. John Major was always there, keeping a low profile coming along quietly, sights firmly set but never indicating just how high they were aimed. Waiting, never expecting, always delivering first-class results whenever opportunity gave him a new task, and ever prepared for the next one – his fate is his own creation.

3
THE MODEST MAVERICK

'I absolutely hate authority of any kind.'

'**T**HE LIFE OF POLITICS IS so exciting,' John Major says, giving the quote that so aptly fits his own life. He is holding a copy of *Can You Forgive Her?*, one of Anthony Trollope's political novels about the Palliser family which are among the Prime Minister's favourites. He wants to identify the source of the quote and finds the relevant page quite quickly. 'Ah, yes,' he says, 'this is it. "Mr Grey . . ." '

He looks up and across at his Press Secretary, Gus O'Donnell, sitting opposite. Gus grins. 'Mr Grey?' he says, eyebrows going up sharply. He begins laughing. John Major, joins in. Their laughter is irresistible. It rings around the drawing room of the Number 10 flat. As we all know, the Prime Minister has a particular objection to being referred to as a 'grey man' and no one knows better than Gus O'Donnell about his efforts to persuade newspaper editors to stop their reporters referring to him in this way.

The grey image has been a deliberate camouflage he no longer needs. He joked about it while standing next to his newly installed, waxwork at Madame Tussaud's the day before his 48th birthday: 'He's greyer than me,' he said, tongue in cheek.

While John Major has been stealing through the political jungle he has found greyness a discreet disguise; a monk's drab habit to disguise a warrior. But the real John Major is grey only on the surface. True, he seems the complete Englishman, all good manners and cool responses. His voice carries little inflection as he delivers his comments on political events. Although he is growing more forceful in Parliamentary debate, revealing some attack at Question Time, he does not usually express himself dramatically or emotionally. He is not a personality with a capital P, not flamboyant, not it seems an angry man, not a tub thumper or an orator. He appears to those who are fooled by superficialities rather boring perhaps, and of course those other misnomers, ordinary and classless. None of these things are remotely accurate as descriptions of the man, only as a summary of the disguise that covered him while he worked his way from the bottom of the heap to the top, as unnoticed as possible.

It's not a bad ploy. The Koran advises citizens of power and wealth to adopt a modest lifestyle and eschew publicity so as to avoid incurring envy. John, without necessarily reading the Moslem holy book, has adopted its very practical advice from his own sound instincts. Hence he is almost universally liked, and as William Waldegrave, who is not one of his close friends, told me, 'I think I have seldom known anyone rise so fast with less feeling of resentment about it.'

If his liking for a low profile has, together with his straight and pleasant manner and apparent lack of ambition, prevented him from creating envious enemies, his eschewal of the limelight also has another motive: he simply hates publicity. That was not always the case and in fact is not invariably so today. Both in his youth, campaigning for the Tories in what was electorally for them darkest Brixton, and now, he is in fact master of the photo opportunity. Witness his speech from the top of a captured Iraqi tank in Kuwait immediately after the Gulf War. A man who really hated the limelight would have played it with much less drama.

During his period as a councillor in Lambeth he made a routine Saturday morning tour of a council estate into another photo opportunity by turning up dressed for his own wedding, in his morning suit. Although it was still several hours before the ceremony, he and his best man Clive Jones, another South London councillor, were unable to resist the opportunity for some photo publicity in the local paper.

In his early Parliamentary career, he kept his publicity to the constituency, avoiding the tricks of backbenchers trying to gain national prominence. As a whip he was best off as a grey figure. But he was unable to avoid controversy soon after he took over his job as Parliamentary Under Secretary at the DHSS when he asked for and managed to get increased cold weather payments for pensioners. The story ran for days across the media. That was unavoidable and he disappeared again as soon as he could. But reviewing his career it seems his profile became lower as his status became higher. In the TV appearances during his time at the DHSS, as Parliamentary Under Secretary of State in 1985 and Minister of State for Social Security in 1986, he looked very much younger, his hair not yet so grey, and more handsome. He had visibly more attack. Later, under the burden of more onerous responsibilities, he seemed to disappear. This may have stemmed from lack of confidence, or from the growing sense that the higher he climbed the more likely he was to be constantly observed and criticised. The latter had to be avoided for two reasons: first it might slow his career advancements and secondly he is ultra sensitive to criticism.

He is also very shy. Jeffrey Archer says, 'I remember once at Chequers about eight years ago when John was in the Whips' Office, a Wren – because they serve you at Chequers – came up and said: "Can I have your autograph, Mr Archer?" And I said, "Of course." John was standing next to me, and to tease him I turned to this Wren and said, "Do you know who this is?" She said, "No." And I said, "You'd better get his autograph because he will live here one day." John blushed and went away.'

From 1987 onwards, John Major's name was increasingly in the headlines and political columns. By the time he became Foreign Secretary and then Chancellor he almost seemed to be looking for somewhere to hide. TV cameras seldom showed him other than in profile and his voice, conveying the nitty gritty of another economic decline, was monotonous, his words terse as he enunciated the precise and simple facts, never rising to reporters' bait, seldom showing anything other than quiet patience, and when questioned aggressively, on TV or in the House, carrying his point by repetition rather than counter attack.

No wonder he was dubbed boring. His image was extremely drab. But, Robert Atkins comments, this drabness was, 'A heavily cultivated image.' TV only accentuated it. In newscasts, his face with its large eyes behind fairly thick glasses and the unusual mouth that seems to smile even when he is not smiling at all, even when he has his teeth grimly clenched, seems to have a painted on expression, as unchangingly benign as a toy animal's. He seemed the kind of chap who wouldn't say boo to a goose, who wouldn't step out of line, who might even be a wimp, who would be about as much of a threat to a rival as a nursery teddy.

Endless commentary about the dullness of John Major has been written, spoken, and made the subject of not always kindly jest. Even so, he refused TV training when a Minister and seemed intent on being the same uninspiring, rather plodding self. 'I am what I am, and nothing will change me,' seemed to be his theme. And, oddly, he has not changed. His friends say this proudly. Old friends and more recent ones say he is the same as he always was, as friendly, gracious and unpretentious as ever. Any attempt at artifice, even for the TV cameras, might start the process of pretence, of acting, of distancing the real from the public man. Perhaps he senses this and resists its contagion. I am what I am. He already has his hair cut at Trumper's, the Mayfair establishment esteemed by other political leaders such as Michael Heseltine and Nigel Lawson, and of course Mayfair gentlemen. Commenting on the ideas of those who want to make him over in a new image – different hair, suits, voice

– he says, 'I'm just plain plug ugly.' He is content to remain unenhanced. Though in fact far from ugly, and not at all in need of artifice or improvement, he is very wise. His very unpretentiousness contributes to his appeal.

He also has true modesty. He does not believe himself a great achiever, says he thinks of himself as someone who moves cautiously from one thing to the other – the tortoise again. He is not, in his own estimation, a high flyer but someone who tries harder and gets there by dint of hard work. When he became Chancellor, he told me that Nigel Lawson was the most economically literate Chancellor Britain had had for decades. The implication was he himself would be lucky to appear as good, let alone perform as well. And this though Lawson had never worked in the City other than as a financial journalist! He clearly admired Lawson's displays of economic virtuosity in a guarded way.

But then he usually has something good to say about everyone. He never seems to complain or criticise or malign any one individually. He only criticises in general terms, never directly. 'You see, some people are very narrow and shallow about this. There are some Labour politicians who do this, but it would be indelicate to name them. They think the art of politics is just to produce telling wounding phrases that are basically geared to the person rather than the policy, and that's all there is to it. But that isn't what there is to it! What politics is about is getting something done and making sure what is done is what you *want* to be done. What matters in the end is whether you can deliver the policy that you want and whether you can persuade people to accept the policy that you have delivered – that's what it is about. The rest is actually frost and bubble.'

So he avoids the telling, wounding phrase, even in cross-party combat. And where his own colleagues are concerned he is elegantly, almost orientally, diplomatic, saying little, always giving the positive comment, and changing the subject with polished abruptness. He may not be able to hide his feelings about the people concerned, giving away in tone of voice, expression or body language how he feels about the person mentioned, but his tact is almost impeccable. It is one of the secrets of his success, one of the ways of never making an enemy by never descending to the personal.

He is aware of how skilful he is in these matters – it is all quite conscious. Yet he does lack confidence in his own credentials. On another occasion, asked about his learning process as Chancellor, he said with a slightly defensive edge, 'I'm not a trained economist.' Perhaps deep down, and despite his much quoted opinions on education, he has not eradicated the popular notion that formal training implies competence.

But overall there is a certain confidence in his own person, his ability to master anything with enough application and observation and hard work. But he views himself as a plodder rather than the high flyer his friends, colleagues and past associates describe. 'I try,' he says quite often. This is not false modesty, but real.

One reason for his popularity is that he seems to have no ego problems. One ex-colleague from Standard Chartered Bank, Peter Seager, told me, 'John is not in favour of the cult of personality.' The phrase is a Marxist favourite, but John Major's dislike of ego display emanates from a deeper source. He has an at times almost touching humility. This is nothing to do with his feelings about qualifications or their lack, or with his fitness to rule. He explained, 'I don't think I like the idea that there are some people who are destined to tell others how to live their lives.' Yet he came to believe he was as capable as his Cabinet colleagues of being that first among equals, the Prime Minister.

Now he finds it irksome that there are critics who do not see his abilities. He is irked not because he has an ego to feed but because he knows he will be impeded in his work if his skill and talent and experience for the great task of Prime Minister are denigrated or not perceived.

The limitation is in the observer not the observed. Those close to him, and indeed the political insiders, have long known about John Major's special gifts. Jeffrey Archer summarises them as being, 'A tremendous ability to work, an immense ability to read a brief and understand it, and an immense political skill as a negotiator. And maybe his greatest skill, if you put him in a room with twelve people – and I don't use twelve lightly with the position we have in Europe – eleven may come out with a different opinion to the one with which they went in. He has this gift for easing you into what he believes, getting people to see the other side of the story, and it's a very rare gift. It's a skill he has developed but he does it all with immense knowledge, immense charm, and total honesty which takes them all by surprise.'

John's skills no longer surprise the insiders. While his rise may have surprised outsiders, it has not amazed anyone with whom he has worked closely.

Now, however, the need for a low-key persona designed to avoid attracting jealousy is gone and John needs a more widespread appreciation of his gifts. Modesty is now a barrier. So many people are fooled by arrogance and bombast. Quiet people are often overlooked while the noisy, even if less able, receive praise because they never cease selling themselves. Now, as Prime Minister, a spot of panache would not come amiss. But has he got it?

He began his campaign for the leadership with a new and devastating weapon: his smile. Once, he confessed, a woman MP told him to smile on TV. He did not take her advice until November 22 1990. Then – wow! What a smile. As natural and as exuberant as a delighted schoolboy, John Major smiled at cameras, waved, and bounded joyfully out of Number 11. He seemed vibrant with energy and self-confidence. He was not immodest. His language was still cautious, fair and straight, but he seemed to be suddenly in his element and enjoying himself.

What the nation was now discovering had been known to those close to him for a long time. In his lighter moments, John Major is energetic, humorous and warm; when not uttering terse statements on the economy, he can be verbally bold, quick and decisive. As for the TV cameras, after the leadership vote he beamed straight at them. No more the careful profile and dry economic dirge. He exuded energy and enjoyment of the now clean fight for the top job. No wonder the opinion polls shot up in his favour. The over-exposed Heseltine looked jaded and old hat. John was an unknown pushed into the limelight. It was like discovering a new star.

After his election, his honest, open and compassionate persona now began to be seen direct to camera more often. There were interviews in armchairs in Number 10 with David Frost where the Prime Minister smiled, laughed and expanded under Frostie's questioning in the most charming and natural way. Now it was possible to begin seeing what the Westminster insiders, his constituency members and close friends knew all along – that here was Mr Charm himself.

That direct-to-camera broadcast at the outset of the Gulf War made a lot of people, previously unaware of him except as the bearer of bad mortgage news, conscious of the new Prime Minister's sincerity and compassion, of his human side. The TV staff who recorded the broadcast are even more enthusiastic witnesses to the impact of his one-to-one presence. When he arrived he was introduced to everyone by name – camera men, director, PA, lighting and sound operatives – the whole crew. He made one recording and then decided he had been moving his hands too much and would like to do another take. So they did another and then they all sat down and watched the two takes. The Prime Minister then asked each member of the crew, by name, which recording they preferred. Everyone said they liked the first one best and he commented: 'If you all think so, then that must be the best one.' He went up to each person and shook hands and said goodbye to them, again addressing each by name. They were overwhelmingly impressed.

But then, this is how John Major deals with the entire world. He has a very special presence that comes across in direct personal contact but seems missing from his TV persona. It seems that if he could meet the electorate of Britain one by one or in small roomfuls, no one would ever cast a vote for another party.

Nobody who meets him face to face can reconcile the impact of his physical presence with the tedious tone and style of his former public posture. The real John Major – of which the protective grey plumage is still, make no mistake, an integral, if habitual part – is someone who absolutely must make you like him. He wants to be liked and to that end uses charm, a lot of charm, but a charm which is in no way synthetic.

One Cabinet colleague says he has never quite been able to put his finger on the secret of John's charm, but of course it stems from another genuine quality in the man: he is considerate. He thinks about the other person. He is one of those rare, and usually very important, people of whom it is often said that when you talk to him, he listens to you and concentrates his attention on you as if there were no one else in the room.

But can this really be true? This is a politician after all, and anything that looks like honesty in such a person is surely open to suspicion. Playwright John Chapman said one night, 'He doesn't act. All other politicians do.' Either that or it's the best act in town.

His charm is pretty potent and helps to make this complex and often contradictory character a very surprising one. But it is a natural part of his make-up, and indeed connected with his honesty. Not everyone is able to capitalise on being themselves. John is too big a person to try to impress with anything other than his own true qualities. But with qualities such as these he does not have to.

Is it, as so many people have said, his ordinariness that impresses? Jeffrey Archer says, 'He's both an ordinary man and an extraordinary man and that's why he'll make an excellent Prime Minister.' But Archer is half wrong. Extraordinary John Major is, but never ordinary. The impression of ordinariness is due simply to his humility and the naturalness with which he behaves.

The first thing that comes across on meeting him is his immense and completely genuine consideration for the other person. He has quite unconsciously and absolutely naturally the kind of graciousness that aristocrats are often made to learn as children. There is certainly a touch of noblesse oblige to him, but he is never patronising, never putting distance between himself and others, or pulling rank. That is, unless they try to put him down or treat him arrogantly.

Then there is the modesty and very obvious lack of ego. Such humility can give an impression of vulnerability, but in his case modesty and humility are the ultimate secret weapons. Vulnerability in a PM has surefire appeal for the electors, especially women, and the female vote may very well go disproportionately Conservative as a result.

His honesty is a point of honour. Truth is very important to John. He has that sort of 'Father, I cannot tell a lie' touch, and as human beings go, is probably as honest as they come. As politicians go he is utterly clever with his honesty, avoiding the lie yet concealing, by simply blocking, information on anything he is not ready to divulge. Ask him a straight question and he may simply reply, 'I don't want to talk about that.' Or he may say, 'I don't know,' or else may change the subject. These are diplomatic devices to preserve truth's integrity. But he doesn't lie, doesn't prevaricate, doesn't exaggerate or fudge. He told me, 'I would never, never dissemble,' and it had the ring of conviction. He has tact, however, and the truth may not always come blazing forth. He knows when to keep his counsel. But then that too is one of the secrets of his charm. And of his success. Like a woman who wants to keep her lover interested, John Major keeps his mystery. And his secrets.

He does seem universally liked, adored almost by friends, not disliked even by those who are not his personal cup of tea. When told a critic or two had been found but no enemies, he laughed. 'Keep looking,' he said. 'I'm sure they're there.' But they are hard to find because he does not seem to have been pushing and shoving others out of the way to get to the top, and has been promoted by obvious merit rather than by knifework. His anger, when he expresses it, seems to be just and rational and contained, his points argued with quiet determination rather than fireworks.

His enemies are emerging from among envious MPs and ex-Ministers, journalists and gossips. Others, from further back when he was less well schooled in controlling certain aspects of his character, are also appearing. Glen Knight, one of his contemporaries at Rutlish School, is someone who did not like him. He says, 'There were three of us who travelled to school on the same train. I got on at Tooting. We'd do anything to avoid being in the same carriage as him. He was so boring! He used to want to talk about cricket all the time.'

Cricket is of course an enduring passion and many of John's close friends are equally enthusiastic about it. Jeffrey Archer first took him to Lord's and subsequently they have gone together often. He has often told the story of how one day, as they walked around the ground, John, then Chancellor, turned to him and said, 'Goodness, Jeffrey, almost as many people know me here this year as know you.' Archer says, 'And it was a genuine joke. He was having a little dig at me.' He does this often, with a straight face, then watches rather clinically for the response, like a child prodding a snail.

David Rogers, who has known John since the early Seventies, is also a cricket enthusiast. A tall, intelligent man with large eyes, poetic grey curls and a stooping gait, he tells how he visited John in the Foreign Office and at one point during the afternoon, a message was brought to the Foreign Secretary. He says, 'The Foreign Office is very old-fashioned and a guy comes round with messages on a tray. This happened and John took the message, looked at it and said, "My God, these figures are disturbing. May I show David?" So the guy came across to me and I read the message which said, "England 135 for 7".'

Rogers, now a political consultant and someone who has mingled in high Tory circles for three decades, says, 'A lot of people are conscious about their position. John is not. And he's so courteous. I remember Rab Butler used to say that, "The great thing about being Prime Minister is to give the impression that time is on your side. It never is but you've got to give the impression that it is. I've never seen John hurried or harried or worried by anything. He's always got so much time. I remember when he was Chancellor, I took Bob Gregory (a financial public relations consultant) to see him. I explained to the desk who we were and then John came and said, "Oh,

I know these two old rogues, I'll take them upstairs. Don't worry." So we went up and talked and had a drink and all the rest of it. Then we left and John, in his shirt sleeves, took us down to the pavement, still chatting, and we had another twenty minutes chat on the pavement.'

His friends tell of his warmth and humour and of his loyalty too. Jeffrey Archer particularly remembers the occasion during the summer of 1987 when Archer resigned as Vice Chairman of the Conservative Party and also brought a libel suit against the *Daily Star* newspaper. John was Minister of State for Social Security. Archer says, 'Before I went through that very unpleasant trial several years ago, he came to lunch. It was after the resignation and you'd never have known I'd been through anything. We went round the garden as if I was on the way to being a Cabinet Minister. And that is a great quality. He doesn't run away from you when you're down. I won't forget that for the rest of my life.

'I remember him saying to me as we passed the Folly, "Well, it's a time that most politicians go through at some level or another, if you think about it." He hasn't gone through it yet. He said, "Oh, politics is a long game, Jeffrey. You and I are in it for a long time." '

Other friends tell similar stories. Peter Seager, a former banking colleague, says, 'He is so sympathetic if you have a problem. The bank has been having a difficult time lately and I'm retiring early and he wrote me such a wonderful letter.'

All this adds up to Mr Nice, though it's not necessarily an advantage to be thought of in this way. For nice, read boring. Being nice in a predominantly male world is perceived as being wimpish. Nice means weak. Real men, surely, are daring, grasping, audacious, unpredictable conquerors, victors in the race for gain? Men who show gentleness, patience, modesty and honesty may in the long term achieve more popularity than their more macho peers, but can they convince that they have strength?

So far, opinion surveys since December 1990 show that John Major appeals more to both men and women than his predecessor in her latter days, and more than his opposition counterparts. And one thing is certain: John Major has somehow managed to come out on top of one of the hardest games in the world, politics. So how did this so apparently mild and modest creature do it? Can one really be this nice and make it to the top?

He is of course absolutely determined and terribly tough. After Cecil Parkinson had described John's techniques for getting his own way in a meeting while he was Chief Secretary at the Treasury, I coined the title 'Velvet Steamroller' to describe him. Parkinson laughed. 'Yes, that does fit. When he's negotiating he always does his best to offer you something too. But then when you've agreed, he tries to get it back.'

Barbara Wallis, a small, blonde and brisk lady who is John's friend and former Lambeth Council colleague, now his constituency secretary and Norma Major's diary secretary, knows him very well. She told me, 'I would hate to be in competition with John for anything he really wanted, because he would be sure to get it. He would be so much more skilful.'

John's steely quality is best remembered by those who dealt with him as Chief Secretary. However his negotiating ability, as described by Cecil Parkinson,

Jeffrey Archer and others has never been in dispute. He seems from a long way back to have had the ability to go into a meeting that was stacked against him and come out having got his own way. Will Manser, who was his assistant for a period in the Seventies at Standard Chartered Bank, says: 'He would go in so well prepared, so well briefed, and argue his case with such logic, that he would simply persuade the others that he was right.'

David Rogers remembers how John would deal with neighbourhood problems. He comments, 'We lived on a small estate, about fifteen houses, (with) a small wood and a meadow. John was on the residents' committee. The usual sort of problems would crop up: some people would want the unmade-up road made up; others would want it left. Some people wanted improvement in the boundary walls, or to employ more gardeners. John was so good because he would defuse the problems before they came up. Rather than let them go on at the committee stage, he'd go and talk to someone a week beforehand and say, "Look this is coming up, we can sort it out, can't we?" '

Friends say John has always argued rationally and with an armoury of facts, always pleasantly, and always with great determination. He used this technique in Cabinet and with Mrs Thatcher. But most of all he used it as Chief Secretary to convince senior Cabinet colleagues that their departmental budgets had to be reduced. During his two years in this post he became known for his toughness. His hotel room in Bournemouth in October 1988 became known as 'The Slaughter House' because that was the room where he took on Secretaries of State and sliced their budgetary proposals into salami. But they all say this of him: that he would negotiate and that he would do so with an understanding of their needs, often coming up with suggestions for other ways of getting more out of reduced allocations. He did what perhaps only the best banker would do for a client, and did it well.

His close friend Robert Atkins says, 'He won't get angry but he gets very determined and he will fight a corner and argue it through. Of course there is the famous occasion with the lady (the Whips' dinner row) but other occasions as well with Ministers. He had more rows with the lady when he was Chancellor than any Minister has done before or since. They were very private rows and she would go completely hot whereas he would be cold and determined.' That cold, steely determination is a surprise to people who see the Mr Nice image writ large. He is too decent to earn the adjective ruthless, but his capacity to prevail has something of that irresistible force about it.

This was evident to his colleagues during his days as a whip, a job at which he excelled. It was no wonder John Wakeham recommended to the Prime Minister in 1987 that John Major should take over his job as Chief Whip. That combination of determination, toughness and negotiating brilliance, packaged with an extremely pleasant manner, those qualities of the velvet steamroller, are perfect for a whip. The lethal charm of honest John overlayed the surgical skills with which he plied his task. These can be equally perfect for a Prime Minister, but in the Whips' Office they are more covertly deployed.

A whip's work is along the basic lines of a good Welsh sheep dog, combining intelligence with rounding up skills. In the past, whips operated rather crudely. 'Arm twisting' is how the Americans describe what happens when the President's men work their way through Congress, piling up votes to push the Executive's measures through the legislature. It can no longer be described so indelicately in Britain.

As always, the whips still keep files on every MP: they know his views, his history, his leanings, his lovers, his weaknesses and his vices. They know, to use another happy American phrase, 'where the bodies are buried'. John Wakeham describes the importance of the whip in today's Parliament and how much the art of whipping has progressed from those bad old days of favour swapping and blackmail, to a more sophisticated level. 'The nature of the whips and what the whips do has been changing steadily over the years, as the nature of the backbenchers has changed. There was a time when the whips were stricter, like the officers in a good infantry regiment where they maintained discipline. They saw that people did the right thing and they were very subtle over appealing to the old school tie.

'Gradually it has changed and in some ways Francis Pym (a former Chief Whip, now Lord Pym) is the man who has changed it the most, by saying, "Look, our backbenchers are more intelligent than this and are more interested in the policies, therefore you need in the Whips' Office two things: one is a good steady influence to keep people calm in emergencies, and you also need some young lads who are interested in the policies and can understand them in order to explain them to the backbenchers, keep them up to date and informed on what the government is doing." ' So John Major's skills and personality were a great asset. As John Wakeham says, 'He has a nice personality which doesn't rough people up the wrong way, another good attribute of a whip. As a junior Member of the House he dealt well with senior backbenchers who might bear a grudge . . . they've all got to be handled. My recollection of John was that he was (a) very likeable and everyone got on with him, and (b) in terms of the issues he dealt with, really understood them better than most.'

Each whip has his own area of jurisdiction, say the Treasury or Environment, and so specialises in legislation in that area and in knowing the attitudes MPs take to different aspects of policy. Whips are intelligence officers on the one hand and propagandists on the other. The Whips' Office is part of the Executive and its job is to get the legislature to support the government's bills. This means opposition MPs are sometimes approached as well as those of the government's own party. Deals can be struck. They may be simple deals, such as bringing the business to a close sooner, or more sophisticated trade-offs of a political nature.

Within the Conservative Parliamentary Party's ranks, whipping involves as much intelligence as persuasion. But also, John Wakeham says, there are simple little ruses such as arranging an air ticket for a Member who claims he can't get back from overseas in time for a vote: 'You get on to BA and fix a ticket for them. Then you ring them up and say, "I'm delighted to say I've been able to get you a ticket. You can now come back." ' Sheep dog techniques still apply.

Knowledge of hidden secrets and the veiled threat are, however, important parts of the game. John Major was very good at this. Indeed, Wakeham says, 'He was the best I had.'

William Waldegrave also remembers John's work as a whip. The rather self-consciously bright and slightly nervous Rhodes Scholar, appointed Secretary of State for Health in Mrs Thatcher's last reshuffle, and who kept his job after John's election to the leadership, despite attempts by political commentators to suggest he would be chopped, told me: 'I first met him when he joined our little dining group that used to meet at Tristan Garel-Jones's house long ago (The Blue Chip). But I first saw him in action when I was a Junior Minister in the Environment Department. He was a whip and I was involved in all those desperate battles to abolish the GLC. Anyway, we were involved in one of those very controversial pieces of business of abolishing the GLC which was fought with tremendous energy and vigour and toughness by the Labour Party and their backers outside. It was pretty rough politics and it was a difficult bill to get through. I began to think I was doing frightfully well because this very dangerous and difficult bill which I was leading on was just going very smoothly along and we were meeting all the objectives, there was no trouble in committee. It was only after we were about three-quarters of the way through that I tumbled that in fact it wasn't anything to do with me at all. It was that (John Major) was an absolutely brilliant whip.

'What a whip has to do is to be able to make deals which absolutely stick and to be particularly trusted by the man on the other side, but also tough . . . if the other man reneges on his deal, to be able to punish it. Nobody ever double crosses John twice, I can tell you, because he is very, very tough. He's got quite a lot of what my old boss Lord Rothschild would call tungsten carbide in his backpack, some very good hard substance indeed. It's quite a good test being a junior whip because you're left on your own for endless committees in the middle of the night, getting the business through, and somehow he managed to be on extremely friendly terms with the other side but deliver the business. And there was never any sort of thought in the Labour Party that they would try and play games with him. I was extremely impressed by that. I remember saying to someone, "Watch out for that fellow." '

Perhaps one would have expected Labour MPs to recognise the nature of John's toughness more quickly than William Waldegrave, a peer's son and a distinguished scholar, perhaps unattuned to the kind of grit that can develop in someone who, though equally intelligent, grows up on the wrong side of the tracks. When asked about his toughness, John Major replied, 'Well, if you learn your politics in Brixton it's there, or you don't survive.' Surprisingly, some Labour Members took longer than many Tory colleagues to appreciate the street fighter's toughness under the genteel pleasantness of John's fair dealing.

When he was Chief Secretary, this should have been becoming daily more clear as in his speeches on the economy he often made accurate bayonet plunges at the opposition spokesmen John Smith and Gordon Brown. Neither were keen to talk about this. Perhaps these stabs were so surrounded by a mass of detail and so concealed under the somewhat dull style of delivery that they were not always recognised for what they were. Does he think they have noticed? He said quietly, 'I think so.'

In closer encounters, there is less doubt. Major is a man who moves in for the kill without warning. Bryan Gould, Labour's smoothest purveyor of Designer Socialism and a politician of cat-like stealth and sensitivity, noted for his deft footwork in any fight, came out of an early encounter with John somewhat bloodied. Gould tells the story: 'I took not the slightest notice of John Major. I remember in 1984–5 sometime, I was winding up a debate and this rather obscure chap came up and asked me how much time I wanted. I remember thinking he wasn't very bright.

'Then, when he became Chief Secretary and I was shadow Trade and Industry Secretary, we were both invited on to "Newsnight". We exchanged a few words in the Green Room and I went into the discussion with him believing that he didn't know very much. He was nice and pleasant before we went in but turned out to be much less nice in the debate. He pulled a couple of fast ones, made debating points based on incorrect information. I remember thinking, "Well, next time I'll be better prepared." But there hasn't actually been another occasion outside the House.'

However, when as Labour Environment shadow Gould attacked the Government in a censure motion on poll tax in March 1991, there was a certain enmity in his manner and words of accusation against the Prime Minister that perhaps show he has not given up waiting for that opportunity to get back at John Major.

Where does this unobvious, but now legendary, toughness originate? John Major's childhood was largely that of an only child thanks to the eleven- and thirteen-year gaps between him and his older siblings, Terry and Pat. The first ten years were spent in the comparatively middle-class area of Worcester Park. He attended a local primary school, was a member of a Wolf Cub pack and seems to have done all the things little boys usually do. But his present-day toughness is a product of his early days there and in Brixton, coupled with his sensitivity and intelligence and perhaps also a deep sense of betrayal stemming from so many bruising encounters with life in those early years.

One day, I asked him: 'Has the iron entered into your soul and if so when?' He looked back with eyes which narrowed a fraction and I saw hurt there. 'Yes,' he said and looked uncomfortable. I pursued the matter and he fenced. After some moments of probe and parry, he said, unhappily, 'It was on my seventh birthday.' The answer had the characteristic precision of the man, but that he should know the day so well revealed the pain in the boy still living in the man and emphasised the power of some event beyond any normal birthday upset. Perhaps a birthday more than any other is a day loaded with expectation. Some catastrophic disappointment must have occurred that this day branded itself so enduringly and so painfully into his memory. Characteristically, in order to protect others, he wouldn't tell me what happened. 'No,' he said, squirming, 'I can't tell you because it would cause offence to my brother and sister. No. It wasn't anything anyone did. It was a circumstance.'

From this experience he says he learned a fundamental truth which is now part of his life's philosophy. 'Events are unpredictable and can take a nasty turn,' he has commented in interview. 'You ought not to take too much for granted. Once you take things for granted something will go wrong. You get complacent or other people get angry. You need your antennae working all the time if you're going to preserve a set course.'

John Major learns fast. If he ever allowed himself to drift and accept the status quo without question, he does not now, has not since he was very young. He is a learner because he knows that is the way to compete, to be strong, maybe stronger than everyone else. And he needs that. He needs to be stronger than others. He needs it in the way a peace-loving nation needs arms – to deter aggression.

Those antennae, his radar and satellite surveillance, his intelligence services, are partly provided by his friends. Though he is undoubtedly extraordinarily, unerringly perceptive, he also values highly the advice of informed and trusted sources. He needs eyes and ears among the grass roots, people who are free and able to explore, see and listen in a way that he, protected and preoccupied, is not. He constantly consults people he has known for years, people he trusts, people whose judgment he values. He keeps in touch because he knows how dangerous it is not to. And he prefers his own sources, those people of many years' acquaintance, to anyone who might have come lately to the scene. Though again, whoever comes his way is evaluated. He knows the value of intelligence. He trusts his own judgment and his own ability to discern true from false. He is starkly accurate in his observations of others. His antennae, whatever their nature, are evidently well attuned.

This extraordinary sensitivity to the world around him is also a source of vulnerability. He feels much and has not hardened himself. Whatever experiences he has endured he has learned from, his suffering has added to his strengths: but he has, it seems, never forgotten the pain. He has never forgotten the experience of living in the Brixton house with the other tenants cheek by jowl by the bathroom door and by the gas rings which were their kitchen, just outside the doors of the two rooms his family rented in that Victorian terraced house. That is too real, too strong an experience of loss of privacy and the security of a roof over the head, ever to be buried or forgotten. So real an experience that his first action after becoming Prime Minister was to ensure more hostel beds were made available for the citizens of 'Cardboard City' before Christmas.

The very thought of people sleeping rough, people without homes, people without security, is enough to make him suffer all over again his own youth's great insecurities. The privations would not have seemed as tough if he had been born to them. The hard part was to learn them after ten years of life in a middle-class neighbourhod as an almost only child with his own private space, his toys, his books, a garden in which to play.

He will not complain about that time. For someone like him, there is always more to be gained from any experience than to be lost. His whole attitude, his whole response to life, is to make the best of any situation, learn from it, never forgetting his goal and moving on resolutely towards it. Is there, though, a tendency to hang on, not only to the lessons and the gain, but also to the pain? Perhaps. But without the pain he has known, and without its memory, how could he feel for others the way he does?

The cost of hardening oneself against pain is often to numb oneself against all feeling, even joy. The person who successfully hardens themselves to their own pain or the memory of pains past, must surely also have learned how to anaesthetise themselves against others' griefs. John does not do this. His consciousness of others' suffering is forever with him. Often his face shows his feelings before the words can emerge.

When asked by Peter Snow on 'Newsnight' from the Gulf, before the war, whether he thought people at home had been sufficiently prepared for the losses that might result, he simply looked at the interviewer for a moment.

In that look was a wordless cry of compassion for the people who waited – mothers, wives, fathers. His answer came, measured and honest, without the glibness of a politician's statement, and the compassion never left his eyes. On his return, he told Jeffrey Archer, 'They are so young. It's terrible to think one might be sending them to their deaths.' Such thoughts become a leader. But it was John Major the father who thought them: he had identified personally with all those families of servicemen. His own son, he told friends, was only a year younger than some of our soldiers.

But his sensitivity is also an Achilles' heel. He seems to pay too much attention to criticism, to the sometimes wide of the mark practice shots of newspaper columnists. He is unduly sensitive to everything that is written about him. Visibly cringing, he admitted, 'I absolutely hate reading anything about myself.'

He is made very angry by untrue stories in the press and by opinion pieces that seem angled against him. He hasn't understood the game of guesswork, and smoke without fire of gossip and rumour mongering, the pastiche of opinion with report and hard facts with mischief, all delivered with the authority of gospel, with which many newspaper columnists are obliged to scrape a crust. He hasn't understood that some kinds of journalists behave like beaters on a shoot, putting up birds for the guns to shoot at when there is little hard news. He hasn't understood it because he is not that way himself.

He is inordinately accurate in his remarks, uses language with a surgical precision and a curiously dated pedantry, yet always means exactly what he says and says exactly what he means. Sometimes the impact of what he says is lost because of his drab delivery. Reading his words it is possible to see exactly what he intends, to detect barbs which might have passed by without the theatrical emphasis of voice and timing. Even the remark he made to the House about Saddam Hussein, 'Whatever his fate, I'll not weep for him,' was delivered in a flat and uneventful tone. Accompanying the words, however, was a sudden hunching of the shoulders and thrusting forward of the head, and behind them, in his eyes and hardening tone, the glint of steel, the sharpness of an anger that began to emerge more and more often in his statements as the war progressed. His description of Saddam as a liar, a torturer of his own and the Kuwaiti people, carried a dark venom. Under the flat voice lurked the violence of his contempt for one who did not rule with mercy and whose misuse of power broke every rule of responsible governance or decent civilised behaviour. It might still take a microscope for some to perceive it, but John Major is a formidable enemy.

His style is overtly conciliatory, but his methods are robust. He was perceived during the war as offering a softer approach. His critics on the right were angry at the opportunity he seemed to give Neil Kinnock to appear statesmanlike. This was not borne out in opinion surveys after the war which showed Kinnock's stock had declined against Major's. Detractors of Mrs Thatcher compared his statements on the Gulf with her tone during the Falklands. Not only was it a different war, but John Major expresses his feelings less obviously than does Mrs Thatcher. Her anger quickly erupts. She expresses herself more emotionally. John Major's emotions are carefully reined in, like a dressage horse.

His feelings were no less powerful than those which drove Mrs Thatcher to inspire the Allies' actions in the Gulf. Would he have had her force of impassioned determination to ensure President Bush began this international venture and that the United Nations debated and passed their resolutions? No one can be sure. But one thing is certain – that when it comes to what is right and decent and honourable, John Major is in the front rank. Mildness of manner does not mean mildness of feelings. He simply keeps his feelings and his plans secret, and if it comes to revenge, enjoys it cold.

Anger against untruth at home is as strong. Once he is angry he engages the antagonist with a terrier-like tenacity. When items that are wrong appear in the media, he makes sure that editors know but does not leave it there. One Secretary of State who was himself the subject of malicious press rumours alleging he would be sacked, was telephoned by the Chief Whip, Richard Ryder, who told him that the Prime Minister had asked him to reassure the Minister that there was absolutely no truth in the rumours that had appeared in one newspaper that morning.

The Prime Minister, the Chief Whip reported, was extremely angry at the incident. Such is John Major's reputation for honesty and keeping his word that the Minister in question was visibly reassured. The journalists, however, would have a less easy ride. 'He will pursue them relentlessly,' the Minister told me. He conveyed an impression given more than once by other friends. John Major forgives, but he never forgets.

This relentless pursuit of his adversaries is a characteristic few may yet have experienced. John Major, after all, has been the man everyone liked to like. He has followed such a course of anonymity and good manners that there are still a great many people who have hardly realised what lies behind the public persona, and a great many more who consistently underestimate him in every respect. Now, this man, having made a profession of private popularity, having practised the kind of public modesty that prevented envy, is anxious to be properly valued. He is distinctly angry at being undervalued, and misjudged, and insulted, and talked of as grey and boring. Now that he has attained the job of his dreams, he wants the world to know that he can do it, that he is indeed someone with whom to reckon. He is impatient to be explained so that his good qualities may be valued and yet, still loathing publicity, still fearful of exposure, still uncomfortable in the spotlight, would dearly love to be left, like Garbo, alone.

Even in high office he spent evenings alone, perhaps eating at fast food restaurants and cafes or bringing in takeaways from Chinese or Indian restaurants to eat at Number 11 Downing Street, in a way that shocked more epicurean colleagues. He might well have preferred some company but everyone else had somewhere to go and his family home was in the constituency. These restaurants' cuisine is also not necessarily what his colleagues might prefer, though certainly there is plenty of this kind of grub in the House of Commons' various cafeterias. The nasty caffs have also been the focus of fine photo opportunities, revealing the high office holder in his native haunts. When asked why he was not perceived hitting bookshops as often as the greasy spoon cafes, he said, 'Oh, but I do. Or rather used to. I can't now.' Then he joked: 'Of course, I keep reading that I don't read anything other than the *Beano*.'

He was referring, tongue in cheek, to the snide and sneering commentary of certain snobbish journalists. He can afford to laugh. Self-educated he may be, but he is more widely read than many university graduates. His greatest advantage is that his reading has never been confined by an academic course, only directed by his own avid interest in politics, its processes and people. He makes a point of surrounding himself, he says, with first-class minds, books included. He reads avidly, an omnivorous diet, from political biography to the novels of his friend Jeffrey Archer. He loves political novels, those of Trollope and less well-known authors. He refers constantly to his books in conversation and in doing so comes alive, almost like someone who has just heard a wonderful piece of gossip. He leaps up and searches his shelves with a sure feeling for each book and its place. He hates people to borrow his books and not return them, is still grieving for all the books that vanished from his collection in Nigeria after he was injured in the road accident. His books are his friends, have been perhaps since the days when he had few minds of equivalent stature with which to associate.

At least from the age of eight: 'I certainly remember reading a lot. No Christmas was complete without a few books. I'm always happy to curl up with a book.' He has thought of writing a novel, tried and given up a few times. He has a novelist's perceptions and sensibilities. Perhaps all he needs is a plot like his own life. And time.

He is thrilled to receive books as presents and word may have travelled abroad of his predilection. At Number 10, he showed me a present from his trip to Bermuda, going out of the room to find a quotation and returning with a set of three clothbound and gilt-lettered books. He set them down with pride: '*The American Commonwealth* by Bryce, my newest acquisitions, a first edition from President Bush.'

His reading should have reduced the sense of discomfort he has almost always felt when dealing with the formally educated. His sometimes shaky self-confidence is always alleviated by reading himself into the subject. When facing something new, he is comforted by knowing he has grasped the facts and the essence of a subject, and this he does fast. Modest he is, and yet growing in self-confidence as each successfully held high office has strengthened his self-image. Those close to him are sure of his gifts, his intelligence and the appropriateness of his experience. His severest critics are among those only partially informed about him: some political writers, senior businessmen, and those whose judgement is what John himself hates the most, superficial. Too often in his life he has found that people judge him dull because he has been modest. It is commonplace, from schooldays onwards, that the arrogant and the opinionated are too often taken for clever while the quiet and undemonstrative personalities are treated as dull of mind as well of manner. A sparkling personality attracts constant interest. John Major is too cautious to want to cavort in the limelight. However, things are changing. Before the leadership election, public perceptions of him were connected with the fact that he was Chancellor, but he was not much exposed outside this area.

When the opinion polls began questioning voters on November 23 after he announced he would stand for the second ballot, he trailed behind the other two candidates, Hurd and Heseltine, on public perception of his performance on most issues other than the economy. But by the Sunday, November 25, after only four days in the public eye as a candidate, he had overtaken the others. By March 13 1991, three and a half months after he became Prime Minister, Gallup was able to publish a poll showing that 99% of the public were able to identify John Major. In this he led a field of political and non-political celebrities including Desert Orchid, the nation's favourite racehorse! Another poll, conducted by MORI (Market Opinion Research International) between February 22–5 1991 showed that his popularity was running well ahead of his party's.

While the Conservative lead over Labour had slipped five points since the previous month (when

the war rather than domestic issues were dominant),
John Major was perceived as doing a good job by
63% and was also more popular with younger voters
and those from lower socio-economic groups than
Mrs Thatcher. Evidently people in these groups
were now begining to know enough about his own
socio-economic background and to identify with that
and his comparative youth.

Public perceptions of his abilities can however be
changed if the attitudes of newspaper columnists and
editors grow critical. During the early months of
1991 a stream of articles appeared in the *Daily* and
Sunday Telegraph, prompted by fears that Major's
leadership would bring wet or more socialistic policies
and change the Thatcherite direction. Much of the
commentary tended to be disparaging, referring to
him as grey – Our Unknown Prime Minister –
and vaguely sneering in tone, more personal than
political.

David Mellor says that, 'John doesn't mind people
who don't agree with him, and I don't think he minds
if people don't like him. What he dislikes is people
who patronise him and look down their noses at him.
There's a certain kind of journalist that is capable
of aggravating him by appearing to curl their lip at
him and he doesn't like that. There is one particular
journalist on the *Telegraph* who got right up his nose.
John is not someone who frankly, bless their heart,
some scribbler should patronise, because John is a
man of achievement.'

The journalist is Charles Moore, who so offended
John with an interview he wrote for the *Daily
Telegraph*'s pre-leadership election coverage that the
Prime Minister has since refused to speak to him.

The article, published in question and answer form on November 26 1990, the day before the ballot, contained questions distinctly insulting in tone, such as, 'On the poll tax, you are more closely identified with it than either of your rivals. There isn't much you can do about it, is there? It is the most unpopular thing about all the Government's policies and you're the least qualified to reform it.' And, 'People wouldn't say you had Mr Heseltine's star quality or Mr Hurd's presence on the world's stage. What is it that you can contribute that they don't?'

Robert Atkins refers angrily to the same interview: 'Charles Moore treated him like dirt in the interview and in the article.' A week or two later John met Moore at the *Telegraph* Christmas party and conversed amicably with him. Moore was evidently anxious to make amends but he is unlikely to interview the Prime Minister in the near future.

Like so many of those close to John Major, David Mellor thinks he is a remarkably able and fine character. He says: 'I think you can't be a complete saint, but John is as basically decent in thought, word, and deed as it is possible to be to get where he has got, and certainly the way that he handles himself now, the total absence of any swell-headedness, the total naturalness with which he conducts himself, is a sign of someone who is at peace with himself and who believes he can do it.'

So, his friends and colleagues feel, it is time for John Major's achievement to be recognised and his abilities to be properly valued. He also reluctantly feels the time for discretion and publicity-shy modesty is past and that it is important that his gifts be recognised more widely than among his own circle of senior politicians, MPs and civil servants. Yet he still shrinks from the thought of revealing himself in any way. If only he could be recognised for what he is, and then be left untroubled to achieve the things that he wants and intends to do.

He is used to being misjudged, and is in fact deeply and quietly angry at various underestimations of him from long time back. But these have served as a spur. Part of the drive which has propelled him forward is the absolutely determined intention to prove the world wrong about him.

This anger has lent powerful impulsion to his career, and as Prime Minister he feels it even more keenly. Everything he wants to do, every dream and hope he has stored up for so long, is now about to be given material form. His empowering anger stems from every small hurt and slight that somehow he has absorbed. Yet this is the man who is said to have no side, to be without any chip on his shoulder, who says he is utterly unresentful of wealth or success or gain by others.

But that can be true, just as it is true that he wants to set the record straight about himself and is as angry on behalf of others as on behalf of himself. He is angry that others should have to go through what he went through. He is angry on behalf of the collective suffering of humanity. He believes that suffering can only be put right by the continuing pursuit of liberal economic policies that create the wealth with which to improve the lot of underprivileged people. Before he became Prime Minister he said, 'Unless you are economically dry, and unless you have the economy right, it doesn't matter how socially conscious you are unless you have the resources to do anything about it.

And,' he added with that quiet, determined anger, 'words do nothing for people in need.'

So it would seem that his economic and political wisdom is being challenged by people who have no real conception of what he intends to do, or of how his grand design for Britain is directly linked to the formative experiences of his own youth. They cannot comprehend his objectives because they have not understood the virtually unique pattern of experience which has created this particular Prime Minister.

Until those experiences and the inheritance of his early days are understood, his political goals will be misinterpreted. In his case there is no doubt that the child is father of the man: John Major the boy is father to the present-day Prime Minister.

The more he is misjudged and misunderstood, the more his old anger is rekindled. Rebellion against authority is deeply rooted in his character, a direct response to certain elements who set themselves up to judge and dismiss him. The evidence of this goes back a long way, certainly as far as that school which, through his mostly negative experience of it, engendered the bite and the drive and the anger he used to push himself forward, year after year, through disappointment after disappointment, to press on when everything seemed hopeless. When he would just as soon give up, that anger, that rebellion against authority, drove him on. The rebellion is both in his being and in his nurture. John was surprised that his rebelliousness was evident but when asked about it he admitted that he was deeply rebellious and that it causes him to provoke deliberately anyone who seems smug or complacent. But: 'I've got better

at dealing with that side of myself as I've got older,'
he confided.

The steely self-control which is another important
quality of the man may not have been as evident in the
boy, but now it helps to keep that provocative urge
under control. Perhaps being so controlled creates
strains which snap his self-discipline. He gets wildly
and explosively angry, especially with his family.
But then, people who keep themselves tightly reined
during working hours often relax their self-discipline
when they are at home or with friends. Another factor
is the low-grade pain he endures constantly from his
injured leg. People who suffer constant pain are often
prone to outbursts of anger. If he endures it while he
works, perhaps ignoring it, he may be more likely
to give way to it once among people who love him.
It is quite natural for someone in pain to seek that
extra sympathy from loved ones. He neither admits
to himself nor tells them what he wants, but becoming
upset at little things is his means of saying he needs
their extra special concern.

Another factor in John's anger is that his family is
often difficult to handle. Many high-powered men
experience a problem with the fact that, unlike
employees, children refuse to fall into line and instead
of doing what they are told come out with their own
needs and demands, emotional or temporal. And the
pressure is worse if the man is away most of the time.

But some of the problem is due to John's character.
His friend Robert Atkins says that John has the most
awful moods. 'He can, with close friends, be a very
angry man when he wants to. And he really makes
very provocative, rude remarks. But he only does it
with very close friends.'

At Rutlish School, he seems to have given rein to this side of himself more persistently. Glen Knight says he smoked in the playground and did anything else he could to provoke the prefects. John replies indignantly: 'It's just not true. I have never smoked. Never in my life. I've always regarded it as a most revolting habit. It killed my mother and it is, absolutely hand on heart, bible in pocket, untrue. I saw a piece like that in the paper – reminiscences from an old school friend. It was fantasy.' However he does say, 'It's certainly true I used to taunt the prefects. That was fair game.' Once he did this – and Knight says he did it almost every day – he would have to stand facing the wall for the rest of play time.

Can he have done this so that he would not have to associate with his schoolmates? Glen Knight, evidently not disposed to praise him, says that he and his two friends who travelled on the train together from South London and were often joined by John, were a year ahead of the future Prime Minister. Such were the rules of the jungle at Rutlish that, Knight says, 'If he came up to us in the playground, we would be really embarrassed. You just didn't associate with people who were in a different year.'

Was John lonely at school? He says, with that touch of sadness that invariably accompanies references to school, 'I did have some friends but I don't know where they are now.'

He may not have appeared so with his rebellious and provocative manner, but he was always ultra sensitive to sneers and goads. He comments, 'School was hard. I was not comfortable because there were things like having to be given money towards my uniform, that sort of thing.' He adds with a flash of anger, 'And I hate authority. I hate being told what to do.'

The anger and the hurt produce a linked response. So perhaps the sneers of certain arrogant journalists today, challenging his well-earned authority as Prime Minister, remind him of the sneers of loutish schoolboys in the days when he was himself subject to another authority. Old anger not fully expressed may be one good reason why his rage at press barbs today sometimes seems disproportionate.

Characteristically, he does not blame the school for his failure. He says, 'It was me, not the school.' That seems one-sided. However, perhaps it is no bad thing his school masters misjudged his intelligence, failed to capture his interest and managed not to turn him into an academic success. Educationally better qualified and the conventional path to success open before him, he would have led a much narrower life, more limited in experience and fields of knowledge. He does not think exams are important, but one disadvantage of having limited his academic achievements in those days to six 'O' levels is that he has had to go on being misjudged for this very lack of educational qualifications. Part of the problem is the way the educated establishment believes that anyone without a formal education after the age of 16 must be handicapped. Since John Major did not go to university, especially since he was not an Oxbridge graduate, he is to be discounted. He has been aware over the years of subtle slights: the turning away of a head, the slight sniff, the look along a long and not necessarily aristocratic nose. No wonder he hates snobs as a class on their own while being biased against no social grouping. But his fate in this respect is the fate of so many self-made men in Britain, where academic attainment, inherited wealth and reputation are still valued more than self-made success.

But the snobbery of others often drives those who know themselves able, to prove their ability by doing' it the hard way. Success then becomes the ultimate act of rebellion, the maverick's revenge. From the back street billionaire to the British Prime Minister, the motivating force is that combination of intelligence and courage with angry determination and a rebellious disrespect for convention. Sometimes these qualities push their owners beyond the legal limits – the entrepreneur becomes buccaneer, the political figure a reformer or revolutionary who disregards all opinion other than his own – but they also, more often, prove that brains and talent will win through, provided they are joined by a good measure of determination and will-power. This John Major himself believes. 'I just think people are too bedazzled by academic qualifications. I don't like these barriers.'

Some pictures of him show a certain set of jaw as if he is clenching his teeth together. That set of jaw and mouth reveals his characteristic gritty determination. This is the boy who rose at five and went to bed after midnight so that he could make up for his failed school career. How much anger, how much determination drove that teenager, who not only had to help support his family but also prove to the world of authority that the misfit, the maverick kid, could do it his way? How different from the average spoiled brat. Indeed, how different from almost any child. In those days he may have seemed a rebel whose cause was a minority one. To fight his way to the top in the Conservative Party, of all political groups, and to do so from the lower ranks of urban unskilled youth, shows the power of the maverick child in the modest man.

He has spoken of the times he almost gave up, when someone else, a friend and advisor, gave him encouragement and hope to go on. His disadvantages were severe. Not only was he a boy without qualifications, the only proof of intelligence in that society, without even skills or a trade and from a poor part of town, but he was that boy in that time, late Fifties and early Sixties England. This was the England (not Scotland or Wales where values were different, even if life was still quite tough for the likes of John Major there too) of the old school tie, ossified by class, the England of the last dying kicks of Imperial pretensions before the winds of change. Those winds when they came, not just to Africa and the colonies but also to the green fields of that English Jerusalem, thankfully blew away much of the stuffy rigidity that decreed that class and family connection were the only routes to power. But they were only partially successful. Had they completed their task, there would be no need now for a John Major to speak of meritocracy and a country where class should be no barrier to the energetic, the enterprising, and the hard working.

The revolution, such as it was, was a parody of itself, often rebellion for rebellion's sake. The motor which drove it, the desire for meritocracy, never quite turned strongly enough, becoming mired in egalitarian dogma. So it became necessary for a new group of meritocrats to hand crank that engine back into life.

Harold Wilson was the man who invented the political language of the early Sixties, who perceived the trends and lauded with calculated passion the dream of a meritocracy forged on what he called 'the white heat of a technological revolution'. The latter ran out of fuel fairly fast and the Socialist meritocratic ideal foundered under a new aristocracy of trade unions' barons.

People like John Major were forming their own political viewpoint while waiting on the sidelines as Wilson played to the death the game of Big Unions and Big Industry. Research shows that most people retain throughout life the political beliefs they form in their late teens and early twenties. In their politically formative phase they are likely to have their views conditioned by the debates and received viewpoint of the time in which they live, and are termed a 'cohort' by psephologists, those experts in political opinion formation and trends. Each cohort becomes an electoral generation, tending to respond to a particular set of ideas and ideologies and a particular party, moving slowly through the electorate as they age. In the Seventies, Major and his political contemporaries emerged from the shadow of Wilson's failed attempt to replace one class rule with another, as their own breed of meritocrats. The likes of Norman Lamont, Kenneth Clarke and others of a group of Sixties Cambridge graduates whose favour Major has since found, were imprinted with the ideas and words of earlier Tory thinkers such as Macleod. They spoke, in the post-Heath Seventies, in practical tones of a Tory meritocracy where those who could would rise, and those who could not would be caught in a safety net of state compassion. Post-Heath, these disciples of meritocracy found Thatcher and followed her flaming torch. Thatcher gone, they are at home with Major, the slow burner who nevertheless cooks unobtrusively.

Margaret Thatcher, educated as a scientist and with a mind therefore not confined by education within preconceived political and economic schools, developed Tory philosophy beyond anything that had existed in the Sixties. Inspired by Professor Friedrich Hayek's *The Constitution of Liberty*, his other works and thought, she clearly defined an ideology for democracy and free enterprise based on the dynamics of individual choice. These ideas were not alien to Tory philosophy though deviating from recent decades of pragmatic centrist consensus government, yet they produced the most practical system of all for a Tory revival. Her radicalism took time to take effect, but gradually the understanding dawned that the survival of Conservatism as a philosophy meant the sacrifice on the altar of change of conservative politics.

The Major cohort of maturing political thinkers, now mostly in their forties, found their true home in Mrs Thatcher's garden of economic renewal. As the post-Heath realisation dawned that the state was suffocating free enterprise, and that individuals must be encouraged to build prosperity, the Major cohort found its voice.

More or less of one generation, that of the Forties, this cohort's members were born to a post-war world impatient to be off with the narrow barriers of the old, and came of age politically in a time – the Sixties – which joyfully shrugged off stale values. Is this the source of John Major's aspirations towards a classless society? He more than any of his colleagues has lived a disadvantaged life and knows what it is like to break free by merit. He is himself living proof that meritocracy is a workable system. His aspirations for the collective are a projection of his own individual experience. His life's work and his life's experience are focussed in one aim.

He knows how class mobility can and should be realised and his mission is to make this possible nationwide. To be such a product of one's experience, and to see and interpret the world and one's work through its lens, is not unusual. What makes John Major special and has brought him to power is timing: his experience and his political aim are exactly where the nation's need is now, and exactly at the point where recent history has programmed mass consciousness to the possibility of transcending class. People are ready to move forward beyond its artificial barriers. First, there is a change of consciousness, then the leader appears who can deliver the goods: that is a fundamental law of political and historical change, whether by revolution or evolution.

More prosaically, John's Major's sentiments about the classless society have caught the imagination of so many. What he meant was not so much classlessness as class mobility, and his life story showed that his words were not mere rhetoric. He more than most of his Parliamentary peers, on both sides of the House, understands the terrible frustrations and impatience of people trapped in situations which limit their freedom and confine them to low status. He said recently, 'I've learned a great deal about the difficulties people face when they feel trapped in situations that they don't think they can do anything about. That's the great thing that has happened in the last ten years. A whole series of policies has made it easier to move from the sort of circumstances one saw in Lambeth.'

How could he ever forget the decrepit housing, low skills, unemployment, racial bias and social deprivation he saw around Brixton? John Major, thanks to his skills, learning power, his determination, anger and maverick spirit, fought his way through barriers of education and social class that have been much weakened in the thirty-two years since he left Rutlish School. But he can never erase the pain of that journey while there are still too many others struggling with the same limitations.

No wonder he now seeks and wants so passionately, under the Dr Cool bedside manner, to build a world in which class is no barrier to achievement, in which it does not prevent people from using their talents and skills to the maximum; does not prevent them from enjoying a lifestyle or a living that convention might suggest belongs to someone else; does not, whatever their success, expose them to the putdowns of people who think themselves superior by birth rather than worth.

John Major and many of his cohort realise one thing above all: that class freezes a society and locks away its energy. A class-limited society is like a champion racehorse with its two hind legs tied together. Such a society does not create or grow or compete, it simply indulges itself. John Major is one of the few unfettered from pursuing his objectives. He broke through, not because he thought he could rise above the system but because he was born and raised outside it and because he was, still is, that rebel whose cause he still upholds. He fought his way through the jungle of class at a time when it became easier to do so, in one profession which makes it easier than most to rise by talent alone. But he has done it with the spirit of the maverick. As he said, 'I realised I would have to do it all from the outside.'

So this outsider who ran along the rails until he broke through and led the field, this dark horse, had a life strategy. But if it was the spirit of rebellion that empowered him, how come he chose the Conservative Party and not Labour or even the Liberals?

A close examination of his background and the influences on him of his parents' attitudes will show that he was programmed as a believer in competition, in excellence, in free enterprise, in effort rewarded and self-reliance. Even so, what better place for a true revolutionary than in the heart of the Conservative Party? Karl Marx would have approved of that. But as a strategy it would have had to be, as it has been, long-term.

John joined the Tory Party at a time in which his views and his background as a boy with no social or educational credentials put him in a minority, socially and financially. The chord of the One Nation being struck by Macleod and Butler, that theme around which Tories of John Major's ilk could rally, was not yet dominant in the party, though it strengthened and took hold in opposition in the Sixties, in response to the changing political climate fostered under the then received ideas of egalitarianism promoted mainly by Labour and Liberal politicians.

But the day of the Tory meritocrats was yet to come and John, a Tory through and through, seems to have wanted to prove something to himself by doing the hardest thing possible, coming up on the outside. Yet he has only succeeded because the spirit of the times through which he has passed evolved in line with the progress.

This convergence of John Major's career with the times in which he lives has to be more than pure coincidence. Destiny? If, as Robert Atkins says, John is too much of a pragmatist to believe in destiny, it may still be argued that destiny too is pragmatic when it provides the right man for the job at the right time.

Timing is one of his talents. His sense of moment is part of that process which he calls 'keeping one's antennae working all the time'. Had he spent his childhood in easier circumstances he might have a less well-developed system of radar. The streetwise are usually much more alert, looking for danger, watching out for tricks and trends, picking up on anything that might be an opportunity. John Major gives the impression of being more gentlemanly than street sharp, but he is both. As he told me, he spent much of his childhood 'in a rough world'. He at least would never make the remark of his predecessor to her Cabinet the morning after her betrayal, that 'It's a funny old world.' John Major knows only too well that the world is harsh and brutal, unjust, untrustworthy, and not funny at all. He is aware enough of that to know how to watch out for himself. His survival reflexes are honed to perfection.

His sense of timing is as immaculate as that of the ace batsman he dreamed of becoming. His mind as quick and decisive. He can respond verbally in a moment. Yet he prefers to deliberate, and his conclusions and public decisions are delivered only after long and considered evaluation of all the aspects of a situation. There is an underlying streak of rashness, but he has contained it like an alcoholic who keeps a sealed bottle of spirit in his house to test his will. It manifests now as a controlled capacity for swift response and a predilection for impulse, but caution is the prevailing force. This caution reveals itself when he answers questions. His responses have the rhythm of a conveyor belt, each word following the next with measured exactitude. He is so concerned to say only what is necessary, to give nothing away, to be as truthful as he can without being revealing, to be precise in language and to convey his meaning without error.

He is concentrated and deliberate and when he answers, it is as if he stares for a moment into the depths, his voice emerging like an echo.

He is as cautious with his emotions, and as discreet. But he reveals his personal feelings without being able to prevent it. These feelings are of a different order from the strong surging passions that sometimes turn his voice into a growl as he taps his political anger, as for instance against inflation which he says: 'I hate because it savages those who are worst off.' No, his private feelings are what he tries so hard to protect from hurt and from discovery. Yet he cannot hide them. Naturally honest, his feelings plainly show in momentary alterations of his features. They are precious to him and buried whenever possible. Yet he is courageous enough to face them and examine them for their worth.

He is, in some soft and hidden place, a romantic with feelings that are old-fashioned and demure, although this goes against his very male strength and the boisterousness that makes him so much a man's man. Yet this softness is what makes him

strong, what makes a man of feeling greater by far
than any imaginary macho hero. For only strong men
cry and if John Major were to do so, it would always
be for others, not himself.

Yet despite this gentle side, relationships with
women are not easy for him. 'I do like women,' he
commented while blushing bashfully. Yes, of course,
but like many men he is afraid of the shadowy female
side buried in his own psyche. Women seem to him
to be powerful creatures that could take him over,
and he has known many who were or are extremely
powerful, from his own mother whom he describes
as 'small but dominant' to Mrs Thatcher. Perhaps
this is why women are more acceptable to John when
they are mother figures, matriarchs. Even Norma is
a year older. It is as if, not uncommonly among men,
he seeks out replicas of his mother's strong presence
to guide and advise and reassure him.

Female peers are harder to deal with. His childhood
without a contemporary sister, his teens at a boys'
grammar school, his first years in politics, limited
his association with female peers. He has a great need
for harmonious relationships with others and so with
women, especially again the older women in whom
constituency gatherings abound, he is immensely
successful. His charm and natural courtesy have
great allure. He is adored uninhibitedly, and not
only by women. Some of his greatest fans are men
in whom he inspires intense loyalty and by whom he
is much admired. Some of his caution with women
of his own standing professionally may be due to a
lack of self-confidence. Yet women generally seem
to like him, seem to spot that vulnerable quality in
him and home in on it. So he attracts perhaps that

mothering touch in all women because that is what he unconsciously seeks.

That same caution applied to his political life may also be due to lack of confidence. Again he feels at a disadvantage educationally: he does not have the automatic arrogance of those who believe they are well educated because of the names of the establishments they have attended, or the numbers and classes of their degrees. It is natural for him to feel this after the years of having it drilled into him that he was not qualified to do anything reasonably responsible. The experience enhanced his natural caution.

His body language can reveal uncertainty. With every change of job, his posture revealed a certain fear of getting things wrong. He confided, 'Thinking about doing something, I worry. Doing it, I'm fine.' His system is to master the facts, to brief himself. He says, 'I like twenty-four hours to think about decisions.' Yet he has no reason to lack confidence. Close colleagues are all in awe of his abilities to read, memorise, grasp facts, analyse situations and problem solve – all these qualities the mark of very high intelligence. Former banking colleague Will Manser says, 'John has a photographic memory. He only has to look at a page and he can remember what's on it.' He gains confidence through familiarity with a situation. His first and only budget as Chancellor in March 1990 was criticised for being over cautious and seemed to lack boldness. But by the autumn he was rampant, the toast of the party conference, having talked Mrs Thatcher into entry to the ERM. It was on this rising tide of confidence, his own and others', that he took the prize in the leadership elections just over one month later.

There was by the autumn of 1990, in his developing management of the economy, the first glimpse of something he usually keeps well hidden – a gambler's touch. Not the sort of gambling enjoyed by Nigel Lawson, his predecessor, an ace poker player in his youth and an optimist about economic trends. John Major is a secret gambler, a cautious gambler, the sort who studies form and works out a system. He only bets on certainties, but he has the sort of persistent application to his task that can work out the odds to a micron of exactitude and the intuitive judgment to know just when and how to place his bets. Initially his caution insists he be sure of his ground. He plays his cards very close to his chest and with a poker face. He never stops figuring the odds.

Perhaps that old recurring lack of self-confidence lies behind his secretiveness. He prefers not to reveal his aims because that might expose him to criticism. Or is it just that he leads a private life of the mind, and almost certainly of the feelings, and prefers that no one else has an inkling what he intends? Robert Atkins, one of his oldest and closest friends, comments, 'He is secretive. He goes into a corner and keeps very private when he wants to be. I remember when we were on holiday in Spain he said, "You've known me longer than anyone, you know some of my moods." But he said, "Everyone out there has no idea what I really think and what I really stand for, and they're going to find out and they're going to be so surprised." '

4

THE MOULDING
PROCESS

'My father's attitude was that if there was something
you wanted to do, there was absolutely no reason why
you shouldn't do it.'

'The Americans are right. It's what you can do, and
whether you can deliver what you want to deliver,
that counts.'

PERHAPS EVEN AS HE WAS born, John Major
awakened to that determination that is now
his hallmark. The will to survive is not bred
but born in one. It comes with the package. What
happens later determines the form it will take. The
will to win, the will to create, the will to destroy,
the will to dominate, the will to endure – will is
paramount and inherent.

Any child needs to be strong and determined to
help propel itself into the world. The moment of
separation from the mother's body is the first
assertion of its individual will. In the moments

and hours after the birth, however, the baby is acutely aware of its mother's emotions, and scientific research has shown how much that happens during the first days and weeks after birth has a profound impact on the later development of the child's character.

John Major had a particularly traumatic entry into the world. His mother was ailing before the birth, and after it both she and her baby nearly died. John still bears the marks of the blood transfusions he received then. If physical scars remain, so also might the memory of emotional ones. John's early experiences were evidently of struggle: struggle to be born of a sick mother, struggle to survive severe illness immediately after birth. Established theory says that fighting to be born and survive like this can condition the individual's whole approach to life. Someone who struggles to be born and survive birth tends later to tackle life with an inbuilt tendency to choose the hardest path forward or strain in situations where less effort would suffice.

Certainly, the facts of John Major's life seem to support this theory. The circumstances surrounding his birth and in subsequent weeks must surely have had an effect on him. Because of their respective illnesses, physical contact between mother and child at this point would have been negligible. It seems unlikely that bonding between John and his mother would have taken place under those constraints. This would have had a powerful and enduring effect on the child's later response to life. It has been scientifically shown that where early bonding fails to take place, the mother–child relationship is never quite as close as it might have been and a great deal of effort is required to develop any sort of closeness later.

As John was growing up his mother suffered from asthma and bronchitis in the winter time and was often ill in bed. When she was well she was very active in the family garden ornament business, and he may well not have enjoyed as much of her attention as he would have liked. He does not remember much about this period but says, 'She was working with my father a lot of the time. She was always busy. I was always busy. So we didn't spend hours sitting there. The person I did spend time with was my father.'

John's relationship with his mother was a loving one. He does not go overboard about it but the affection is plain to see as he recalls, 'I got on very well with her. It was fine. There were no problems.' He says he always remembers she seemed to be there as a presence, but her preoccupation with the business as he began to toddle and talk did limit her time with him. This, following the trauma of his birth and illness, may have been enough to trigger the extraordinary independence, toughness and determination which have been paramount in propelling him through early difficulties to extraordinary success.

Other early childhood experiences could have reinforced these qualities. A most significant fact of John's childhood is that he was, by virtue of the age gap between him and his elder brother and sister, technically if not actually an only child. Only children are known to develop differently from those with siblings of comparable age. They are more reliant on exchanges with adults, more often alone, and therefore develop interests such as reading and solitary games which may accelerate mental development.

Terry Major-Ball says, 'By the time John was five, I was seventeen and my sister was two years older. John was just a little kid while we were already grown up.' But Pat and Terry still lived at home, with the exception of Terry's two years' National Service. So even after the move to Coldharbour Lane, and later when the family was in a Brixton council flat, John was surrounded by adults. Terry may, as he recalls, have been too far removed in age to be able to take an interest in John, but he was still around the house.

Even more significant is the fact of his parents' relatively advanced ages. Although he did play with other children, John's preschool environment was conspicuously adult and mature. No wonder he gives the impression that he was one of those children who is adult in mind. Even childhood pictures of him suggest that the solemn-eyed boy was five going on forty-five.

But the family into which John Major was born had another distinguishing feature. They were, wherever they lived or whatever their financial circumstances, primarily a showbusiness family, so the home atmosphere was never conventional. John Major's much vaunted classlessness stems from the fact that his family, like all such families, did not fit into any existing social stratification. England with its little hierarchies and subhierarchies of class, its petty apartheids of trades, professions, birth and income, could not find a slot for people like this. Like gypsies, they were outside the social system. Class-free rather than class-less, they lived by their talents and stood on their own, special and apart. Chroniclers may waste hours trying to plumb the mystery of John Major's classlessness. It is this class freedom or class apartness which is the real key to his life philosophy, to his social foundations and social mobility; and that is what he wants for others. He wants them to be free to move through society regardless of so-called class, of origin or background. For it is not only some members of the upper classes who would like to maintain their status and keep others out. It was Miners' Union leader Arthur Scargill who berated non-striking miners for being 'Traitors to the working class'. John says, 'He's the worst.' In John Major's Britain no one will owe allegiance to a social class, nor find in it an excuse for failure or a barrier to their progress.

Fuelling this reforming fire, the philosophy of Tom Major, his extraordinary father, permeates John's views and political objectives. Much colourful and anecdotal material has been written about Tom the entertainer, but most important of all the information about him is the fact that he spent the formative years of his youth in America.

Abraham Ball, John and Terry's grandfather, arrived there soon after the ending of the American Civil War in 1865. The great Abraham Lincoln had been assassinated, but his nationalistic fervour still lived proudly on, particularly in the words of his address at Gettysburg, beginning with the immortal sentence, 'Fourscore and seven years ago, our fathers brought forth upon this continent a new nation, conceived in liberty and dedicated to the proposition that all men are created equal . . . the world will little note nor long remember what we say here, but it cannot forget what they did here.'

But the text has been enshrined in marble relief in Washington DC's Lincoln Memorial, and that final phrase: '. . . that the nation shall under God, have a new birth of freedom, and that government of the people, by the people and for the people, shall not perish from the earth', must have been engraved upon every American heart from that time onward. Indeed, to lasting effect on future generations on both sides of the Atlantic through its undoubted impact on Abraham Ball and his descendants.

Blood had been shed on the battlefields and political wounds were far from healed when Abraham Ball went to Pennsylvania. But the post-war boom economics were a healing force. In the North at least began the vast economic expansion on which the US's present great prosperity is based, and on which Abraham Ball also based a happy and prosperous lifestyle.

During the war, British elements had supported the South because of the economic preference of rich Lancashire mill owners for the cheap, slave-picked Southern cotton. Now, though, British money poured in to support America's great industrial expansion, primarily the building of railroads and rolling stock to carry goods from one end of the developing nation to another. Steel, the key to this industrial expansion, was produced near the coal mining areas such as Pennsylvania, where Abraham went originally to build a blast furnace. The British and their money were very welcome, in what was then developing into the industrial heartland of the North-eastern United States; and the American spirit and dream of everyone's right to 'life, liberty and the pursuit of happiness', enshrined in the Declaration of

Independence, infiltrated the credo of the immigrant Ball family. Thus did the powerful pioneering spirit of the emergent superpower have a direct impact on the attitudes of John Major's grandfather, his father, and through them on the British Prime Minister. John's absorption of these attitudes ensured he would become a Conservative whose views harked back to the Whig influence on nineteenth-century American Republicanism.

Terry Major-Ball says, 'My grandfather was a master builder who went to the US to build a blast furnace for Andrew Carnegie's steel mills near Philadelphia. While he was there he started his own building company. My father told me they lived in the foothills of the Allegheny Mountains in Pennsylvania, and spoke of being able to reach out of his bedroom window to pick a peach.'

Some interesting parallels or unusual coincidences link the Ball family and that of Abraham Lincoln. There is the frequency of the names Abraham, Thomas and John, in both male family lines, for instance. There is also the fact that Abe Lincoln's ancestor, Mordecai, of four generations before his own, was a blacksmith who set up a furnace for smelting iron ore in the town of Scituate in Massachusetts, later moving to Chester County, Pennsylvania, to continue the business – iron smelting being the forerunner to steel production in that coal-rich area. Mordecai's sons, including Abraham, the President's grandfather, wandered all over the US. So, after he had grown up and become an entertainer, did John's father Tom.

Like Lincoln, then, the British Prime Minister comes from an apparently migrant male line, and whereas the Lincolns appear to have come to New England from Norfolk in the early seventeenth century, young John Major lived there for a year as a baby when evacuated with his mother during World War II, and is now MP for a neighbouring district of East Anglia.

Lincoln's statue stands in Parliament Square between the Treasury and the House of Commons, another reminder of the many ties of blood and a shared libertarian creed between Britain and America.

Abraham Ball sent his wife back to England to have Tom, who was born on May 18 1879, in a village called Bloxwich near Walsall in the West Midlands. He was soon taken back to the US and life in the Allegheny Mountains and stayed there until he was 16. At this time he returned to Walsall, although he later went back to the US many times where he toured as a circus performer or in other theatrical companies. While in his teens in the US, Tom Ball played junior baseball and also became a baton thrower with one of Philadelphia's brass bands. The imprint of American culture and thought upon him in his formative years was inescapable.

The importance of all this in the life of young John Major is the power of the American vision which infiltrated his mind through the stories his father told him, some of them passed down from Grandfather Abraham.

When John was 5, his father was 69 and with failing sight. John spent a lot of time with him, steering him around the streets of their Surrey suburb. 'My father was a great raconteur, the best one-on-one raconteur I've ever heard. He had a long career to look back on, immensely varied experiences, and I think sometimes he probably embroidered his stories for a young and enthusiastic audience. But I would sit for hours listening and he would talk about everything. He did talk quite a bit about America, about what it was like before he was born. He used to talk about the differences between the North and the South, and he talked about going across the Atlantic in a sailing boat, which he'd done.'

John imbibed a great deal from the annals of Tom's great American experience: tales about the great railroads and the farms and the cities he had seen on his travels; the former slaves and the cotton and the war with the South; the Indians, the folk heroes and leaders, such as Lincoln; the great land with its prairies and mountain ranges, its lakes and forests, its mighty rivers and swamps, that lay like an Eden of opportunity between the Atlantic and the Pacific. But it was not so much the spellbinding stories that imprinted the American dream on to the blank pages of the future Prime Minister's young mind. John says, 'I learned a lot about his attitude, that if there was something you wanted to do, there was absolutely no reason why you shouldn't do it. That was always his view. He did a whole range of things. He wouldn't have been put off by artificial barriers.'

These views show John's father as a true son of America. So how could the boy John escape absorbing similar attitudes as he drank in the stories of life in that energetic land? John agrees that his political views blend perfectly with American ideas of upward mobility, the assumption that anything can be done with enough applied ingenuity, energy and effort. 'Yes,' he said, nodding, 'I'm very comfortable with all that.' No wonder one of a group of American Congressmen who were among the first Americans to meet the new Prime Minister at a London Embassy reception before Christmas 1990 said of him: 'He's our kind of guy.'

So John's class-mobile values were seeded by the American influence in his father's attitudes and reinforced by his theatre family's class-free mores which discriminated against no one. John says his father would never accept anything or anyone just because they were supposed to be someone special. 'He was no respecter of persons. I don't mean he was impolite: I don't ever recall him being impolite. He wouldn't be intimidated by position or authority.'

John's own views of others were probably formed around this time. Always polite, always gracious, considerate and tactful, he is only angered by snobs, by those who do assume they are superior, better than others, educationally or socially. He hates that. He does not tolerate that sort of person, whether they attack him or anyone else. His view is: 'The Americans are right. It's what you can do, and whether you can deliver what you want to deliver, that counts.'

Terry Major-Ball says, 'I don't think John realises how much his background has influenced him.' And it is true that he seems an astonishingly exact product of his background. However, it is more attitudes he has absorbed than precise views. He has said that he did not agree with his father's views on race, and on other matters he does not recall hearing distinct viewpoints at home. 'My father didn't talk about politics. I guess he probably voted Conservative. I don't know. I never heard party politics talked in the house. But all his instincts would have been Conservative, my mother's as well, and I'm pretty certain they voted Conservative, although I never asked them.'

Stories were what Tom told John. But stories are the most powerful way of conveying ideas, more powerful than any polemic. 'He talked a great deal about his experiences on stage. He had all sorts of stories about how theatrical artists of the past derived their names. Nosmo King was from the "no smoking" sign on a railway carriage window. He talked a great deal about his days on the stage. He talked about people a lot. He was a true judge of character. I used to be fairly certain that he would be able to judge whether someone was a hundred shillings to the five pound note very quickly. And my recollection is that he could.'

Tom Major dropped the name Ball somewhere along the line while touring with theatrical groups and medicine shows. These latter were entertainers hired by itinerant vendors of patent medicines. Something akin to modern TV advertising, they offered theatricals to attract customers who, once gathered together as an audience, would be sold various remedies.

Tom had had other names, too, which is one reason why Terry, who has been researching their father's life, has had difficulty now and then picking up the trail.

The great showbusiness tales Tom told John were from the Naughty Nineties of a hundred years ago, the glamorous era of the music halls. Terry says, 'We once found an old trunk. It was full of letters and press cuttings and theatre programmes autographed by Marie Lloyd and famous names of the day.' That and an acrobat's costume of their father's, quartered with a Stars and Stripes design, were lost when the Majors moved from Worcester Park to Brixton. 'There was so little room,' Terry says. 'All my mother's furniture had to go eventually because it got woodworm where it was in storage.'

Faint echoes of Tom Major are still alive today in the memories of the Beverley Sisters – identical twins Teddy and Babs, and Joy, another sister – who can still recount what their mother, once a glamorous musical hall player, said of Tom. The sisters, a well-known trio of singers who were household names of the Fifties and Sixties, and still perform today, are the daughters of Victoria Mills and George Coram whose musical comedy act Coram and Mills played at the Hackney Empire during the Twenties, at the same time as Tom Major.

The twins, Teddy and Babs, told me how their mother realised she had known John Major's father. Babs says, 'When John Major was made Chancellor, nothing about him had really been seen before.' Suddenly there were a great many articles about Major which picked up on his father's background. Teddy continues, 'Our mother, who although she was ninety was very sharp and alert, suddenly said, "I used to work with his dad." We wondered if our mother's mind was suddenly playing tricks. We just couldn't believe she and the Chancellor's father had worked together!

'Our mother then told us what an attractive man, and how charismatic and wonderfully intelligent, Tom Major was. She said she used to stand in the wings of the Hackney Empire and watch his act every night, so that our father became quite jealous and wouldn't let her watch any more.'

The sisters have been in touch with Terry Major-Ball to help with his research. 'He's been working jolly hard,' says John. 'Huge areas of my father's life were a total blank. I knew astonishingly little about him. He was just always there. In my first real memories of him, he was seventy.' Although there were the wonderful stories, 'By and large my father tended to look forward, not back. He would talk about the past but certainly his instincts were to look to the future. I never heard him complain of the things that had gone wrong, not once did I ever hear him do that, even when his health cracked up.'

John Major's own style is also to look forward rather than back though his preoccupations are, understandably, with the immediate. When he was Foreign Secretary, he said, 'I don't think about the future, the present is what matters.' He also refuses to complain about any of his own life's experiences. He says he does not regret anything, not even the accident which almost cost him his leg. He views it, and everything else which might be regarded as misfortune, as part of life. How can he complain when he has fused disadvantage and opportunity to bring him to this point of triumph? But there is regret at the untrue comments that have been made, the things that have caused unnecessary hurt to himself and to others, and for his family's distress at the untruths about his father's life, which appeared in some newspapers.

'I knew some anecdotal stories about him and then I saw them in print and I couldn't actually prove them right or wrong. There was a particularly vicious piece which appeared the day before the (1990) Budget. It suggested that my father was a charlatan and that my parents weren't married. It was in the *Sunday Correspondent* colour magazine. At this point our family knew that what had been said wasn't true but we couldn't prove it. That gave Terry a great incentive to find out about my father's life, and he's done so. Now he's managed to paint it in by various means, months and months of work in libraries and back through old newspapers. Whole years of what my father was doing, and where he was, when he went to South America, whereabouts he was on tour, that he actually did have a farm in Shropshire for a while . . . things that we had vaguely heard about but could never prove. Terry has been filling in those blanks because he was angry at the insinuation that my father would have told fibs.'

The Prime Minister is very protective of his family. It was, after all, a very united family that stood together when things were hard. His sensitivity is again in evidence as he speaks of them and particularly of his parents. His mother, he says, is the one people forget about: 'They are so obsessed by the fact that my father appeared in the circus that they've forgotten her.'

The importance of mothers in the lives of prominent people is usually overlooked. But it is often the mother's ambition and drive, especially if unexpressed in her own life, which is somehow lived out through her child's. Prominent individuals, especially those in the theatre or in politics, usually have extremely strong-willed, often dominant, mothers. John Major is no exception. He told me, 'My mother was the rock around which the family revolved. My father made the big decisions but my mother ran the home and our way of life. She ran the business, too, for many years, when my father was ill.'

Terry says, 'Mother was an extraordinary woman. I still remember her vividly. As a young boy, I never envisaged life without Mother. Even when she was not well enough, she would go out getting orders and collecting money. She was a very forceful woman and very successful at everything she did.' Perhaps it is not surprising that with a mother like this and a father who was, according to Terry, 'Both strong physically, a big man, and a strong personality,' at least one of the Major brood should grow up with enough push to become Prime Minister.

John's father was a strong force for discipline in his life, someone who demanded and exacted high standards. John remembers that, 'If I went home from school and told my father I had come second, he would never praise me, but would say I must come first.'

Terry says, 'My father was never one for whom there was any second best. Something was either perfect or it had to be thrown away. He got this from his own father. I remember he told me that he worked for his father for a time in his teens before coming back to England. His father would look at a wall of bricks he had built and if there was any cement smeared on it the wall would have to be scrubbed down until there wasn't a scrap of cement to be seen on the brickwork. My father was the same. When we lived in the bungalow, there was a pile of garden ornaments at the bottom of our garden. Today they might have been sold as seconds but Father wouldn't have that. They were either perfect or they weren't for sale.

'He was not a Victorian father, I didn't have a Victorian upbringing, but I had a Victorian attitude towards my father. I worried about not pleasing him. And if I did anything wrong, I worried even more terribly that I would be out of favour with Mother.'

John too refers to his mother's strict outlook on life. 'She was quite prim in some ways, quite puritanical. I don't mean physically puritanical, I mean puritanical about behaviour. She had a clear sense of what was right and what was wrong and would expect that, there was no doubt about it, there were some things you just didn't do. She didn't bother to rationalise why you didn't do them, she just knew it wasn't the way to behave and you didn't do it. You didn't realise what a strong personality she was. She was very tough.'

John also told me his mother was rather authoritarian. He did not generally have battles of will with her, but, 'When I got older, in my teens and she was really rather ill, there were frustrations when she didn't realise I'd grown up, but very minor.'

The pressure of living up to such exacting standards in childhood is perhaps one of the reasons why John Major ultimately became a high achiever. Workaholism and attainment are not necessarily linked but in John's case they surely must be. He, like others whose parents demand relentless striving for excellence, is unable to rest. Attainment of an objective is never a cause for relaxation. He simply prepares for the next task. People like John Major take their work to bed and away on holidays – if they have them. Even in their leisure hours they tend to be driven constantly to improve themselves.

This kind of behaviour carried to extremes may lead to unhappiness since whatever is accomplished is never enough. Parental training has stressed that there is always room for improvement. Confidence is never very high because criticism is constantly expected. The only happiness lies in striving towards the next goal. For John Major, and for others like him, happiness lies in the pursuit of the moving frontier. For him, as for other high achievers, it is always better to travel than to arrive. So it is with a kind of wistfulness that he sometimes looks at life out of the window of his career's express train.

Jeffrey Archer says, 'I went to see him the day after he became Prime Minister and he said, "There's life after politics, Jeffrey. Don't forget we've got to go to Australia to see the Test Match." And I think he's looking forward to that more than anything, as we've arranged for years that we will do the Australian tour together.'

An exacting character or not, John is very proud of his mother and speaks of her tenderly. He told me, 'She didn't do anything very prominent. She was a dancer in my father's travelling show. Her act was called Glade and Glen. We've got some old photographs. She was very slender, right up to the end of her days.

'But in those early days, my father was still married to his first wife, Kitty, who was an extremely glamorous redhead, quite talented, who wrote quite a lot of music and appeared on stage with my father for twenty odd years. But they had no children and then Kitty had a terrible accident.

The iron girder safety bar above the stage fell down and hit her and she was in hospital for about a year, mentally damaged, and then died. My mother, who had grown up by then, married my father a few years later. My mother always told the story that before she died, Kitty had said to her that she must marry my father and look after him.'

Gwen Major was born in April 1905, 26 years after Tom, who was 50 when she married him. John's relationship with her appears to have been one in which she offered him a model of femininity combined with steely strength. A mother who combines a bountifully loving nature with drive is a tough woman to replace. John may have found it hard to meet girlfriends who matched up to her, and friends of his teens and early twenties find it hard to recall any at all. John's friend Clive Jones, from Brixton Young Conservatives days, remembers that during the early Sixties John had a girlfriend who was the daughter of a publican with premises near his home in Burton Road.

Terry talks of how his mother 'in a way put me off women. I'm frightened of women'. Terry is happily married but he remembers that when he went off to do his National Service in Germany, 'Mother warned me, "Don't go out with any of those German girls." ' He also says, 'She had strict rules about girls, about how they were to be treated. They were to be treated as ladies.'

John also has a tendency to be shy of women professionally, although being a warm-blooded male, he can be very affected by women as women. The first hail of criticism against him, the day after his appointment as Prime Minister, came when it was realised that there was not a single woman in his Cabinet. He swiftly made up for this by appointing two female Ministers of State and a woman head of the Number 10 think tank. He is, however, as his friends agree, very much a man's man, not at ease with women, though he has been professionally close to, and the beneficiary of, relationships with several older women, of whom Mrs Thatcher is the prime example. Perhaps he can accept women who fill the role his mother occupied of advisor, facilitator and source of supportive strength. Norma, his wife of twenty years, is, 'Very much like my mother in many ways, though not as assertive.' Norma has the sweetness and gentleness of John's mother, and indeed many of her strengths. On another occasion he said, 'Norma isn't like my mother in many ways at all. She's not like her to look at, but she's similar in the way that she protects the family from outside pressure.'

John also has vivid memories of his mother in another light. 'My mother had a greater affinity for people than anyone I've ever met. Her capacity to relate one on one was remarkable, and she attracted lame ducks rather like glue attracts paper. Our kitchen was usually full of someone who was in difficulty and having tea poured into them and common sense poured down them. And she continued this for a very long time. She had a great sense of community property. What was hers was, by and large, available to other people as well. She was very strong-minded about it.'

Margaret Jay, John's agent in St Pancras North for the period 1971–4 when he was candidate there, says that, 'John would always go out of his way to see people who had problems.' The same is true of his record in Huntingdon, and even now that he is Prime Minister he is still personally attending to constituents' problems, insisting that he must even when he could get away with paying less attention because of his demanding executive role. Could it be that his own concerns with the disadvantaged are a continuation of his mother's kindness towards people in need? 'Could the entire nation be just one great hobbling duck,' I teased. 'Be quiet, be quiet,' he laughed. 'I'm not in my mother's class, I assure you.'

Terry too extols his mother's open-hearted qualities with a typical story: 'I was a fairly solitary youth. I used to go up to the top of Worcester Park High Street and walk up and down or sit in the milk bar. I got to know another boy who went to the milk bar and one day I brought him home to tea.

'Mother found out that his parents had died and he was on his own and he stayed the night. The next day, my mother and father went off and bought a bunk bed and moved it into my bedroom, and there he stayed until he was married.

'My mother was the most gregarious woman I have ever met. My mother loved the world and the world loved my mother. Our house was always open house. My mother was a theatrical person and everyone was welcome from the highest to the lowest. I haven't found anyone yet who remembers my mother in a detrimental way. She was very well liked. People have spoken about John making friends in politics, about how he gets his way without badgering them. He gets this from my mother. She preferred to have friends than enemies.'

John, it is well known, has pursued this course throughout his career in politics. Praise of his ability to get on with people, to deal with difficulties and persuade people to his viewpoint, is widespread. Clearly, he seeks to resolve issues without animosity. He has a great desire to be liked, to relate smoothly and harmoniously to people. His loathing of criticism and of being written about insensitively stems from this desire to be seen as likeable and to be on good terms with everyone. He does not avoid rows, however, though his anger is still, except with close family and friends, curbed to a polite level of argument. While he can control the relationship's tone, it is kept friendly. He is, more than most people, averse to disapproval. This may be something he both inherited and learned from his mother.

This, together with his father's perfectionist influence and his school failure, probably goes a long way towards explaining his lifelong desire to prove himself, which seems to have been the most powerful motivating force behind his achievement. It may stem quite simply from his desire for approval. His craving for approval may stem from the early deprivation of loving contact with his mother caused by their illnesses after his birth.

This may also explain that quality of vulnerability which is part of his appeal. But his need for approval, coupled with his extreme sensitivity, could turn out to be his fatal flaw. He focusses unduly on press criticism. He relishes combat with the opposition but is upset by adverse comment from within his own party. It was reported that he was hurt by Tory criticism, which he interpreted as a lack of support, for his poll tax revamp. He shows signs of failing to adjust to the fact that, unlike Ministers whose activities are confined to their own area of responsibility, the PM is never out of the limelight, or the crossfire. He bears ultimate responsibility for all departmental policies and must take the flak from his own side as well as from opposition parties.

Division, rancour, acrimony, are not his style. But, so far, he has not managed to spread his techniques of damage limitation, so successful in smaller circles, to the entire operation of government. Perhaps this will prove impossible. Now that he is in the open, he must get used to being the target he never was while keeping his head well down in a department. If he cannot, he may, by being too responsive to critics, be swayed from his own clear-sighted objectives and the impeccable sense of timing which has always been his strength.

As we have seen, the educational system of the day failed John Major. His above average abilities were not conspicuously channelled in one direction – mathematics or music, for instance – and he slipped through the academic net. Were he a child now he would probably be identified as one of high ability and therefore be placed in a special educational category. High IQ and sensitivity are often linked according to Dr Joan Freeman, President of the European Council for High Ability and Director of the 15-year Gulbenkian Research Project on Gifted Children in Britain, in a forthcoming book, *Gifted Children Grow Up*. Sensitivity can, however, often be a reason for poor performance, even in gifted children. A system that depends on examinations as the main guide to potential is thus fallible – as the Prime Minister has often mentioned.

John Major's sensitivity, both on behalf of himself and of others, is very evident, indeed remarkable. He seems truly to feel for others and to be aware of them in an unusually empathetic way. Empathy is also, research suggests, a feature of high intelligence. No one who is informed in these areas can doubt, surely, that John Major is a man of exceptional ability. Even the uninformed must realise that to have achieved what he has in such a relatively short time, despite enormous early obstacles, shows a high degree both of intelligence and its application. Traits which make his high intelligence readily apparent include his exceptional memory, his ability to grasp issues quickly and get to the heart of problems, and his ability to concentrate long and hard.

As a child at a time when gifted children were assessed according to very narrow criteria of exam results and special talents, neither John's family nor his teachers realised his true intelligence.

The same applies to others today, and keenly aware of the problem, he has spoken out against the assumption that academic credentials are the only acknowledged measure of ability to perform in a job, and that anyone without them should be consigned to the job market scrap heap from school leaving. The argument has come under fire from educationalists and socialists, but it is essentially the same argument as that used to discredit the eleven plus as a means of dividing secondary school sheep from goats on grounds of exam-passing ability. Surely consigning young people to the employment scrap heap at sixteen is as bad?

He explains his views thus: 'I don't like these barriers, the people who come into a particular

organisation in a different stream because they
have a particular educational qualification. If it is
a specific qualification, if you're a chemist going
in for chemistry, then clearly that is a different
matter. There should always be a chance to make
good, to branch out and to gain fair access to
opportunities, all through life. Underestimation of
human potential because of the absence of a piece
of paper is tragic both for the individual excluded
and for the community that loses their undeveloped
gifts.' Under these circumstances, only those with an
extraordinary amount of audacity, determination and
persistence can, like John Major, win through from a
bad start.

So John Major's powerful drive can be interpreted
as the desire to prove himself, to receive acknowledgement of the gifts his school failed to notice, to reach
the pinnacle of excellence exacted by his father, and
to achieve the love, admiration and approval of society
as a substitute for the close bond with his mother
which the circumstances of his birth denied him.
Lest to explain the man's life in this way should
appear insulting or demeaning, it should be said that
almost any high achiever will have a pattern of such
needs and drives behind their success. Contentment
is the enemy of achievement.

John Major's workaholism has been an asset
during his rise, but has potentially dangerous
consequences now. As the first one hundred days
of his office passed, he demonstrated that he is
not the polystyrene Premier. His fatigue after the
sleepless nights of the Gulf War, more than half
a dozen overseas trips since he took over his new
brief in November, and the strains of dealing with

economic problems and the poll tax row at home, culminated in symptoms of exhaustion. His wife told journalists he had been overworking and should rest.

But John Major has been overworking for years without fatigue. He has even said he has an easier time now than he did as Chief Secretary. The difference since he became Prime Minister may be the overwhelming intensification of the need to achieve in this job, knowing that the moving horizon has now stopped. At the peak of the mountain one has to raise the flag, build the cairn – and after that it's downhill all the way. What John Major knows is that his life's work has now reached its ultimate testing point. All the rest was training and practice for that coveted top job. The pressure to succeed and achieve is much greater on him now. In this job he stands or falls in history by his true ability. This is where he really does have to deliver the goods, and it has to be a daunting prospect.

So how does he relax? He has few interests outside his work. Reading, however, has always been a refuge. And it is in books that he has found the companionship of great and like minds, and a stimulus for his own ideas and imagination.

Like many others before him he has been able to extract meaning and inspiration from the highest but also the least pretentious books. He can read a political biography, memoir or philosophy text, but can also gain from reading novels of all kinds.

He particularly enjoys the classics and not only reads but rereads them. His favourite novels are said to be those of Jane Austen and of Anthony Trollope. Perhaps his immersion in the Trollope novels is one of the factors which has affected his manner of speech.

It is undoubtedly a little dated at times. Reading Trollope, it is possible to see how the cadence and phrases of the nineteenth century have impressed themselves upon John Major's use of language. His father, too, being a man of the nineteenth century, may have given John a verbal model that now strikes the ear as old-fashioned, although clear and exact in meaning and economic in its use of words.

When he was a child, John read books like *Twenty Thousand Leagues Under the Sea*. He also enjoyed the Br'er Fox and Br'er Rabbit tales of wiliness in the animal world. Br'er Fox's motto was, 'I think I'll lie low for a while.' Playing grey, perhaps?

One book which John Major has read and thought extraordinary is a novel called *Under the Salt* by Costain about a US Senator who dreams of another life, led in England during the barons' period of struggle against King John for the creation of the Magna Carta. John often mentions the Magna Carta; there is even a picture of him holding the ancient document which was being sent to California as part of the American bicentenary celebrations. His proposal in April 1991 for a Citizen's Charter is a product of his interest in the document signed by King John in 1215 which guaranteed English nobles their right to oppose the monarch, and which was the first step in the evolution of the British Parliament. Perhaps some insight into the Prime Minister can be gained from his fascination with this book. It is based on reincarnation and is also a romantic love story with the idealistic theme that the need and capacity for love and beauty is perhaps the highest human state. The story contains elements appealing to his enduring concern with the rights of man, expressed here in American and English contexts; a concern with the struggle for political improvement as being essential for human progress; and interest in the as yet untapped reservoir of human potential.

One sentence from the book appears to reflect John Major's own early experience: 'Gradually, I became convinced that for some reason, far outside my powers of understanding, I had been sent back into the world. I was here to accomplish something, not to live an aimless life like people around me. When would I know what I was supposed to do about it?'

While he was awaiting the answer to this and other questions, in his childhood and teens, he also enjoyed radio programmes like the 'Goon Show' and 'Much Binding in the Marsh'. Nowadays he likes to listen to reruns or recordings of these. Buddy Holly is a favourite singer, again harking back to earlier days. Not, one suspects, because John Major is unable to move forward with the times, as are so many nostalgia buffs, but because since those days he has probably had no time to get to know any of the current radio and TV shows or find new enthusiasms outside the political world. Political people are usually hard at work while the evening shows are broadcast. They stick to the news programmes featuring themselves and their rivals.

Another influence in his childhood was Mr Swain. He says, 'Mr Swain was a retired senior official of the Post Office who lived next door to us in Brixton. I used to go there, and he was a very gentle, kind man. He used to help me with my homework. My mother and father were a different generation, they didn't understand homework, but Mr Swain did. He was so quiet and undemonstrative, very gentle. It was a rough world and here was a sea of tranquillity.'

John's difficulty then, which increased as he grew older, was the widening gulf of experience between himself and his parents. As a young child the time he spent with his father was a spur to his imagination. He was stimulated and his mind enriched by the great variety of the extraordinary tales his father told. But as he grew into his teens and his father approached his eighth decade, there was a problem of identification. What John missed most of all was a role model sufficiently expressive of the vigour and virility, the strength and power, of a young male. His father, the amazing, charismatic old man who had wisdom and experience and had lived a remarkable life, had now passed on his attitudes and his beliefs, had strung the loom of the child's thoughts and drawn the picture his life would weave. They had sat at home together or gone to football matches over the river at Chelsea Football Club. Now John needed someone younger on whom to model his coming manhood. Who was it to be? Terry was off and away in his own life of an older teenager. There would have been neighbours like Mr Swain, teachers, school friends. But no obvious person for him to emulate. No one who was both old and young enough to be a role model.

Where then, if there was no one at Rutlish whom he could admire and follow, would he turn for a male image? Who would be strong enough, heroic enough, clever and male enough, for a boy to strive to imitate? His mother – strong, assertive, dominant and always busy – may have confused him, for his male role model, his father, was becoming more passive while she, the female, showed strength and control. Gwen dominated and controlled the domestic scene in which Tom Major now became an invalid. For John, then, the teens were a time of confusion. His status changed by the move to Brixton; his academic ability open to question by his failure at school; his only male role model weakening and becoming helpless through blindness; alienated from snobby school fellows and rejected by his teachers as a drop out, to whom did he turn for some confirmation of his identity and his male self?

This is where cricket and cricketers became so important to him, chief among them Len Hutton, later Sir Leonard Hutton, the great English batsman of the Fifties. And there were others like Peter May, Freddie Trueman and the Australian Richie Benaud – all strong, resourceful, successful and masculine, and above all heroic as cricketers. Cricket had to be important, and the men who played it heroes. So John clung to cricket as if to a liferaft. He supported Surrey, the home team for his old stamping ground of Worcester Park, and still does. Nostalgia? He has moved so fast and so far that supporting Surrey for cricket, Chelsea for football, listening to the 'Goon Show' and returning to South London for the odd takeaway, are all he has to remind him of who he once was. All he has of roots.

Is there confusion still about his identity? In a way. It is part of the price to be paid for his dramatic rise. To move in three decades from a poor and uncertain life in Brixton to the tenancy of 10 Downing Street and Chequers, and all that this entails, is like travelling to another planet. This is migration, vertically through society rather than horizontally to another location. As studies show,

migrants with roots have a stronger sense of their
own worth and are more stable and successful than
the rootless. John's family, his cricket, his old haunts
across the river from Westminster and his home in
Great Stukeley (see Chapter 6) are the stabilisers in
his rocketing flight path.

Workaholic or not, John Major has watched a lot
of cricket lately; more, Norma says, in the last two
or three years than ever before. This seems strange
because the last two or three years have been the
busiest and most demanding of his career. Perhaps,
under more pressure, he needs more time to goof
off? Or perhaps he just needs to identify again with
his forgotten heroes. Watching those white-flannel
led figures, their movements choreographed by the
gravitational dynamics of a leatherbound ball struck
by willow, is not only temporally to lose himself and
his cares in the game's slow motion geometry, but also
to seek out and find the lost hero in himself.

Jeffrey Archer tells a well-rehearsed tale of the
Prime Minister's encounter with an old icon. He
told me, in raconteur's style, 'We were at Lord's
one afternoon when John was Chief Secretary and
were sitting in the box together. "Look who's over
there!" he said. "My hero, a god!" "Yes," I said.
"I spoke to him about three years ago when he got
the freedom of Sheffield and I had the honour of
meeting him." John said, "I'd love to meet him."
So I said, "Come over with me." He said, "I couldn't
do that." So I said, "All right," and left the room
and went into the MCC tea box where Sir Leonard
was sitting. "Good afternoon, Sir Leonard." And he
said, "Jeffrey, how nice to see you," which was very
flattering.

'I said, "My guest today is the Chief Secretary; he'd love to meet you." He said, "Oh, I'd love to meet him." So I went back to John and said, "Sir Leonard would love to meet you," otherwise he would never have come. So, I took John over and they had an hour together. And when he came out after the hour, John was like a schoolboy. He said to me, "I will remember that for the rest of my life, and I will thank you for the rest of my life." '

The power of his heroes in white flannels has made cricket itself a psychic symbol of great importance to him. The associations of the game with the dream he once held, before he surrendered it to that other dream of going into Parliament, take him back to his youth.

As Glen Knight remembers, John talked about cricket all the time then. Because cricket was a gladiatorial field of which he dreamed, waking and sleeping; because cricket in his life was both a refuge and an inspiration. A cricket game was a complete escape from the handicaps of life in Brixton with no money and ageing, ailing parents, where nothing and no one else seemed really to connect. It was a possible future for a boy who showed some talent and skill with a bat. And so the game and its heroes became deeply embedded in his psyche. Even though he took a trial with Surrey at some point but was not accepted, cricket remained at least psychologically a way out. And, in a way, it symbolised a kind of heaven denied to a Brixton boy. A heaven such as Rupert Brooke described in 'The Soldier', the famous poem foretelling his death in battle:

> . . . A pulse in the eternal mind, no less
>   Gives somewhere back the thoughts by England
>   given;
> Her sights and sounds; dreams happy as her day;
>   And laughter, learnt of friends; and gentleness,
>   In hearts at peace, under an English heaven.

Yes, cricket has all this, the sanctuary and sanctity of an England that is all blue skies, green lawns and summer days, punctuated only by the sound of leather on willow, the roar of the crowd as the batsmen run, and the clink of teacups in the background. For a poor boy in Brixton, and for a workaholic Prime Minister who carries the burdens of state, this image and its reality must have undiminished charm and persistence.

David Rogers remembers an incident that reflects on another aspect of the importance of cricket in John Major's life. He and John used to travel on the train together back and forth from Beckenham. He told me, 'We were coming back one night, it must have been June or July, about eight o'clock or so, quite a light evening. Just before you get into the suburbs proper, you come out of London, the train stops and there are all these playing fields. There was a cricket game in progress and the batsman was out and someone was coming to take guard. I said, "He's looking round to see where the fielders are." And John said, "No. He's looking to see where the spaces are." And I thought the whole of his life was there. Not seeing where the people were but seeing where the spaces are.'

5
THE POLITICAL ROPE TRICK

'I think the thing I resent most is people telling other people they can't achieve something and they can't do it . . . Don't believe them. You can do it if you're prepared to put in the effort, and if you have the luck, and you have the persistence. Don't believe the people who tell you you can't do it.'

'Nothing makes me more determined to do something than someone telling me I can't.'

THE BRIXTON ROAD IS A wide, dusty thoroughfare, lined on one side by stately terraces of early Victorian elegance, and on the other the same, interspersed since the Sixties with the rain-stained concrete cliffs of council blocks. It is little more than a mile up this road from the heart of Brixton, where the shops and the street market and the railway converge into a congested and colourful mêlée, to the Oval cricket ground, where the teenage John Major indulged his passion for the game of gentlemen.

Beyond the Oval, under a railway bridge, still

going north, one comes suddenly upon the Thames at Vauxhall, and from here, where the grey stream runs deep between high stone walls, you can see a mile downstream to Parliament.

Even on a fine day this landscape is grey and desolate. The wind blows off the river on to ugly office blocks while the streets leading off the Albert Embankment deep into Lambeth, at night now the muggers' territory of fear, are adrift with litter. But in 1959, when on his sixteenth birthday John Major joined the Conservative Party, this was a freer, friendlier place, undivided by tensions of race or extremes of wealth.

He remembers, 'It was coincidence that it was my birthday. I was at home. We then lived in Burton Road, and this tubby boy with a bicycle knocked on the door and asked me to join. His name was Neville Wallace and I think he became legal representative to the NFU eventually.'

This Brixton of the late Fifties was a place where the innocence and make-do-and-mend enthusiasm of post-war Britain was still alive and well. Life had a certain simple, old-fashioned rhythm. The corner grocery shops closed at half-past five and the pubs opened promptly at the same hour. They were mostly of the spit and sawdust sort, but with Victorian windows and mahogany bars, and fireplaces that burned real coal in winter, they were cosy and convivial homes from home for those whose dwellings lacked such comforts.

Follow the Brixton Road from the Oval southwards and you come to another railway bridge under whose black bulk double decker buses squeeze on their way to and from the southern suburbs of Streatham and

Norwood. Heavy traffic bound for and from the south coast shakes the streets and casts its smoke and dust over the shoppers. To the left, just before Coldharbour Lane where John's family first found a home in Brixton, is the street market with its packed stalls of fruit, vegetables and colourful clothes. On a Saturday the market is thronged with bargain hunting crowds. It was in this same place, thirty or more years ago, that John Major, as an early school leaver, first gave public voice to his political opinions.

Clive Jones, his old friend from those early days of street politics, remembers they used to have not so much a soap box as a set of steps with a platform on top. From these, John harangued the Brixton market shoppers with his views: Conservative, of course, and in that poor working-class neighbourhood where Tory meant Toff and Them, and Us meant Labour, distinctly minority.

Having entered this world a refugee from a more comfortable one, having passed through a period of alienation and isolation in a 'rough world', having left school where he found cold comfort and no soul mates, he had at last found like-minded companions. Suddenly he was one of a group with a common purpose, bravely proclaiming Conservative views amid overwhelmingly Labour territory.

This called for verbal guerilla warfare. After years of rebelling against school and feeling out of place, now John Major found something he could legitimately fight for, and in company. As Clive Jones, who campaigned in the neighbouring Lambeth constituency of Vauxhall, told me, 'We had had local Labour government for as long as anyone could remember. We were never on the defensive because we had nothing to defend so we were permanently on the attack. It was an uphill struggle.' For John, this rebellion with fellow activists was novel and challenging – and crucial. Out of school and with nowhere to go in life except up, it brought him a sense of belonging, of comradeship at arms against the common enemy of the Labour status quo. Had he not gone to Brixton, he would not have developed politically in the same way. He would not have met Marcus Lipton, would not have gone at his invitation to the Commons that day. He would, he is sure, come what may, have drifted towards politics, but he would not, in a more conventionally Tory area, have experienced this rough and tumble or have grown accustomed to being the challenger, the minority rebel, as he did in this most Labour of areas.

In a Surrey suburb's quietly respectable streets, he would have lacked the challenge to make street corner speeches or the adversary on which to hone his budding skills. Besides, where the Tories were likely winners it would have been best to use the conventional approaches of canvassing and coffee mornings. Hustings speeches would be saved for elections and not made for the hell of it. In Brixton, there was not only a challenge but anything went. No one at Central Office cared what the local Tories did, within reason. It was a Labour area, there was nothing to lose and everything to gain from winning attention for one's views. So this was showbusiness politics and all the fun of the fair.

In this graveyard for Conservative candidates, the superficially quiet, polite John Major was able to vent his need to rebel and provoke, and to develop his political strengths and relish their use. The attack element is still in him even if later he has concealed it under a silken smoothness. But he can fight more roughly too, and though few have really experienced his street fighter's armature yet, they surely will. The adult John Major combines the courteous gentleman and the street-sharp political fighter under one thin skin.

This ground in which John Major tried to cultivate the first flowering of his political career seemed hard and stony, but it had a hidden spring which often watered and refreshed his aspirations. He has, throughout his career, been fortunate in encountering not only circumstances but people who have inspired, guided, taught, groomed or promoted him. When he first joined Brixton Conservatives, no help was in sight, but for the moment he did not need it. Out of disadvantage came advantage. It was inevitable among an embattled minority that anyone vocal, articulate and intelligent, and willing to give the time to seemingly hopeless and unrewarding work, would rise swiftly. Teenaged John came quickly to the fore in this small group of defenders. At first his rise was encouraging. He became involved with the Young Conservatives and almost immediately held office. Between 1960, when he was 17, and 1964, when he reached his majority and stood for council, he became successively Treasurer, Vice Chairman, Political Officer, and then Chairman of Brixton Young Conservatives. Later there were other offices including Chairman of the Association.

In the earliest days, especially, his political work gave meaning to his otherwise dead-end life. It blossomed rewardingly and, in contrast to the lack of career satisfaction, provided encouraging stimulus and opportunity. During the Fifties and early Sixties, politics was heady stuff. People, especially young people, had much less money than is usual today, so going out to theatres and restaurants was a very rare treat rather than a normal event. TV was in its infancy, and other lounge lizard pastimes such as booze and billiards were hardly substitutes for the ready made opportunities for meeting people, partying, and just plain having fun among thousands of young people joined in a common cause.

Jean Lucas, who became John's mentor from about 1967, was Conservative Agent for Clapham and then came into the Lambeth area as an organiser for the North Lambeth group of constituencies, which comprised Brixton, Vauxhall and Clapham. She remembers the Fifties and early Sixties as a particularly enthusiastic and exciting time in politics, especially in the Conservative Party.

'There was this tremendous energising enthusiasm that a lot of the Young Conservatives had.' She feels that this mood, during the Fifties particularly, was a continuation of people's 'Passionate interest in getting Britain right after the war – people were mad about politics. There were huge meetings. I had 280 Young Conservative branches to look after when I was organiser in the South Eastern area. I produced people like Peter Walker, Paul Beresford, some MPs, judges, company directors. They were all really vibrant people.'

The Young Conservatives throve as a social as well as a political forcing house, a place where young women might meet promising young future politicians, as indeed Norma met John, though slightly later. There were many links between constituency groups, and the

oment of triumph: the Majors outside Number 10, jubilant
ter John's leadership victory.

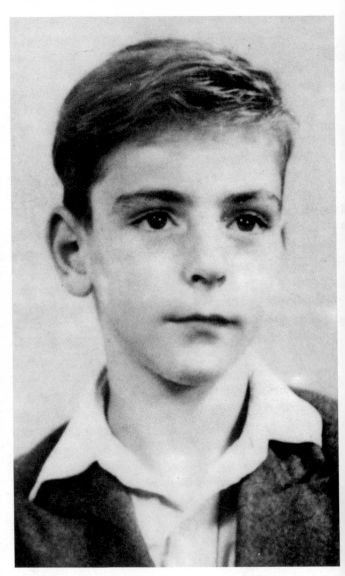

An eight-year-old John Major.

Rebel in white flannels: John at fifteen with Rutlish School cricket team (centre).

(Rex Features)

Tom Major, the vaudeville performer, in action (left).

(Manni Mason's Pictures)

Above: The humble suburban bungalow at 260 Longfellow Road, Worcester Park, Surrey, where John Major spent his first decade, before the family were forced to move to Brixton.

(Yoshinari Yamamoto)

Right: John playing the game of his childhood heroes outside the modest four-bedroomed house that he says is 'the home I always dreamed of having'.

(Syndication International Ltd)

gust 1984: two old political buddies, John Major and Robert
kins, indoctrinate their sons—both named James—in the
ort they love.

(Ewing-Reeson Photography)

John Major with George Bush at his first summit in December 1990 in the misty heights of Camp David, the US presidential retreat, where they discussed the Gulf crisis. John says, 'I get on very well with Bush. I'm very comfortable with American ideas of class mobility.'

(Official White House photograph)

hn Major standing on a captured Iraqi tank addressing
itish troops during a surprise visit to liberated Kuwait a few
ys after the Gulf ceasefire in March 1991.

(Syndication International Ltd)

aptured Kalashnikov brings a smile to the Prime Minister's
e.

(Syndication International Ltd)

So if she sells sea-shells ... sea shore,
I'm sure that the shells are sea-

John Major charms another generation of prospective voters in his Huntingdon constituency. Perhaps he means to go on and on...

(*Manni Mason's Picture*

Greater London Young Conservatives was a further level where the more ambitious and active political juniors might meet each other, discuss policy and encounter a wider circle of the up and coming, meet MPs, hear Cabinet Ministers speak. To anyone as interested as John Major in a political career, Greater London activities were a natural progression from office holding at constituency level. He went to some GLYC events but there were snags: 'I had the opportunity to get on the London Executive of the Young Conservatives, but I couldn't do it because I couldn't afford to travel around London and I couldn't afford a car.'

There were many frustrating elements in his situation, then, but still the stories from those days convey an exuberance and enthusiasm that is gone from today's world. Perhaps politics, even now, is one of the last remaining areas of contemporary life where there is still the possibility of passion, through the ferment of ideas and espousal of causes.

The Conservative Party is traditionally more responsive to practicality than passionate ideals, more cautious than radical. But the party has been transformed by Margaret Thatcher's leadership, for she conveyed and forged a practical doctrine out of a passionate commitment to ideas and ideals. Mrs Thatcher's generation, politicised under Churchill's leadership, was fifteen or more years ahead of John Major's and she would have been in her twenties while the Fifties frisson was in full swing, though young enough to be motivated and mobilised by political passion.

Perhaps we are only now experiencing the impact of the later years of that apparent Renaissance of

Conservatism, ignited by Churchill and taken up by Iain Macleod, as Conservative politicians, whose views were moulded during that enthusiastic age, now come to power.

The Fifties was a successful period for the Tories. From 1951–64 they held office continuously. So it is conceivable that even in solid Labour areas like Lambeth, a few remaining bubbles of campaigning enthusiasm continued to float merrily above the dilapidated tenements and austere council blocks. Harold Wilson's first Labour Government, elected in 1964 with a majority of four, changed the tempo and the tune of national politics. A grimmer note began to emerge and the bubble of Tory enthusiasm burst. But there was still, even then, a lightness of political being, a sparkle and a gloss to politics as socialism's latest manifestation led the debate. But, not long after Wilson went to the country again in 1966 to secure himself a much larger majority, and by the time in May 1967 when John returned on crutches from his aborted trip to Africa, the Conservatives were the beneficiaries of a swing in public opinion.

Robert Atkins first encountered John Major in those heady days of the early Sixties at Greater London Young Conservative meetings. 'Greater London Young Conservatives were a great force for change in the Conservative Party at the time. The GLC was formed in 1964–5 and (John) was really only on the fringes of that, but nonetheless an important fringe. Then there was a great punch up in Streatham, which is in the Lambeth borough, in 1968 over some fairly nasty right wingers who were frightfully raucous and were also campaigners in the Greater London YCs against a wide variety of things, like the Immigration Act. John was fairly forceful in having them chucked out. I was involved in Haringey doing similar things.'

An upsurge of fairly alarming Powellite racialist followers in its ranks disturbed the Conservative Party's mainstream. The extremists were vocal, received much press coverage, and there was a groundswell of support for their views, especially in areas with large Caribbean or Asian populations. Opinions vary as to John Major's role in disciplining Lambeth's racialist elements. Clive Jones who first met him around 1963 remembers the story differently.

Clive, a large, jovial character who now lives in a flat in a small terraced house in Dulwich, still very much the grass roots activist involved in local politics, describes some of his friend's early political history: 'We were both around the twenty mark and enjoying our politics. He was living in Burton Road with his family. His father was dead but his mother was still alive and his brother and his sister and brother-in-law and maybe one or two children were living there too. The house was on a rather nice private estate, the Minet estate.' Both Clive and John had stood for the council in 1964 when John was only just old enough to stand. 'The election was in May and he was 21 at the end of March.'

'Both of us enjoyed it all very much,' remembers Clive, 'and had lots of thoughts of going to Parliament.' Clive subsequently stood for Parliament in Vauxhall, but was never Central Office approved, did not progress to further winnable seats and subsequently gave up the attempt to become an MP. Two years after that first council election, in December 1966, some nine and a half months after Labour's election victory on

March 31 1966 gave them a majority of 97, John went
to Africa.

Was this a sign that he had given up his dream of
going to Parliament? 'Oh, not at all,' he says. 'It was
that I felt I needed to go abroad. I had never travelled
and I particularly wanted to go to Africa. Leaving the
country when a Labour Government was in seemed a
very logical and sensible thing to do,' he continues,
tongue in cheek.

Clive resumes the story: 'After his return from
Africa we renewed our acquaintance and became
rather good friends, which is how I ended up being
best man at his wedding. Anyway, he didn't go back
to living with his family then. He was living in a
bedsitter at 14 Templar Street, in Myatts Fields.'
This was very convenient for the City where he
was still employed by Standard Chartered Bank.
However, in April 1991 BBC's *Panorama* programme
questioned whether John had actually lived at this
address and claimed he had not been resident in
Lambeth at the time of his election to Lambeth
Council in 1968. This claim was refuted by Downing
Street.

It was during this election that Enoch Powell made
his 'rivers of blood' speech, warning of trouble to
come if coloured immigrants to Britain were allowed
to increase in numbers. He advocated repatriation to
avoid what he predicted would be racialist bloodbaths
at some future date. Some South London Conservatives had been capitalising on the grass roots' response
to his sentiments. Hitherto, Clive says, 'Because of the
nature of the area we were in, housing was always the
predominant issue.' Now race also became the issue in
an area which had a large immigrant population.

'There had been a considerable influx of mainly Caribbean immigrants into the Brixton area in the late Fifties and Sixties. But people would have reacted to anybody moving into the borough. It wasn't the fact that they were dark skinned or that they happened to be West Indian. Anyway, it was not long before we were elected to the council in 1968 that Enoch made his "rivers of blood" speech. The three candidates in the northernmost ward in the borough put out a leaflet saying, "We back Enoch, don't you?" Well, they won the ward.' The group was reprimanded. But, Clive adds emphatically, 'John wasn't involved in any shape or form in bringing action against them.'

Ken Livingstone, who was later elected as a Labour councillor for Lambeth after the Tories lost in 1972 and then elected to Parliament in 1983, speaks admiringly of John Major and, like Robert Atkins, subscribes to the mythology that John, devotedly anti-racialist, was a key mover in opposing the use of Enoch Powell's views as a vote grabber.

Clive Jones says: 'I was one of the people involved. We had a few members of the Conservative group who were very far to the right, and I suppose with hindsight we shouldn't have selected them as candidates. After the election, a statement was produced which they invited a number of us who had been elected to sign, and I was one who signed it.

'Basically it said that we needed a ban on (immigration) into Lambeth as we (had) enough problems with housing and so on without any more people coming in. The way it was read was as anti-coloured. I suppose that some of us were rather naive and didn't realise the way the statement would get used, because

of course it was publicised. All that actually happened
was that the leader of the council had us into his
office – don't do it again – and that was it. John
was not involved at all. As far as I'm aware he was not
even asked to sign it. He just wasn't involved in any
way.

'The only time he was, and this is something I have
documentary evidence for, there was a sort of right-
wing group which was almost a branch of the Monday
Club which I had been involved with prior to the
election. It had died because lots of the people were
elected to the council, but at the beginning of 1970
it started to revive itself and put out a statement. I
was Prospective Parliamentary Candidate for Vauxhall
and John was Chairman of the Brixton Conservative
Association and both of us went public disowning this
statement. I've got the press cuttings bearing that out,
and that's the only time as far as I can recall when
anything public occurred involving race.'

John Major was now a force in South London politics, Chairman of the Constituency Association, and
also in 1970 Chairman of the Housing Committee
of Lambeth Council. It was yet another example of
his being in the right place at the right time. In
Brixton, he had risen swiftly among a group that,
because of the unpromising nature of the constituency
for Tories, contained few really ambitious rivals.

The swing against Labour, even the speeches of
Powell, had, despite John Major's opposition to any
form of racialism, helped to thrust him into local
government. It was not only that he was elected as
a councillor, but as part of an overwhelmingly large
group: 57 out of 60 total councillors were Tory.
Barbara Wallis, who had stood for Parliament in

the Labour-held seat of Feltham in 1966, and had been a councillor in Willesden, was in 1968 also one of the Lambeth Conservative councillors. She recalls only 14 had ever had any experience of being on a council before. It was a moment of euphoria and also of chaos. But for John Major, able, coherent, determined, ambitious and hard working, then as now, it was a heavensent opportunity to rise to the top. After the first two years he was clearly, despite his youth (still only 27), one of the ablest and a leader in every sense.

According to Ken Livingstone, John had also benefited at this time from the influence of Bernard Perkins. He was an experienced local government officer who, Ken Livingstone says, 'could take an inexperienced young lad and knock some sense into him and turn him into a decent local politician.' John was no less a fast learner then than he proved to be during his Parliamentary career. Watching, listening and evaluating, he would have absorbed experience like a sponge, his sights always set on becoming an MP, and yet at the same time concentrating on doing a job he enjoyed, and doing it well.

His period on Lambeth Council matured him as a politician and gave him an edge he could not usually have hoped to get as a Conservative in a strong Labour area. As part of the majority group, he was not just a backbencher in opposition to a Labour-dominated council, but actually in charge of running the borough.

During his period on Lambeth Council he gained experience especially in the areas of social services, housing and finance. Involvement with these functions in Lambeth has provided him with the strong foundation of hands-on experience in working-class

areas in which most Conservatives, whose electoral
strength lies in better off suburbs, prosperous country
constituencies and rich inner city boroughs, lack
the grass roots touch. After his election in 1968
John, then one of this great mass of inexperienced
councillors who would initially be making up their
working plans as they went along, served on both
Housing and Finance Committees. In 1969, now
progressing in banking as an employee of Standard
Chartered, he was promoted to Chairman of the
Accounts Sub-Committee. But he also became at this
time Chairman of Housing, Lambeth's most creative
area of operations. During his time as Chairman, a
pioneering Housing Advice centre was set up which
gave advice to residents on anything from how to find
rented accommodation in council or private sectors
to how to go about purchasing and financing the
purchase of their own home. Some council house
sales also took place during his period as Chairman
of Housing, though this was not yet so popular a
policy as it turned out to be during the period
of Conservative Government under Mrs Thatcher.
There were, however, numerous creative and inno-
vative enterprises in the area of housing during John
Major's time on the Housing Committee.

Clive Jones says, 'John was the first of that 1968
intake to get a chairmanship. As I was on the sub-
committee of housing management when he was
Chairman we would meet the tenants' association
groups in the Town Hall or the housing department.
We would help tenants get the finance for house
purchases. The council would grant mortgages.

'We also actually built for sale one little estate
in Flodden Road on the borough boundary with

Southwark. We built a small estate there, about 17 houses, but we also had in Lambeth a number of places where there were rows of town houses which the council had built and we were offering those for sale to sitting tenants. The housing department identified as many as 500 properties, not in blocks so there wouldn't be any management problems, and we moved people in when those properties became vacant, transferring tenants who wanted to buy.

'We used to do housing estate visits, what we called "Taking the housing department on tour". We used a tenants' hall if there was one on the estate, or a hall near an estate, and we would literally take the housing department – senior officers, senior councillors – invite tenants from the estate or a couple of estates, whatever was nearby, let them come along and explain everything we were doing policywise. And of course it gave them a chance to have their beef at us.

'There was one particular site on Streatham Hill that our Labour predecessors had purchased but hadn't started any redevelopment (on). We handed it over to a housing association. That was something that was new, and all these are things that John was involved in.'

'Another thing we did was to establish links with new towns. Peterborough was one and Swindon another. I remember the Peterborough councillors coming down for a presentation to the Housing Committee. We approached those particular links as another way of solving the Lambeth housing problem. They were expanding. They had not only homes but jobs.

'We were recognised as being one of the most forward-thinking housing authorities in the country. I mean, even the Labour Party got to hear of us. They wouldn't acknowledge it but I think they did admire what we were doing.'

Ken Livingstone agrees that he and other socialists admired John Major especially because he would stand up and say: 'We've got to help people.'

It cannot have been coincidence that, after all this, John eventually became MP for Huntingdon where so many migrants from Lambeth had settled as new town dwellers. With every day he spent on Lambeth Council he was building up the dossier of qualifications and a bank of vital experience that would make him the perfect heir ten years hence to the once squirearchical shire constituency turned new town area, and building up an electorate of ex-Brixton new townees while he did it.

But for years before this sudden and unexpected opportunity, and its consequences, things had looked bleak for him. 'It all looked hopeless, absolutely hopeless. When you're sixteen, seventeen, eighteen and nineteen, and you're a Conservative in Brixton and you don't ever win anything . . .' He never actually gave up. But he had moments of utter hopelessness. The political wilderness is hard on those who languish in it. The tide of fortune seems so much more a force in politics than in business or any other professional career because the will of the electorate is such a vital factor. Anyone in the wrong place, or even the right place at the wrong time, is consigned to watch that tide running on another shore, to be marooned, out of office, out of influence and out of the only thing that matters in politics: a measure of power to enact, create, reform, abolish or amend the statutes and, through them, history.

To an energetic, creative, intensely and instinctively political animal like John Major, passionately ambitious for political progress as well as for a role to play in it, the experience was deeply frustrating. But, though he felt marooned again a few years later, in the mid Seventies, he was not fated to languish long without encouragement.

Perhaps, in addition to his own clear ability and personal qualities, it is his gift of discerning the best qualities of the people around him that has enabled him to find some important ally at each crucial turn in his career. Of all those who helped him in those struggling Lambeth days, he is especially grateful to Jean Lucas who became Conservative Agent and organiser for the Lambeth area during the mid to late Sixties.

'Jean Lucas was an immense influence. I can't tell you how helpful she was from time to time when it looked so hopeless. Jean used to drive me home and I used to sit in her car and talk about what could be done and how we would go, step by step. She was very encouraging. She used to say that things were changing, and "you can do it".'

What was altering was not just the movement of the nation's viewpoint back towards the Conservative Party, it was more that things inside the party were changing. It was becoming more possible for people without background and personal wealth to move forward in the party. The whole Sixties shift in attitude to class was making it possible for grammar school boys, even working-class Tories like Norman Tebbit, to be selected more frequently as

Parliamentary candidates, and grammar school boy
Edward Heath became Tory leader.

Parliament was always John's real objective. Jean
Lucas says he had not considered standing for council
other than as a distraction, but she persuaded him that
he should stand to get the experience of contesting
a seat. With his ability to know a good source
of advice when he meets it, he was persuaded,
encouraged, and nursed along. She was a kind of
political mother to him. A number of years older,
vastly experienced about grass roots organisation, a
very competent Agent. Energetic, intelligent, a good
judge of people and politically astute, she is crisp,
succinct, a penetratingly accurate observer of the
political scene. This petite, vigorous and attractive
woman, dedicated to her career, was a driving force
and an inspiration to the Conservatives within the
Labour-dominated heartlands of South London. She
could recruit and harness young people's energies,
motivate and organise their efforts, and she could
pick winners. John Major says, 'I'm not alone. There
were lots who would have been through the Lucas
influence. She was a very influential Agent, one of the
best I think there's ever been.

'She's got a good instinct for people collectively,
what is worrying them, a very fine political instinct. It's
a great shame she was never in the House of Commons,
she would have been superb.'

Jean first really noticed John Major in the period
after his return from Africa. 'I was aware of him
in the period around 1964 when he was Young
Conservative Chairman in Brixton, but I really only
became conscious of him around 1967 when I formed
the North Lambeth Conservative group. Previously

I'd had my head down with Clapham only, but then I came across John who was Chairman of the Brixton Conservative Association Political Centre Committee. He was obviously the brightest and most intelligent of the Brixton lot and so I did tend to ask his help and advice on things I wanted to do.'

She also recalls those earnest talks in her car: 'I used to take him home because he had this gammy leg and he didn't have a car. He would sit and talk and I used to keep the engine running for a bit, and then eventually I would switch it off. I'd think, "I want to go home. I'm tired, I want to go to bed." And John would carry on talking, talking about local politics or about national politics or how he was going to become an MP. One night in the car he asked me, "Will I? Do you think I will be able to get to be an MP?" ' He obviously lacked confidence then that he could overcome the combined disadvantages of his situation. 'I'm a great confidence booster,' Jean laughs.

'Marion Standing was his first supporter. She was my trainee and also Agent for Brixton. She went to North London and then I came in, the older woman who could help John. During that time we were building up his biography. He didn't really want to get on to Lambeth Council because it did represent something of a contest between his aims for his job and his interest in politics. We had already discussed this to the extent that I was saying, "You have to get yourself a good job, John, and you have to get a little money behind you before you can afford to launch too deeply into politics." That's why he stood for Ferndale which was a difficult ward and not one where he was certain to get in. But then, of course, he did get in and he decided to take advantage of the opportunity and really give it his best.'

All the while in those early days there was another inspiration. Robert Atkins says, 'Iain Macleod was very much the driving force in terms of the party and our attitude to it, very much the guiding light even now in John's and my philosophy.'

John has made it clear that it was Macleod and Butler who were his lodestars in the late Fifties and early Sixties. 'Not Macmillan,' he insisted with double emphasis: 'Not Macmillan.'

Atkins says, 'John thought Macmillan was a complete fraud. I disagree with him on that. I don't think Macmillan was a complete fraud – a fraud maybe, an actor, a poseur – but John thought he was a complete fraud and had very little time for him.'

Macleod vibrated chords of sympathy in the Young Conservatives of John's era. He spoke warmly of them as 'a political movement which would be the envy of any political party within the Western world'. His ambition for young people was 'to give them more equal opportunities of proving themselves unequal', and he said this in the days when egality had come into vogue under Wilson's Labour government. Macleod in fact scorned Labour's egalitarianism which was perceived, on the right of British politics, as an attempt at levelling down by reducing opportunity. He was an enthusiast for extending opportunity, and this of course is the basis of Tory meritocracy.

Macleod identified himself as a liberal Conservative. Edward Boyle in his introduction to Nigel Fisher's biography of Macleod wrote, 'He was a libertarian who believed that there were fairly strict limits to the functions which any government should attempt to perform. Nevertheless, he also believed equally firmly, that within these limits, government was there, "to be used as an instrument of action" (I quote from *The Making of the President: 1960* by Theodore White). And this leads to the consideration of the question: why did he have the reputation, rightly, of being a liberal Conservative?

'The first answer is that Macleod was deeply concerned throughout his political career over two key domestic issues – poverty and unemployment. He had compassion.'

While he was concerned for fairness, both at home and in the colonies (he was Colonial Secretary), he spoke out against racialism, but he was also a bitter critic of union militancy. John Major says, 'Anyone who thinks Macleod was a soft, mushy, centrist Tory doesn't know him. He was merciless with his political attacks on opponents from time to time, quite merciless.'

Macleod's magic was in his oratory, according to John Major. 'There was always a drama about a Macleod speech and there were several things one felt when one heard (him). Firstly, it was pure drama. He had a style of speaking that I don't think would work today. He spoke very slowly – the great deep bell-like voice and absolutely immobile head. The reason he was immobile was, of course, his physical disability but it was very compelling. You always felt better at the end of a Macleod speech. You always felt several things. He was saying exactly what he believed . . . he always pitched his argument around principle. He didn't say it was principle, but he pitched his argument around principle. There was always a good reason for what he had to do, and from time to time he was bitingly funny as well.'

John Major's own speechmaking is not his strong point. His delivery often lets down the content. In this he has not been much influenced by Macleod, despite hours of listening to records of Macleod's speeches with his friend David Rogers. Rogers was Macleod's speechwriter during the Sixties, up to his death after his appointment as Chancellor in Edward Heath's new government in 1970. He became John's neighbour during the mid Seventies and used to travel on the commuter train up and down from the City with him. Rogers helped John with the ideas of speech construction he had used with Macleod. He says a speech always has to have two negatives and a positive – two attacks on the opposition and one piece of positive praise for one's own party. 'Also, you have to find a rhythm. You need to have a favourite poet and use his style.' The great orators always have a rhythm to their words, non-rhyming lines of poetic prose. Rogers says, 'John reads a lot but he doesn't have a poet he loves.' He recalls, though, his friend's complete fascination with Macleod, saying, 'John used to ask me a lot about Iain Macleod and how he worked, and I remember saying, "Iain and I used to have breakfast twice a week on Tuesdays and Thursdays and we ran the week from there. Some weeks there was nothing at all to do." But I also remember that Iain's great ability, which I think John has taken on board, was looking after people you've sacked from the Cabinet or the staff, and looking for people you've got to sack.'

Macleod's ideas perhaps, more than his style, influenced John Major during the formative period of his political life. In the late Fifties and early Sixties, Macleod struck a special chord with John's own experience when he spoke of creating opportunity for the young to prove themselves unequal. And John Major, the man who is now first among equals in the highest office of government, has proved that even when opportunity is unequal, with determination and hard work, the able will rise.

Like his disciple, Macleod had plain origins: he was a doctor's son, but his grandfather was a Scottish crofter. Like John Major, he was more pragmatist than idealist, but had similarly strong beliefs. One was that Gladstonian one that it was the duty of the Conservative Party to raise the condition of the people. His most famous legacy to the cohort of present day Ministers, whom he inspired with his own meritocratic messages, is in the 'One Nation' concept expressed in speeches and a pamphlet.

Macleod also said that: 'Britain should play her full part in the great movement towards European unity.' But that was when British involvement with Europe was more theoretical than practical. In fact, none of the Major cohort's adulation of Macleod implies a departure from Thatcherism. Macleod, though strong on compassion, was economically dry. Mrs Thatcher was in his Treasury team in 1970 and cannot have differed from him in ethos, herself a libertarian and a meritocrat both by creed and experience, and a practical Tory idealist for whom getting the economy right and getting the able out of their socialist lethargy was a priority that does not deny ultimate compassion. Likewise, there is no cause to assume that a Macleod or Major's emphasis on compassion implies high public spending or taxation leading to deficit-led inflation. There is no fundamental difference of direction though there has been a perfectly natural evolution of emphasis.

Nevertheless Macleod's slightly eerie legend haunts the Prime Minister's dreams of action, a ghostly muse who can only be exorcised by the generation whose views he shaped so powerfully; by their continuing progress towards that compassionate meritocracy which he inspired through his emotion-loaded rhetoric.

Unlike John Major whose timing is impeccable and whose message is so attuned to his time's trends, Macleod himself was a hero ahead of his time, who died too soon to make his will manifest. Perhaps Macleod's ghost will rest once his political children have made his dream materialise.

After Jean Lucas, whose advice he still seeks today, Margaret Jay took over John Major's political education. She was his Agent at St Pancras North before and during the two elections of 1974. When John was selected for St Pancras North in 1971, he began doggedly working himself in there. Mrs Jay remembers him as being very cooperative, willing to do anything and go anywhere he was asked.

'He was always open to reasonable suggestions, was good on the doorstep, always polite in arguing his case rationally. He didn't do case work as such but I know he went out of his way to see people who had problems. He was also starting to learn about public speaking. He was always very nervous but he overcame the nervousness. I knew he was nervous but I wouldn't say a lot of the public or the people that he spoke to (realised).'

In public meetings he displayed the same gifts as he does today. Margaret Jay says, 'He had the facility to win arguments, and he could slap people down without annoying them and still keep their respect.'

There may have been some doubt in his mind at this stage, working two or three evenings a week and Saturdays, at a solid Labour constituency, as to whether he was doing the right thing. Mrs Jay says, 'He did speak to me about his ambitions. Because he had a very good job at the bank and was set to go great distances, he asked me on more than one occasion if I thought he was right, when he had a wife and children, to think of giving up this good safe job for politics. His wife of course has always been very supportive. I said to him, "If it's in your blood, you won't be happy if you don't. Give it a go." And I always felt he would go to the top if he did succeed in getting into Parliament.'

This advice was crucial at a time when John was seemingly at a crossroads. Several of his friends picked up the same sense of doubt as he spoke of concentrating on rising in the bank and being a family man. There were minor problems with James, the younger child, who was very late beginning to talk. There were financial pressures from very high inflation rates under the Wilson/Callaghan government. And then there were the difficulties over getting shortlisted for constituencies, later eased when Jean Lucas discovered the candidates' department mix up of the two John Majors.

He had already declared his political interests at the bank. Peter Seager, an ex-colleague from the late Sixties and early Seventies, remembers with amusement an incident that occurred soon after John became Chairman of Housing in Lambeth.

'After John came back from Africa he had gone into foreign exchange dealing and there was an occasion in which a reporter actually penetrated the inner sanctum and asked him his comments on some local housing issue. His then general manager was not particularly happy about this intrusion and John was asked whether he was more interested in politics or in dealing. And he said, "Politics." So he was then told, "Well, if you're going to take an interest in politics, perhaps this area is not for you." Because dealing is very intense. There's a lot of late work, unusual events, and I think he and they felt another area would be more appropriate.'

Soon, John lost his seat on Lambeth Council and started to spend his evenings on the doorsteps of St Pancras North. He entered his wilderness period and for a while experienced the doubts and concerns of which Margaret Jay and others have spoken. It may have seemed that he had to choose between the bank and politics, but in fact the two soon began to run in parallel and encourage John's political hopes anew.

Anthony Barber, Edward Heath's Chancellor, had retired from politics and moved to Standard Chartered Bank as its Chairman. Barber, now Lord Barber, had retired with a peerage which had been criticised at the time since his policies while Chancellor in 1971–2 were widely held to have been responsible for the massive inflationary surge which hit Britain by 1974. 'The Barber Boom' as it was called was infamous, but there were other factors in that Seventies inflation, such as decimalisation of the British coinage, the disastrous harvest of 1971 in the USSR, driving up the world price of grain on which were based animal feed prices and others, and the hike of Arabian oil prices following the Yom Kippur War of 1973.

Barber, who had not stood for re-election in 1974, was Chairman of the Bank in 1975 when John Major came into contact with him as the new press officer. Brian Haynes, a public relations consultant with a company called City and Industrial Publicity Services, who handled Standard Chartered's public affairs, was also involved at this time. He remembers, 'The bank used the public relations department as a management training ground – you got a man, got him trained, and then if in two or three years he was any good, you moved him on. John came into the department from administration, I think, as number two, and it was about this time that Lord Barber became Chairman. John used to talk to me about going into politics but the biggest thing we had to discuss was Standard Chartered's purchase of the Hodge Group. This was headed by a Welsh financier called Sir Julian Hodge who was, as a result of the purchase of his group, one of Standard Chartered's biggest shareholders and on the board.

'When the bank came to take it over, one of the general managers was given the job of sorting it out. He phoned me to say we had problems. The whole affair was a disaster. Shortly after, John became the Public Relations Officer and he inherited this mammoth problem.'

In the early Seventies trouble arose in Britain's secondary banking system and new legislation was brought in to tighten the banking regulations.

Haynes says, 'About this time, a law was passed that anyone trading as a banking institution had to get a licence granted by the Bank of England, and it emerged that the authorities did not want Sir Julian Hodge to join Standard Chartered. The simple solution was that Hodge had to go. John flourished (in) this situation. He obviously had the front to do the thing.'

Haynes explained that the Hodge Group, concerned with hire purchase finance and other ventures, had been involved in enterprises which the Bank of England considered unacceptable under the new rules. Sir Julian also founded a Bank of Wales of which his friend James Callaghan, the Labour Prime Minister, now Lord Callaghan, was a director. The press took a keen interest. Esther Rantzen's programme broadcast an item. John Major, meanwhile, was the public relations officer working with Haynes to limit the damage. Haynes remembers, 'We had quite a hairy time of it, and eventually we had to orchestrate. After months of wheeling and dealing, Hodge departed. He will probably deny this, but at the time he blamed John Major, about whom he seemed very angry.'

Sir Julian Hodge, who now lives in Jersey, has very courteously stated in a letter to me that he does not know John Major and did not meet him during his association with Standard Chartered.

The story, however, Haynes believes, 'Shows how John was first blooded in PR when we had to deal with an extremely damaging, high profile situation which put him in the front line of the city, the financial press, TV and so on. It was really tough and he thrived on it. He really loved it.'

It was during this period that he learned the public relations skills he has since employed adeptly on his own behalf. Mostly not so much to attract publicity, with the exception of his knack for the photo opportunity, as to avoid it. Brian Haynes agrees that part of his own task as the public relations consultant was to teach the bank's internal PR people the tricks of his trade. The main problem was that as soon as he had them trained they were moved on to another department of the bank. Haynes says that he found John Major had a great aptitude for PR, learned fast and performed like a natural. He had a keen sense of what to say and what not to say, and his extraordinary ability to deal with people enabled him to forge excellent personal relationships with financial journalists.

This period was valuable also because it developed the link between John and Lord Barber. During the Hodge business, Lord Barber had been often enough in contact with John Major to come to appreciate his diplomacy and gift for persuasion. So, when a trip to Manila to the International Monetary Fund conference was proposed, he opted to take John with him. 'It was clear that if he'd stayed in banking he'd have gone a long way,' comments Lord Barber. 'He's a high flyer. He's reliable, he's straightforward, and coupled with ability that's worth a lot. I had to take someone to Manila and I thought I might as well take someone who was agreeable as well as competent. Anyway, although I thought he was destined to go far in the bank, I realised on this trip that his first love was politics. I've often talked about the dangers for a relatively young person with a family and no capital, but he was one of those people I encouraged to go on with politics. I could see how keen he was and I realised that once he'd got a safe seat he'd clearly have no trouble getting into the Cabinet. (Though) I didn't realise he'd be in the Cabinet so soon or that he'd be Prime Minister.'

Later, after John was selected for Huntingdon, Brian Haynes says, 'Barber gave a lunch to which he invited Francis Pym, or so the story goes. He said to Pym, "This young man is going to be an MP. When he comes in to the House, keep an eye on him and show him the ropes." Consequently when John entered the House, Pym showed him around.' Lord Pym himself modestly plays this down. 'We were from neighbouring constituencies so it was quite natural that I should show him around. I don't remember that I helped him particularly.'

There is no certain knowledge of the degree to which Barber helped John Major advance his political career. Lord Barber told me that after John had been elected, 'I put in a good word for him here and there with Mrs Thatcher. I remember talking to Margaret Thatcher about him one time, saying he had the right ideas. He was right-wing on economics but compassionate.' Barber was not involved in any way in putting in a good word for John at Huntingdon, however. The selection process is strictly for the constituency party and any attempt to lobby on a candidate's behalf could easily rebound. But Barber helped in other ways.

John's friend from banking days, Ian Cameron Black, now godfather to James, remembers the situation at the bank after John was selected for Huntingdon. He says, 'To be honest I don't think Lord Barber was a fairy godmother to John, but it could be that John was very discreet and just didn't tell me about that.' Cameron Black, who is now retired, says he joined the bank in 1969 and worked with John in the business development department before going to Hamburg in 1971.

While in this department, he says, 'We were both on first name terms with Michael McWilliams who became the Bank's MD, so obviously that was helpful to John.' When Cameron Black returned from Hamburg he and John were once more together in Group Credit Control. He says that in this period, the mid Seventies, John was despondent about the frustrations he had been experiencing in his search for a constituency, and had promised the bank's then Managing Director, Sir Peter Graham, that he would not apply for any more. By 1976, when Sir David Renton decided to announce his retirement as Huntingdon's MP at the next election, John was Head of Public Relations and the business over the bank's licence was behind him.

Cameron Black recalls, 'John then decided, when Huntingdon came up, that he would apply. He was so upset that he hadn't got anywhere since 1974, he wanted to prove to himself that he could get on a short list. Of course, he was through like a shot and he then had to apologise to Peter Graham that he'd gone back on his word. Peter Graham accepted it because he knew how much John would like to do it. So John went on to half time and half salary, and then he was transferred into the department in which I was.'

The reason for going on half pay and half time was to be able to devote more attention to nursing himself in as David Renton's successor in Huntingdon. This was a constituency of some 370 square miles, with 5 urban areas and 80 villages. John Major should have had no serious worries as the seat had a majority which never seemed to fall far beneath 10,000 votes, but he is a worrier, taking hard his life's early lesson never to take anything for granted. During 1977, he bought a three-bedroomed semi in the pleasant village of Hemingford Grey and moved up there with Norma and the children. He went religiously to constituency events and organisational meetings and began the long task of being introduced as the successor to the man who had been Huntingdon's MP since 1945, and who had fought and won ten elections there.

Sir David remembers that the new man worked very hard. He says, 'I have a house about two villages away from Great Stukeley and they came and stayed with us there several times before they found a house of their own.'

Sir David and his wife Paddy made the Majors feel at home, but while the preponderance of London overspill new townees fitted his own Lambeth and St Pancras experience, John Major did not immediately satisfy the expectations of some of the East Anglian landowners who were also very influential as leading members of the local Conservative Association. There was among them a feeling that the Association had departed from the norm expected for a county constituency. They would have preferred someone like the Marquis of Douro who rang more bells with aristocratic, landowning interests. They disapproved of John Major because he was a townie and had no money or background. His wife, while pleasant, did not seem the sort of woman who would hurl herself into local society, whereas Paddy Renton, as the daughter of an Irish peer, had all the right credentials.

But David Renton says, 'I soon discovered that after he had met a number of the leading founder members – the squirearchy is not extinct in Hunting-donshire – three or four leading landowners thought he had in an effortless way acquired a knowledge of their problems and an understanding of their work.' He had, of course, been beavering away as usual, absorbing local knowledge and making himself master of the relevant facts. Sir David says, 'I found he was a fluent speaker, well-informed, well-read, with very clear ideas about finance and economics. I found that he and Norma fitted naturally into rural life.' Even so, he was apprehensive, afraid local voters would also feel he was not the right candidate to follow Sir David. His habitual pre-performance lack of confidence haunted him right through until the votes had been counted.

His adoption was in December 1976 and the election did not take place until May 1979, so for more than two years he lived in a kind of limbo, losing his place in the bank's promotion process and meanwhile subject to bouts of jitters about whether he would ever become Huntingdon's MP. Ian Cameron Black's story is that, even before this, 'John was going nowhere at the bank.' He told me, 'You read in the papers that John's career at the bank provided a great stepping stone into politics. We laugh every time we read it, because it is nonsense. Barber, Graham and McWilliams gave him tremendous support, and indeed probably encouraged him, although they were of course aware that he was diverting the time he could have been spending at the bank.

'But, in that sort of institution, you get to the top usually by playing safe, by doing what has been done before. Otherwise you get promoted because you have made a mistake and you are moved to get you out of the job you were doing. So you get there by being safe and dull and unimaginative and blinkered. These people, your middle management, are intensely suspicious of someone like John or myself who are free spirits, and there were no doubt very considerable undercurrents which John felt with his very acute sensibilities: people saying, "What is he doing talking direct to the Chairman?" And although the MD said, "We leave it to you to decide what is part-time – we are not going to check up on you," nevertheless the people in the departments expected John to sign in and were counting the hours he was there.'

One ex-bank employee, now a financial public relations consultant, told me, 'I was at Standard Chartered at the same time as John Major in the Seventies when he was looking for constituencies. I remember he never seemed to have anything to do.' Other employees seemed to think John was being paid while he nursed his constituency on a whim of the Chairman. No wonder Cameron Black says, 'John felt awkward and uncomfortable, and yet he was bored to tears by what he was doing because there was no scope. The man who is called Director of Public Relations now has a vastly bigger job than in fact John's was.'

After he was adopted for Huntingdon and went part-time, John worked with Cameron Black in the Credit Control Department. 'People didn't realise we were close buddies,' says Ian. 'It was pure coincidence we were working side by side. I even had an extension on my phone so that I could pick up his calls. I took a lot of messages for him and in fact finished off a lot of his work. But it was very much hack work, writing papers for the board, and he was rather bored doing that.'

But there were other things to do in the furtherance of John's political career. There were influential people to meet. Margaret Jay was able to help. After St Pancras North, she became Agent for Douglas Hurd's Oxfordshire constituency. Hurd, a former diplomat and Heath aide, was at this time opposition Foreign Office spokesman. Mrs Jay remembers that, 'John was still a candidate at this time – I can't remember exactly which year it was, '76, '77 – and he was very anxious to meet Douglas. I remember he and Norma came to spend the weekend with me and I managed to get Douglas Hurd to come to dinner with us. And I think possibly from that he met Douglas again. Douglas was probably able to give him more help than I was.'

His brilliant connection with Lord Barber was a considerable asset. Friends think that perhaps he learned a great deal by osmosis from observing Barber and seeing how he dealt with influential people. John had after all no previous experience of dealing with powerful figures. He had only watched from afar during his days in the Young Conservatives and later as a councillor. Now, before he became an MP, he was being exposed to a much bigger league, and watching, listening, he learned and absorbed.

When he became Huntingdon's MP with an increased majority, he had a few moments of euphoria and then characteristically began putting his mind to the problems ahead of him. He had first to adjust to the life of the House. Francis Pym and other East Anglian MPs helped and guided his early days there. Someone has to show new members where the coat pegs, loos and cafeterias are, and such is the warrenlike structure of the House with its amenities sprawling along rambling corridors and rising up and down staircases on different levels that one can easily become lost, time and again. John adjusted quietly. He had the companionship of another new member, his buddy Robert Atkins of Greater London Young Conservative days. He also made friends quickly with David Mellor whom he first met at a function for new members. The 1979 intake was large and relatively youthful by Tory standards. John's political cohort was well represented and joined those like Norman Lamont who were already in the House.

Iain Macleod's and Margaret Thatcher's young meritocrats now replaced the older, more traditional Tory MPs. Their presence critically shifted the balance between the old and the new Conservatives, which had been changing since the early Seventies. The troops Mrs Thatcher needed for her revolution now predominated on the Conservative benches, and John Major was among them.

Now the life of politics really began to take hold of him. For the first time, he was a full-time politician and his horizons, which had been limited simply to getting himself elected, could advance towards hopes of office. But there was no sign of a rapid rise. His first appointment took time, though after the years of frustration, of longing and struggling to become an MP, this may not have been a problem.

He had plenty of adjustments to make now that he really was MP and out of Sir David Renton's august shadow. Pleasingly, the word of mouth from the constituency was strongly favourable to him. As

Andrew Thomson, his then Agent, recalls, 'He is a magic, magic man.'

There was a great deal of work to do there. Andy Thomson remembers that Barbara Wallis, John's friend from Lambeth council days who became his secretary at Westminister, and is presently his constituency secretary working at Number 10, laughed at them. She told Andy in 1981, after John had been MP for eighteen months, 'Andrew, you and John are still fighting this seat as if it were a critical marginal.' Thomson says, 'And we were. Even for the two and a half years before the 1979 election, John and I were very, very active on Friday, Saturday and Sunday. Meeting after meeting, function after function, interest groups, tennis parties . . . you name it, we were there. We really worked hard.'

Although it seemed Huntingdon was by now one of the safest Tory seats in the country, John Major could not take his big majority for granted. He had to go on proving he was worth every vote and more. He still must, even today: with the workload of a Prime Minister and international leader, he is still attending functions and dealing with constituents' problems. Baroness Blatch, who lives in the constituency with her family, told me, 'He is still coming to functions almost every week, but the trouble is we can't put it on the invitation now because of the security.' He surprises them arriving when they least expect it.

His present Agent Peter Brown, who came to him in 1982 from Norman Lamont's constituency of Kingston after Andy Thomson left to become Mrs Thatcher's Agent in Finchley, says, 'Now I have tremendous difficulty with him because he has so many calls on his time. I have said to him,

"You don't really need to do that," but he insists. He really hates to disappoint people and always puts the constituency first, always has done, and likes to do the best for them.'

He was not offered a government job until 1981 when he became Parliamentary Private Secretary to the Ministers of State at the Home Office. PPS is the lowest form of appointment, a job that entails keeping one's Minister well informed on issues and views in the Parliamentary Party. A good PPS is a spare pair of eyes and ears, invaluable because of the workload that chains the Minister to his desk and keeps him away from the lobbies and bars for much of the time when Members are circulating freely.

From then, things moved more swiftly. Next, in January 1983, came the job of Assistant Government Whip, another very junior but more testing post. While in this job, he became well trusted by John Wakeham, the Chief Whip, the more so since, after the Brighton bomb which injured Wakeham and killed his first wife, John nursed the Chief Whip's constituency for him until he was recovered. 'He looked after my constituency for the best part of six months for which I was jolly grateful. He did all the correspondence and work for me, and was really good.'

Wakeham was an important ally who, close to Mrs Thatcher, helped her begin to appreciate John Major's qualities. After the famous row Wakeham, who was her Chief Whip for eight years, was able to give her advice as to his junior's abilities and suitability for various jobs. John progressed in the Department of Health and Social Security from Parliamentary Under Secretary of State for Social

Security, to which he was appointed in 1986, to Minister of State (for Social Security) in September 1986. By the time Wakeham proposed him as his successor as Chief Whip though, Mrs Thatcher had had more opportunity to observe him performing in Cabinet sub-committees involving the DHSS, and had decided already that he was good enough to be given a very important job. So in 1987 he became Chief Secretary to the Treasury, in control of public spending, and was an outstanding success.

Now he came into continuous contact with Nigel Lawson, Chancellor from 1983–9. A headline in the *People*'s Sunday magazine described him as: 'A Lawson unto himself'. It is common wisdom at Westminster and in Whitehall that, in the words of a Cabinet Minister, 'Nigel ran the economy entirely by himself.' But John Major was a loyal and effective number two whose views on the economy's management were in harmony with the Chancellor's, even if his opinion on some of the fine detail diverged from Lawson's. So while Lawson managed the whole economy, raised revenues from taxes or cut them, changed tax law and allocated the revenues, controlled interest rates, exchange rates and international economic treaties, John Major's role was to oversee public spending and keep to the limits imposed by the Chancellor.

What was their relationship like? Lawson has refused to comment or to be interviewed about John Major. Was Lawson difficult to get on with? 'I didn't find him so. I know he has that reputation but I found it a perfectly agreeable working relationship.' But, until his underling succeeded him as Chancellor, perhaps Nigel Lawson had no cause to see him as

a rival. There was, of course, the fact that Mrs
Thatcher's favourites were eventually known among
insiders. When John Major became Foreign Secretary, she was certainly talking of him as her heir.
But before that, while he was Chief Secretary to
the Treasury, his position as a possible heir was
less evident.

However, Mrs Thatcher's other favourites were,
during this period, begining to fall by the wayside.
Parkinson had never really made a comeback after the
Sarah Keays débâcle and had proved a flop both at
Energy and Transport. John Moore, while Secretary
of State for Social Security, after his callous remarks
over people on unemployment benefit wasting their
money on drink and cigarettes, had quickly vanished
into the wilderness. There were rumours that John
Major had helped both Parkinson and Moore on their
way with judicious comments to the lady, but there
seemed to be no voices raised in their defence so
his advice would seem to have reflected the received
wisdom among other Cabinet colleagues.

Mrs Thatcher was evidently shaping up as John's
most glorious Fairy Godmother yet. Nigel Lawson,
though, would have responded differently to John
Major's rise, for Lawson was himself a candidate for
the succession.

During the heady period from 1986–7 when Lawson seemed as cunning and skilful as a magician
in his handling of the economy; when he bragged
that Britain's economy was now the strongest in the
Western world; when he attended finance meetings
of the world's leading nations as an elder statesman,
the most senior finance minister of the G7 group of
nations, and even bluntly told the US to cut its deficit:

at this time he was flying high, immensely admired and widely tipped as Mrs Thatcher's successor. Things had yet to go badly wrong for the economy, and all was set fair for an election victory earlier that year in June. John Major was yet to enter the Cabinet. Only after he did, coincidentally, did Lawson's star start waning. The economy began to fall into decline during 1987 and interest rates had to be raised again, to be forced down once more after Black Monday for fear of a world recession. But Lawson's image as Britain's most successful Chancellor for fifty years prevailed despite the developing economic problems.

Once John Major became Chief Secretary after June 1987, he became a handy ally to the Chancellor. His brilliant work at cutting public spending was of enormous help, enabling the wizard to pull more tax cut rabbits out of his hat. Likewise Lawson's enormously powerful position, and the respect in which he was still held, gave John Major the strength to deal confidently and decisively with public spending. The Treasury's power became even greater among the departments of state in a government which was already Treasury-dominated. It was the economy and its successful management, after all, which determined the other Ministers' budgets. John Major's power as Treasury Secretary was much enhanced by this situation. So Lawson's then glittering coat tails gave him a very useful ride on his way to Number 10. In return, he rewarded his senior colleague with loyal support in Cabinet on issues such as the ERM which Lawson wanted to enter early, and the poll tax to which Lawson was opposed.

For the two years between John Major's arrival as Treasury Secretary and his appointment as Foreign

Secretary in July 1989, the battles between Mrs
Thatcher and her Chancellor over interest rates
and the exchange rate dominated headlines. Even
so, there was a subsidiary battle. There were the
other headlines warning of plots between Howe and
Lawson to remove Mrs Thatcher and replace her
with Lawson. And there was Mrs Thatcher's little
speech about looking for her successor from among
the younger generation, skipping Lawson and his age
group. Was this a warning, a threat or a promise? Was
Lawson ambitious for the premiership? It was said
he was. But, when the crunch point came and he
resigned, it was the young John Major who inherited
his then job of Chancellor, and who a year later won
the succession. Only after Lawson's resignation did
the full impact of the economic mess the country
faced become clear. But who was to blame? Major
inherited the mess, but was it not partly one in which
he had concurred? He has not made it clear where
he disagreed with Lawson and where he supported
him. Not that it would have made any difference, of
course. Lawson listened to no one. He did what he
thought best, ignoring the Treasury and the Bank of
England, the Prime Minister and her key advisor.

So now Nigel Lawson, having played his part in
removing Mrs Thatcher, having supported Heseltine
in the leadership election, has begun to undermine
John Major. He made a point of attacking him over
the poll tax, having already had an article published
in the *Daily Telegraph* shortly before restating his own
views of the tax and setting the record straight on
what he had told Mrs Thatcher. Is this a continuation
of his fight against Thatcherism, merely a desire
to place himself in a positive light after so much

criticism of his financial politics in the media, the City and Parliament, or is it a product of less than gracious feelings about John Major's election to the coveted top job?

When asked if Nigel Lawson might be jealous of him, the Prime Minister replied, 'I don't know.' Surely the only safe answer is 'No'. But when the question was rephrased, he cut in again: 'I don't know.' I laughed and teased, 'Of course you don't know. What is the phrase: "You might think that, but I couldn't possibly comment."' Having quoted the famous phrase from the recent television serial and novel *House of Cards*, I began talking about something else, but he cut in again. 'Nesta,' he said quietly, 'I think you're a witch.' And we laughed and, of course, no more was said on the matter. Three days later, in the House, Lawson made an attack on the Prime Minister and his government for indecisiveness over the poll tax. Later Lawson said that this was not intended to be a personal attack on John Major. Perhaps Lawson feels ill rewarded for the boost his extraordinary Chancellorship gave to the younger man's career. Or perhaps he simply feels aggrieved at his own peremptory act of resignation as Chancellor which paved the way for John Major's success.

When asked if she thought there could possibly have been any jealousy behind Nigel Lawson's refusal to talk about the Prime Minister, Baroness Blatch commented, 'I'm not sure about that because I don't know Nigel well enough.' But, she added, there was a story she could tell me that might shed some light on the situation. In the spring of 1989 there were all sorts of parties to celebrate the Thatcher government's first ten years in office. Lady Blatch says, 'I organised in Huntingdon a dinner for John which started off as a relatively modest affair. We wanted a tenth birthday party with a couple of hundred people. It's another measure of John and the constituency that suddenly we were oversubscribed. It went eventually to five hundred and something and we had to cut off the list.

'We held the dinner in a very glamorous marquee on the lawns of Elton House and Nigel was the guest of honour. It was June 1989 and John was still Treasury Secretary but it was just before the reshuffle in which he was made Foreign Secretary. We had had a huge cake made for him by a Tory member in the constituency. It was shaped like a lovely book, absolutely fabulous, with a ribbon that came down the middle. The best wishes message on one page and on the other a biography of the different Parliamentary jobs he's had, ending up with Chief Secretary. We had a long top table, and the marquee full of people, and I think there is no doubt about it – Nigel Lawson was quite taken aback at the atmosphere and the number of people. It was a wonderful evening.

'He was flown up by helicopter because it was his only way of getting up the A1 on a Friday night. He arrived in grand style. But the thing he actually commented on that did take him aback (was that) this was an Association that John knew and that knew John. And during the course of the evening, a thing that definitely impressed him was that people came up and it didn't matter who, from whichever corner of the marquee, it was "Mildred" or "Joan" or "Maureen" or "Ken" or "John". They knew John and he knew them by their Christian names. There was no one who came up he had not met before. He knew that gathering and more.

'Nigel Lawson was incredibly impressed with that. He actually said he couldn't do that in his constituency. That must have given him an insight into this fellow who was sitting next to him, actually his number two at the time. He gave a very witty speech and spoke well of John and left before the dinner, flown off by helicopter somewhere else. I just wonder what went through his mind on that occasion.'

Perhaps they didn't really like each other? Lady Blatch says, 'It would be dishonest of me to say that I have any reason for saying it, but you piece lots of different things together.'

Two months after this party, John was Foreign Secretary, and only fifteen months later had been Chancellor for a year and was now Prime Minister. It is possible that, motivated by sour grapes, or perhaps shaken by the onslaught of press criticism of his economic managment that occurred during the first few months of 1991, Lawson is shaping up as that new breed of creature in John Major's life: an enemy. If so, and as the Prime Minister shows more and more what he is about, new opponents will probably emerge. There are already a few among the press, mostly self-appointed rather than earned. Thanks to his previous low profile, his belief in attacking policies rather than personalities, the influence of enemies on John Major's career has been hard to spot.

Attempts by media rumour to set him at odds with his greatest benefactor, the former Prime Minister, have caused some discomfort. It is difficult on the one hand to prove oneself one's own man and on the other to avoid accusations of ingratitude for providing that very evidence. However, that most powerful of all Fairy Godmothers, Mrs Thatcher, remains silent on the matter of her hopes for his future policies – though, it is said, with mounting impatience. She must certainly have believed that, despite their disagreements on many details, he was planning to continue along the same political path which she had carved out over her eleven-year term of office. She made no secret of her joy at his election but when asked about his relationship with her, he finds little to say other than, 'It was easy and very friendly and I liked her a lot. I don't know what else to say about her.' And how did they get on? 'It was not a difficult relationship at all. When we disagreed, we disagreed. These things happen. But there was never any stress or strain in the relationship. There was never edginess or mistrust.'

It is not only thanks to Mrs Thatcher and the other fairy godmothers that John has advanced so quickly. It is because of his own preparedness for and alertness to the moment of opportunity at each step of the way, and the fact that, in job after job, he was always able to deliver the goods. The more his excellence was recognised, the faster he rose. On its upward trajectory, John Major's career seemed to accelerate like a rocket freeing itself from gravity as it reaches space. All the loading, all the effort, was in the earlier stages. The further he rose, the easier things became. His ascent seems perfect in every particular. As his Agent said of him, 'He never puts a foot wrong.'

To John Major, aspiring politican since puberty, it may have seemed a long hard road, not only from the back streets of Brixton to the green fields of Huntingdon, but also from Huntingdon to Downing Street. To others observing his career, it seems like a lightning ride on a horse called Lucky. But it was never that. His life is like his work – as solid a piece of craftsmanship and engineering as one could expect to find in any science museum, marked 'prototype'. He is his own original invention, not modelled on anyone, never a fake.

So is his success a fairy tale with doors opened effortlessly for him by fairy godmothers, or is it the result of his own dedicated work? Hare or tortoise? Concorde or Challenger tank? The answer from his point of view will always be the slow, sure plod, the concentration of mind and effort on the sole objective, step by step, the goal always just in sight on the brow of the next hill. As for fairy godmothers, they had to be earned like everything else on his tough road from the outside into the heart of power. Concentration, determination and hard preparation enable one to take advantage immediately opportunity appears. There is no such thing as luck, only opportunity prepared for and pounced upon. That 'tide in the affairs of men, which, taken at the flood, leads on to fortune'.

To the hindsight specialists it may all look easy, but to John Major, the only easy bit was the first step. In all one thousand mile journeys that begin with one step, the beginning is hyped by hope. Only later do adverse weather, rough trails, weary limbs and low blood sugar slow the journey and drag the walker's spirits down. Only John knows the hope and despond, the rough and smooth of his journey to that goal, which, once attained, is, like a wedding, only the start of the hardest part of all. Until now the whole struggle was just a courtship. Being Prime Minister is not the end of the journey but the beginning of its most testing phase.

6

THE MAN FROM
NOWHERE

'I won't leave this place for anything. This is the
home I've always dreamed of.'

THE OFFICIAL RESIDENCE OF THE British
Prime Minister is 10 Downing Street in the
flat on the top storey of the several combined
London town houses that is the nation's nerve centre.
The terrace seems at first sight a tranquil enclave
protected from intrusion behind its own high wrought
iron gates, a hurricane's eye. But, of course, it is a
vibrating heart of energy. Nor is this building just
one of the pretty faces of England's history. When,
on February 7 1991, the IRA audaciously launched
a mortar attack on Downing Street over the roof of
the Horse Guards building from a Ford transit van
parked near the Defence Ministry in Whitehall, it
was revealed that the gracious house was well able
to withstand blasts. The double glazed windows
are coated with shatterproofing material so that the
one mortar which exploded in the rear garden, feet

from the Cabinet Room's windows, had no chance of harming the Prime Minister and his Ministers as they discussed the latest moves in the Gulf War.

Not only are this elegant fortress's walls, doors and windows reinforced against bomb blasts, but beneath the historic Georgian terrace, a system of nuclear age tunnels and bunkers spreads under Whitehall and St James's Park connecting all the major offices of state, including Parliament and Buckingham Palace. Carefully concealed electronic devices discreetly scan all visitors who enter through the famous steel-reinforced front door, brass numerals, letterbox and lion face knocker the sole decorations on its glossy black paint.

British understatement is as evident in the internal and external decorations as in apparent security. Within this fortress, gracious rooms of state are decorated with silk wallpapers and fine paintings, and furnished elegantly with beautiful antiques which gracefully complement the Georgian interior.

There had been buildings of sorts on what later became Downing Street for hundreds of years by the time the present house was built by a dubious political adventurer called George Downing, three hundred years ago in Charles II's time. The present terrace stands on land which has been important from Roman times. The area comprising Downing Street, Whitehall, the Houses of Parliament, Westminster Abbey and the Church of St Margaret's was originally part of the Isle of Thorns, or Thorney Island, formed between two branches of the River Tyburn which joins the Thames at this point. Roman pottery shards were found under the courtyard of Number 10 when it was substantially rebuilt during the

1960s. A Temple to the goddess Diana, protectress of hunters, wild animals and maidens, was the Roman settlement's focus.

But there was more to the place even than that. The ancients were good at building their settlements and temples in places where the earth's energy was strongest. At such places, there was more power for worship, for prophecy, for mental activity, more fertility for crops, cattle and people. In England these subterranean power points are called ley lines. Where the lines join, their power is said to be enhanced. Westminster is a major ley junction where, according to Christopher Jones in his book about 10 Downing Street, legends of 'wonders and mysterious things' seen by the locals were once frequent. Much water has flowed down the Thames since and the wonders have taken a more material form.

Number 10 is one of the three remaining properties (the other two being 11, the Chancellor of the Exchequer's residence, and 12, the Whips' house) in a street that once had at least twenty houses. Now access is closed off at each end. Huge wrought iron gates bar the way from Whitehall and a smaller gate closes what was once a public footpath up some steps from St James's Park. Accredited TV crews keep watch on the famous front door which is opened before a visitor has time to knock by a custodian, who is often in shirt sleeves.

The black-and-white-tiled floor has a single strip of red carpet running its length into another, inner hallway from which the staircase rises. There is a little coming and going, all is very low key with altogether the atmosphere of a large private house from which the owners are temporarily absent but in which the servants are still going about their daily business. This is terribly deceptive but very English.

A pair of lifts opening off the first entrance hall elevates visitors smoothly up four floors to the residential quarters. Upstairs, in what must once have been the attic where servants slept, the flat which sprawls laterally across the two houses which now comprise Number 10 reflects conventional English standards, again of comfortable understatement rather than style or panache. The undecoratorish arrangements of antique side tables and cabinets, pastel walls hung with the work of notable artists, floors covered partly in beige, partly gold Wilton carpeting, sofas in pretty chintz upholstery and simple straight-falling curtains seem cosy but almost too modest. Lacking the grandeur and dignity of the high-ceilinged rooms in the main house, the flat is small-scale and much less impressive than many of central London's upmarket apartments. But then a nation which pays its Prime Minister £70,000 a year, a fraction of the salaries earned by British industry's top executives, may not be surprised to learn that the accommodation that goes with the job is just a modestly appointed conversion.

It is the state drawing rooms looking out over Horse Guards Parade which best convey the sense of true English elegance. The rooms are simply beautiful, but quite unaffectedly so, like a woman with no consciousness of the effect of her beauty on onlookers. The grandeur is assured but unassertively restful, and with a casual poise. The White Drawing Room where so many of the photographs with visiting heads of state are taken before the marble fireplace, the Green Drawing Room (formerly the

Blue Drawing Room) which opens out from it, and the pillared drawing room opening from that, each conveys an atmosphere of being within a private house rather than impersonal rooms of state.

Perhaps Number 10's history as a private residence still permeates its walls. It may take a few more centuries fully to reflect the degree to which this building is now an office of state with a residence merely tucked away in the garret. For the time being, Number 10 is still a lovely house, warm and welcoming and charming, in a very convenient part of London.

Perhaps the flat could be prettier and cosier with a few more personal touches: more fine pictures, fresh flowers, a few more cushions and rugs, and some swags and flounces around the windows. Mrs Thatcher filled it with flower arrangements and hung her own prints. The Prime Minister can borrow pictures from state galleries and use furniture from other state buildings. During the first four months of the Majors' residence, one of the only two pictures remaining in the Majors' drawing room at Number 10 was a state-owned Lowry originally hung there by Mrs Thatcher. For at least three months after John became Prime Minister, picture hooks were the only decoration on the other pale pink emulsioned walls, marking the places where the Thatchers' personal paintings once hung. But by late April more pictures had appeared and family photographs were arranged on a sidetable.

The Prime Minister seems unconcerned and comments gleefully, 'I'm so glad we've got this flat. I'm running out of places to put my books at home.'

Perhaps in time Norma Major will put her
homemaker's mark on the flat's interior. But,
judging from her choice of furnishings and fabrics
in the family home in Cambridgeshire, it seems
unlikely that she will impose a grander style. She
says she prefers the Number 10 flat to Number 11,
the Chancellor's residence. 'It's more me. I don't
feel quite so overawed. Number 11 is a very grand
flat.'

David Rogers remembers that he and Carole Stone
had been helping John with a speech one evening
while he was Chancellor. 'John had to go to a
meeting, so Carole and I worked on a bit and
then left. As we closed the door behind us we
said, "What a cold and impersonal place to come
back to alone at night." When the Lawsons were
there, it was more of a family home with the kids'
bicycles in the hall. But when John was there there
was nothing to show that anyone lived there. It wasn't
a home at all.'

Norma's artistic interests are musical rather than
visual. Her interest in and knowledge of the world
of opera and her abilities as a writer are proven by
her biography of Joan Sutherland. Besides, Norma
says the pressure of time rather than lack of interest
prevents her from devoting herself to homemaking
as much as she would like. In January 1991 she
had made a start at rearranging furniture in the
flat's drawing room, but to little effect. The place
was conspicuously bare of fresh flowers, in marked
contrast to the Thatcher occupancy. Norma told me,
'I don't bother having flowers in the house.' Perhaps,
as Norma spends but two nights a week in London,
she may consider them wasteful or unnecessary,

especially if her husband might not notice these touches.

But there are flowers left by Mrs Thatcher – dried flower arrangements and also the pretty Laura Ashley wallpaper and fabrics in the private bathroom of the master bedroom suite. The whole flat is timeless and pretty. The master bedroom, looking down on St James's Park, is spacious and simply furnished. A free-standing mahogany wardrobe and dressing table have a Forties look. The double bed has an attractive print bedspread. There are stuffed animals on the bed – one a Dalmatian to stand in for the one John says he was disappointed not to be given as a child, the other a white bear to celebrate his first one hundred days in office. Both are gifts from friends.

Norma loves Chequers, the PM's country residence in Buckinghamshire. 'It's a really lovely house, warm and homely.' The house today remains much as it was built in 1565 by a man called William Hawtry whose family had lived on the surrounding estate for 300 years. That estate was first recorded in the Domesday Book in 1086, 900 years ago, as being of the dimensions of fourteen and a half hides. It got its name a century later from its owner, Elias de Scaccario, an Exchequer official. Scaccarium was the Latin for chequer board, and Exchequer accounts were settled on a chequer board table. De Chekers was the Norman-French version of de Scaccario and the estate became known as Checkers. The house was eventually given to the state for the use of Prime Ministers in 1921 by the then owner, Viscount Lee of Fareham, who had substantially restored and redecorated the Elizabethan mansion.

Lloyd George was the first Prime Minister to use the house. Now used for official meetings – lunches, dinners and parties, mainly at weekends – it is kept entirely private. No filming or photographs, no openings to the public, defile the serenity of this august hideaway. Norma Major went there for the first time as Prime Minister's wife at Christmas 1990, and fell in love with it. She remembers, 'I had been there before. The first time was in the early Eighties to a small lunch. I remember stopping off because we were too early.'

Norma has been reported as being reluctant to use Chequers. 'That wasn't really true. I said that I liked Chequers and that I'd like to spend more time there if it were possible, but I can't because of the family.'

The needs of a resident hamster called Psycho, the family's only pet; the commitments of James's Saturday football matches and Elizabeth's horse riding, make the family home at Great Stukeley the preferred weekend base. But, at Christmas 1990, they all went to Chequers and Norma comments, 'We were completely spoiled. It was three days of absolute bliss.' They went back again at New Year to host a party.

But an official residence can never be home. If it were, one might not have the courage to set one's heart there as tenure can be ended suddenly and unceremoniously. As Baroness Blatch, who was at one of the Chequers parties at the New Year of 1991, says, 'Norma is a realist. She knows these things don't last. She knows it's only there for so long, and she will enjoy it while she can.' It is John who is the main reason why Norma may not see as much of Chequers as she would secretly like.

John Major's heart is definitely in another place: in the house set among trees near the Cambridgeshire village of Great Stukeley. This house is the home of his heart, and his sanctuary. It is also his Eden, the earthly paradise to which he retreats from the clamour of public life; indeed, all uninvited intrusion. The square brick four-bedroomed house, sheltered by several acres of trees and lawns, which has been the Majors' family home since 1983 is the fulfilment of a dream for the Prime Minister, a dream that seems as powerfully motivated as the one that brought him to Number 10.

Baroness Blatch describes the moment John first showed her his new house while giving her a lift back from a meeting: 'He said, "Would you have the time to come and have a look at our new house?" Now, he and Norma and the children lived at the time in Hemingford Grey in a semi-detached modern house. Hemingford Grey is rather a nice village, a bit more upmarket than some in the Huntingdon area. But John was in a fairly ordinary semi-detached house and this house in Stukeley was well detached. Not only detached but beyond the edge of the village in a copse. They'd just bought it and it was still empty. So I said I'd love to come and see it and he took me off and we drove into this driveway and went into this empty house with no furniture, absolutely empty, and he stood in the middle of this house and he said, "Nobody's going to know what this means to me. When I think of the high rise flats, the always living cheek by jowl somewhere with endless other people . . ."

'This was his first detached house. I can still see him standing in the centre of it and it meant so much to him. This was a very real, very emotional moment for him, something very special. I think Stukeley means a great deal more to him than another house. To most of us the next house is the next house. But to John . . .'

To look at it's nothing special, this house of dreams. Of weathered brick and square post-war modern design, it stands at right angles to the road, set well back, screened by trees from passing traffic. Even the driveway is so discreet that a stranger can miss it, opening off a tight bend in the road that is also an accident blackspot.

The gravel driveway circles a tree and the doorway is set mid-way along the long brick wall in a porch of country back-door simplicity, stacked with wellies. You enter a short narrow hallway which joins at right angles a longer, similarly narrow lobby from which all the downstairs rooms open. The drawing room spans the house at one end. Other rooms fall to one side or other of the hallway, all of them square or oblong. But the great charm of the house lies not so much in its architecture as in its setting, and it is this above all which appealed so strongly to John with his urban background. From every room a large window looks out on green lawns and mature trees. This secluded paradise populated by birds, rabbits and squirrels was deliberately chosen to give the Majors the privacy for which John has longed most of his life.

The Brixton experience undoubtedly induced this passion for privacy, even though John Major seems to have gained great riches from it in other ways. 'It was not a deprivation but, for a ten-year-old boy, a great adventure.' Yet the one thing his early years there absolutely lacked was privacy.

The sharing of a bathroom and kitchen facilities with other families, the fact that five people were living in two small rooms, must go a long way towards explaining the passion to surround himself with space. In Brixton John shared one room with his father and older brother Terry, while his mother and older sister shared the other. The bathroom was several flights below while the kitchen on the Majors' top landing brought other tenants to their door. Some people brought up in large close families feel exposed if afterwards they are placed in solitary situations. Perhaps John would find himself similarly bereft without his own immediate family: an only child by virtue of his age distance from his siblings he may have been, but he is a warm, affectionate, gregarious individual. It is the madding crowd he seeks to put at a distance. No wonder he feels conflict between his private needs and his passion for political life. Politics is a life of such intense communication, of constant handshakes, shoulders rubbed and backs slapped or stabbed. There are few private moments until the door shuts and the curtains are drawn.

So how wonderful to feel that one might also stretch among the sycamores and beeches, walk the grassy earth and feel the scented breeze, uncriticised and unburdened, free of the need to be a public person, and as secluded as though a great door had closed out the world.

Brixton's teeming proximity sowed the seed of need for space, a need which has grown stronger like some tenacious root over the years of polite neighbourliness in middle-class suburbs which followed. As a public figure, the problem of neighbourliness is that one's every action is noted. One's voice shouting at the children floats over the small distances, and narrow cavities separating one thin-walled house and another.

In all the places he has lived, even the young marrieds'
semis first in Beckenham and finally in Hemingford
Grey, John was surrounded, overlooked, and in close
proximity to neighbours.

Had he not been in politics it might not have been so
important to find that seclusion he craves, but anyone
in public life is inevitably exposed more to gossip and
intrusions into their privacy. John Major is an intensely
private man and constant public exposure has only
exaggerated this sensitivity. He hates to be revealed,
even to the extent of being written about; is too touchy,
too often hurt by small things. Too vulnerable for
comfort?

How differently he might have felt had he been
brought up in some respectably anonymous family
and never entered politics. But the reverse has been
true and John, the son of a well-known local figure,
in a family used to the limelight, had never really been
out of the spotlight – until the house in Great Stukeley
enclosed him within its protective trees.

'It took me five minutes to decide to buy Finings.
I hadn't even seen the inside before I'd made up my
mind. We drove around the turning circle. I looked at
the trees. I looked at the house. I didn't care if it was a
complete shambles inside, I knew we could put it right
and I knew I wanted to buy it. The question was, could
I afford it and the answer was no. So we bought it.' He
smiles. 'Most of the big decisions in my life, personal
decisions, have been made quite quickly.'

Norma explains that Finings was what the former
owner had called the house. He told them a story about
how he had been breathalysed on the way back from a
local brewery. Apparently finings are something to do
with the brewing process. But it does seem strange that

a house that is such a prize possession and refuge should not have been renamed by them for something special in their own lives. Perhaps with houses, like boats, to rename them is to change their luck, and Finings has been a very lucky house for John Major. In the seven years since he moved there, he has gone from being a junior whip to top dog. No wonder he says he never wants to leave it. It is the first time he has really felt at home.

This, then, is where he spent every spare weekend until he became Prime Minister. His walks in the woods with Jeffrey Archer; his Sunday trips to the pub with the family; gatherings with friends – lunches and suppers for friends like Dulcie and Robert Atkins, the Archers, Ian Cameron Black, Emily Blatch and other local buddies, cooked by Norma and eaten around the highly polished table in the small square dining room, facing out on to the green acres of lawns and fields beyond those blessed trees. A house for comfort and reflection, filled with books of all kinds, from political biography to Flashman novels; a house run by Norma, empty of John's presence all week, but there like a refuge come weekends. Then he can return, immerse himself in family life that has its own rhythms and be healed of the week's wear.

A restful place for the workaholic politician to come home to from the front line and enjoy Norma's care, talk football with James and Elizabeth, work a bit or read in the study while they go about their lives, pleasantly aware of his rare presence. A base from which to plan a measured rise up ambition's slippery rope ladder. Yet, planned or not, with each rise on that ladder from Junior Whip to Minister at Health and Social Security to the highest Cabinet rank, his visits to Finings became sparser, limited by trips abroad, more pressured by work on first the black boxes of the Foreign Office, then the red ones of the Exchequer, and now those of the Prime Minister. But this irrevocable process is not without pain or submitted to without a fight.

When he was newly Foreign Secretary in September 1989 John Major sat in his cube-shaped and book-lined study staring out into the rain-drenched garden. His eyes seemed to gleam with a sudden wetness behind his glasses and his colour rose as he said emphatically, 'I won't leave this place for anything.' He went on, 'This is the home I've always dreamed of, a place surrounded by land, where my children could grow up.'

Yes, this is where the rootless boy who moved so often both down and up the housing scale, has put down a massive tap root. This is where his stability stems from and where, while jobs may come and go, the true self still lives. 'This is where anything is that's important to me.' He had already said earlier with a laugh, 'I'll dive back here like a ferret down a hole every weekend.' It was to this end he refused, as Foreign Secretary, the use of Chevening, the grace and favour country house which Sir Geoffrey Howe had been so loath to give up with the Foreign Secretary's office. He never moved to Number 1 Carlton House Terrace, the very grand Foreign Secretary's town house overlooking The Mall, using it only for entertaining. He continued instead to live in a secluded pied à terre on the top floor of a former banking colleague's detached early Victorian villa in a charming Brixton square.

Durand Gardens was hardly Brixton proper, but a
highly gentrified enclave of large detached Victorian
houses, situated off the Clapham Road and literally
two or three minutes by car from the Thames and
Parliament. Number 35, the house in which John
Major lodged, is one of a pair of very attractive,
white stuccoed mini-mansions with beautiful bow
windows set in bowed front elevations. Its owner,
Stan Hurn, says, 'I'm a bachelor and one day I
bumped into John. He'd been living in digs in the
Kennington Road. I said, "Why don't you come and
live in my house?" The whole top floor was already
arranged as a separate flat.' Stan Hurn saw little of
his lodger. He says, 'Bankers' hours and politicians'
hours don't coincide. He used to get up at five quite
often, and of course he mostly came in after I'd gone
to bed.'

Apart from its evident charm, the place would
clearly have commended itself to a man who evidently
needs to feel secluded when he is not bustling
about the business of politics. Durand Gardens is
a world apart, not only from the heavy traffic and
urban poverty of mainstream Brixton, but from the
demented swirl of Central London and the hurly
burly of Parliamentary life. For a man who likes to
dive down a hole for a break from politics, a salubrious
Stockwell square is a lot more of a hideaway than
prestigious St James's. He stayed there for four years.

Before he became Foreign Secretary, however, John
had been planning to buy a London base with his long-
time friend and cricket buddy, Robert Atkins.

The Minister for Sport keeps a cricket ball on a silver
stand on his desk and manhandles it while he talks. 'We
were going to buy a house together because we were fed

up with living in digs. The place we were looking at was quite smart, despite rumours to the contrary. Neither he nor I had any background money and therefore we were finding it a bit of a struggle. We were thinking of our families growing up and wanted a base in London. Then, of course, he became Foreign Secretary and got Chevening and Carlton House Terrace and it all fell through.'

As soon as John was promoted to Foreign Secretary, the peaceful seclusion of Durand Gardens was shattered by the advent of security guards and devices. Stan Hurn's lovely house became a fortress girdled with invisible beams, discreet wires and very sensitive alarm bells. Reporters lurked and police guards hung around the once quiet square, disturbing its story book charm and seclusion. Hurn says that the police were very alert. 'They had to wander all around the house and watch both front and back entrances. Once when I was away, a friend came to feed the cat. By the time he'd got into the kitchen, the police were banging on the door.'

The move to Carlton House Terrace was eventually organised for the day that John was catapulted out of the Foreign Office and into the Treasury by Nigel Lawson's stormy departure. It was hastily cancelled and, finally, reluctantly, he left his Stockwell retreat to live at the Chancellor's official residence. He could hardly refuse to live next to the Prime Minister and come and go through the communicating door to Number 10 for late night or crack of dawn conferences with Mrs Thatcher.

He did not however make use of Dorney Wood, the Chancellor's official country residence much enjoyed by Nigel Lawson. To John Major, the gracious option of these wonderful state mansions meant nothing. He already had exactly what he wanted. For him, the tree-girt house with the mortgage 'that will take until about 2050' to pay off was his safe house. When he was made Foreign Secretary, the sanctuary was seen as the most vulnerable point in his security, and had to be strung with alarms and guarded by policemen. As Chancellor he was already on the IRA's death list, but not so well guarded. But now that he is Prime Minister, the guards have been redoubled. So he is obliged to accept the presence of round the clock shifts of uniformed police officers, highly visible in the driveway, based in their own small caravan.

The reality of their presence became vividly apparent as he sat in his study on a rainy September afternoon. He was still Foreign Secretary and had agreed to an interview. He had not turned on the light despite the gloom of twilight and dark rain clouds. Perhaps he preferred to leave the curtains unclosed and still look out on to his Eden's green comfort. Cognac was poured and the conversation grew informal. Through the window, two policemen and his driver appeared, pushing the heavy bullet-proofed Daimler out of the driveway to a breakdown truck. Into the silence following their passage over the gravel came the steady pouring of rain on to the trees and then his apologetic voice: 'I feel guilty about resenting them but I can't go anywhere without them now, not even to the corner shop.' He seemed to screw up his face as he spoke. This loss of privacy was obviously hurting deeply.

When asked if it was not worth it, for a moment he did not reply. The look in his eyes clearly indicated that this loss of the so recently attained privacy was the greatest sacrifice he could offer for the privilege of high public office.

'It could get worse,' I said. He cried out as though at some appalling news. 'No!' he said sharply, looking aghast. There was a moment of astonished silence at that rebellious note. 'There's one job that's worse,' I said. Then he smiled. He relaxed and shifted in his chair. The tension left him. 'Oh.' He blushed and he seemed to feel foolish. 'Yes, That Job.' It was clear that there would be sacrifices he would make for 'That Job' that were barely tolerable for one to which he had never aspired. So, now, the security is, indeed, much more prevalent. The trees that were his guardians of sanctuary are now filled with a more sinister protection: armed guards patrolling among the trip wires that could set off any number of alarms should any unwanted person come close. The house's once comfortable spaces are cramped by the presence of burly bodyguards.

And yet he goes back there almost every weekend even now, state engagements permitting, when really the demands of office make Chequers a more logical place to weekend. There meetings, lunches, dinners and parties can take place without extra security precautions; servants keep a smooth running establishment. At the end of a long driveway, moated and in much more extensive grounds than Finings, Chequers is the safest haven for a Prime Minister permanently on the alert for terrorism.

If there was fate in the future PM's Brixton childhood, there is something even more fated about this house in Great Stukeley. The same fate, the one having created the other. Those days at cricket matches in Surrey were enveloped in safety and serenity and a similar mood is conveyed by this house among trees and lawns in leafy Cambridgeshire. John has vested all his dreams in this house. He has made this house into a talisman for the life for which he has always yearned. Talismans were used by the ancients to ward off evil and here in his talismanic house, John wards off the insecurities which haunted his childhood. When he is there all sense of being threatened by forces of change and events in the world outside is banished. He literally escapes into this grass- and tree-girt house as if into another world. To John, this house is much more than a house, much more than a home, much more than the place his family stay. It is a kingdom.

And it is a fortress, secure against terrorist attack. It would have been more convenient for everyone else if the Prime Minister had agreed to spend his weekends at Chequers. Especially after the bomb attack on Downing Street, friends have voiced their anxieties about his security. But protection at Great Stukeley has been strengthened. John told me forcefully, 'They'll have won if they stop me going there. I'll keep on going there.' His voice and features expressed stubbornness, and anger. Any terrorist that attempts to attack John Major will be the focus of a relentless retributive pursuit. After the IRA attack on Downing Street, the Prime Minister's voice rang with cold steel when he said, 'They will be hunted and hunted until they are found.'

Lady Blatch believes that the Majors will gradually adapt themselves to the need for change. 'I think when the realisation dawns, John will accept it too. This (the Downing Street mortar attack) has been quite a shock to him. He'd be much safer in Chequers, and sooner or later they're going to have to put the official letter on him to do that. I think now that Norma has taken to Chequers, she's very excited about it. She liked Number 11, she likes Number 10, but she'd go to Chequers willingly.'

Norma Major confirms, 'We are adjusting. Our life is work mostly. We have nice efficient people to support us which I haven't had before – it takes getting used to, using that help. They're there to do things and they do them well and and one doesn't mind them being there.' However, there's still no place like home, it seems. She adds, 'One of the things I find hard at the moment if I go away for a couple of days is that when I get back to Huntingdon, I have to go round and shake it up a bit and make it mine again, which is time consuming. I have to make the nest again. Huntingdon will be even more important as it's ours and it belongs to us. It doesn't matter how much we are pampered, there is something private about your own home.'

Lady Blatch feels that the present domestic problems, with James still at school and living at home and Elizabeth also working from there, must be resolved so that the Majors can be weaned away from Great Stukeley and live their lives more securely. But John's powerful attachment is the most difficult obstacle. He seems to make icons from his past. His home is his source, where he comes from in a total sense, both present and past. The treasured house at Great Stukeley is a wellhead from which he drinks deep at weekends, but replenishing more than mere physical energies among familiar acres and familial rhythms. His need for this place is as powerful as the need of a rootless refugee to say he belongs somewhere. Is it

ancestral, like so much else in the man, a product of
genes, a longing assimilated from both parents who,
after years of theatrical touring, sought a home in
which to root themselves? Dunroamin?

It was not to be for them. Worcester Park, the
seemingly anonymous suburb, could never be the
place where they belonged. A good enough place to
rest, yet it was not to be permanent. Nor even was
the far less comfortable roost on the top floor of the
Brixton rooming house. For who would stay in such
a place if they could better themselves? So as they
moved again, and as, when he was old enough, John
moved through a series of bedsitters, bought his first
flat at Primrose Court, married Norma and eventually
moved away from Brixton, to Beckenham, and then to
Huntingdon, the almost nomadic rootlessness sowed
an insatiable need for a place in which to come to
rest.

It is not love of a particular home that has kept alive his
connections with South London, more a remembrance
of freewheeling, striving yet carefree times with friends
from his happy campaigning days: people like Peter
Golds, Clive Jones, the Lawrence Kennedys, Jean
Lucas. Even his support of Surrey County Cricket
Club and Chelsea Football Club is a harking back.
Surrey is the home team for Worcester Park. Chelsea is
the club supported by theatrical people, and naturally
the choice of Tom Major and his young son.

Throughout his Parliamentary years, John has
homed in on Brixton like a radar-guided missile.
Late night trips to fish and chip shops and Indian
takeaways continued even when he was Chancellor.
When he became Foreign Secretary, journalists were

cheered at the colourful photo and interview opportunities presented by the new Cabinet Minister's
proletarian haunts and tastes.

There was a favourite cafe at Elephant and Castle
where, while working at the nearby Department of
Health and Social Security, he liked to breakfast
on triple beans on toast or eggs, sausages, bacon
and fried bread with tomatoes. Once he became
Foreign Secretary, and the haunt was discovered by
the press, it became off limits. As Prime Minister,
even more the terrorist target, security makes such
excursions difficult. More recently there was the
much publicised stop en route to a Northern engagement at a Happy Eater restaurant where the Prime
Minister chose a typically cholesterol-rich meal. A few
days later the IRA mortared Number 10 and his life
was endangered, but perhaps he's more at risk from
his favourite foods which include takeaway dinners,
hamburgers with fries, his favourite roast potatoes
and other deadly dishes.

These culinary tastes may also be part of his nostalgia
for a gayer, freer past. It is as if by eating cheap, basic
foods and visiting the unpretentious places that serve
them, he can evoke Sixties politicking on Lambeth's
streets, the community of fun and kindling fires of
ambition, the knife-edged excitement and anguished
longing and fear of failure that were all part of planning
a future that sometimes seemed possible, at others
remote.

Could it be that as the ambition is fulfilled, John
Major, like many other great achievers, now longs
for the spirit of that time in which he lived before
success took away the zest for and joy of life? Perhaps
life is more fun when the only place you have to go

is up. By harping on Brixton and the tastes of his youth, is he trying desperately to evoke the memories of past joys to fill suddenly empty spaces left by dreams fulfilled? Or is he continuing his need for rebellion, by eating foods and visiting places which are completely at odds with the tastes and pretensions of the political community of Conservatism. Something of each. John Major remains the rebel at heart and the more his life conforms to conventional mores, the more the rebel has to find some harmless means of expression.

Whatever the reason, Brixton remains the place from which he has to claim he comes. Yet he is really the man from nowhere, just passing through like his parents on tour. John Major has no reason to reject his background or to pretend he was a changeling. He would never do so and does not. He is as clear a product of nurture as of nature. The very unusual qualities of his background have made him exactly what he is: an extraordinary and brilliant man. Yet he is a man whose restlessness has brought him to high office. Neither his ambitious soul nor his extraordinary destiny have allowed him resting place or a sense of belonging. So the importance of Brixton as an icon and of 'Finings' as a refuge and true home of the heart are clear. Between them lies the story of his transition from penniless boy whose loving but nomad family was his only foundation, to founder of his own family and creator of a permanent material home that symbolises and provides everything he previously lacked.

Ironically it is the point at which he left Brixton which marks the real start of John Major's sense of belonging. When a councillor, he bought his own small flat at Primrose Court where, Jean Lucas remembers, he had no furniture, apart from his bed and just one chair. She says, 'I would go up with him and he'd make me a cup of coffee and I'd sit in the chair. If there was a group of us it would be a rush to see who would get the chair.'

Then one day, Norma came on the scene. And that is the beginning of another phase of the story.

7

LOVE AT FIRST SIGHT

'Oh, I thought she was super . . . She had the biggest brown eyes I've ever seen.'

'I thought, "What a gorgeous man!" '

THE BREAKFAST ROOM TABLE IN Lawrence and Aine Kennedy's large house in Dulwich Village is the one at which John and Norma Major began their courtship. The plain rectangular teak table with its six matching chairs confesses nothing of its historic connections with the Prime Minister and his shy wife, but russet-haired Aine (pronounced Awnia) vividly recalls the night she first invited John and Norma to dinner at the Kennedys' Lambeth house, soon after the GLC elections of 1970. She swears she was not match making as has been suggested, and says she was 'really furious' at a suggestion in *The Independent on Sunday* that Norma was keen to get to know John Major and had persuaded her to invite them both to a meal.

She says, 'I just thought they were both such attractive young people. Norma wasn't a close friend but I knew her quite well at that time. I used to see her at the committee rooms and at different functions and we used to talk. I thought she was the loveliest, most attractive girl, and always beautifully dressed. We used to talk about clothes, I remember. She was really interested in (them).'

The Kennedys are contemporaries of the Majors. Lawrence was one of the famous 57 Lambeth Conservative councillors, and a solicitor who still practises in the borough. Aine is a natural hostess, the sort of woman who makes a complete stranger feel instantly at home and cosseted in her house. The dinner party, she recalls in her soft Irish brogue, was 'Nothing special. We were young. We didn't make a fuss. It wasn't formal. We just had a few friends round for a meal.' So John Major, Norma Johnson and Barbara Wallis, a Lambeth councillor previously Conservative Parliamentary Candidate for Feltham, gathered together with the Kennedys around the then new teak table. Aine recalls that Lawrence sat at one end of the table with John at his left and Barbara on John's left. Norma was sitting diagonally across from John.

It was clear, Aine says, that they were very attracted to each other. But both were evidently shy. The discussion was mainly about politics. Norma did not say much but John talked a great deal with Barbara and Lawrence about the GLC elections, the coming General Election and political issues which preoccupied them all at that time. Perhaps Norma was so shy that she used every opportunity to vanish into the kitchen. 'I don't remember an awful lot about the evening,' Aine says, 'but I do remember that Norma was one of the nicest, the most helpful people I've ever had in my house, carrying things out to the kitchen and washing the dishes. Oh, she was a lovely girl.' And, 'No, she wasn't really interested in politics.'

That dinner is a landmark in what became a whirlwind romance. But the whole thing really began on the polling night of those GLC elections. There are various versions of the events that led up to John's marriage proposal to Norma in that spring of 1970.

Norma says, 'I met him on election day which I think was April 3 1970. I was driving my car and picking up people to vote. It was the first time I had done it. I'd been making clothes for Diana Geddes, the candidate. A friend I met at the opera, trainee Agent Peter Golds, was also a friend of Diana's and he said to come and give a hand.'

Peter Golds had met Norma while they were both queuing for Joan Sutherland tickets. He says, 'You were there for hours, often sleeping there overnight, and you tended to get to know the other people who did it regularly.' It was Peter who first introduced John and Norma. He says, 'I came into the main committee room with John and when he saw Norma, his eyes lit up and he said, "Who is that pretty girl?" '

John, who was Chairman of the Brixton Conservative Association at the time and organising the GLC campaign with Marion Standing, remembers it slightly differently. He says, 'No, I was already in the committee room and Norma came in. Peter was a very old and very flamboyant friend, and he had brought a girl to help me canvass. It was Norma'.

John's first impression of her was, 'Oh, I thought she was super. I can tell you exactly what she was

wearing: a two-piece costume – very faint brownish
check – white boots below the knee, creamy blouse,
and she had the biggest brown eyes I've ever seen.
That's what I remember thinking when she came
in.'

Norma remembers, 'John was throwing his weight
around a bit actually. I saw him and thought,
"What a gorgeous man!" ' As she talks, a frisson
of remembered excitement is clearly apparent. For a
moment the conventional comfort of the 10 Downing
Street setting dissolves in her recollections of that
committee room with its blue-edged posters, stacks
of left over leaflets and election addresses, electoral
rolls, canvassing sheets and call back lists spread
on trestle tables among the empty coffee cups and
takeaway containers, with spring sunlight coming
through the dusty windows and everywhere the
bustle, energy and frazzle of a successful election
campaign nearing its close.

From the demure, shy and slightly worried-looking
lady comes a new energy. Suddenly the shyness seems
to vanish. Her voice becomes firmer, her manner
more confident. Her head is slightly lowered and
she looks out from under her lashes in a very
feminine gesture, quite unconsciously re-enacting
the events of twenty-one years before. Her mouth
seems suddenly fuller, almost pouting. In an instant
of complete coquetry her shoulders move under the
shocking pink silk blouse she was wearing with
tailored black gaberdine trousers and elegant low-
heeled black patent shoes.

Sixteen months earlier, on the first occasion I saw
her, a day when she was clearly harassed by a very
full schedule, she wore a very long bias-cut dark blue

skirt, flat shoes and a white blouse printed with a small blue motif – she had seemed an altogether more 'housewifely figure'. Her hair that day was cut quite short, permed and blow dried off her forehead. It was still in the same style when she appeared outside Number 10 the day after John's election as leader. But, by the time of the January 1991 interview in Number 10, both Norma and her hairstyle seem to have undergone a transformation. Her hair is carefully blown back so as to complement her good bones. She is wearing a light but flattering make up of foundation, blusher, powder and eyeshadow.

As she comes alive to her memories, a sudden touch of natural colour appears beneath the discreetly applied blusher. Revealed under the newly acquired confidence of the Prime Minister's wife lies an unexpectedly girlish breathlessness, the stirring of feelings that are probably still triggered every time her husband walks into a room. They were there in the shy glances and smiles she gave in the couple's highly public moments outside Number 10 on the morning of John's Prime Ministerial debut, caught in a thousand photographs.

Every time Norma looks at John the camera seems to capture that same excitement, that same sense of attraction, of being alive to him as a man and proud to be his woman. 'My man,' she called him in one interview. 'I still adore him,' she said in another. And he adores her too, needs her. Two decades on from that first exciting moment, they are each other's most special people. No partnership is perfect but theirs was a love match, and despite the inevitable stresses inherent in any marriage, and especially a political one, they are still true mates.

'It was a couple of mornings after having met her. I was turning the thought over in my mind as I walked to catch the bus to work. It just became perfectly clear, I think.' He speaks reflectively in a way that makes it all seem a very long time ago. Twenty years is almost half his lifetime and so much has happened since that spring morning in 1970.

When John and Norma married, later that year, aged 27 and 28, their life expectations were both so different. John had his political ambitions but to Norma it must have seemed like impossibly high hopes even to dream of getting into Parliament. She envisaged a good married life to a successful banker – but wife of a Cabinet Minister? Prime Minister? Not in her wildest dreams.

Norma's dreams were and are quite different from John's. To many onlookers it has seemed, during his recent rapid progress through the Cabinet's highest levels to Number 10, that he would leave her behind. She seemed bewildered at each new post. When John became Chancellor she told Jeffrey Archer, 'I don't know where to live or what to do.'

'There's a sadder story,' he recollects. 'When John became Foreign Secretary, Norma rang up Mary (Archer) and said, "Would you like to come and see Chevening?" (the Foreign Secretary's country residence.) Mary said she'd love to so Norma said, "Well, let's go and see it together. I'll ring you and fix a date." She never rang and when Mary mentioned it some five months later – by that time John was Chancellor – Norma said, "I never actually went." ' Archer adds, 'I'd have been down next day. But not Norma and John. Norma's very puzzled by it all at the moment but she's handling it very well,

I think. She's such a lovely, genuine, super human being.'

Now she is begining to find new strengths within herself. After a moment of shattering stage fright which, after the events of late November 1990, catapulted her back to Great Stukeley like a frightened rabbit, publicly vowing to live her own life and change nothing to fit her husband's new one, she has adapted.

John, according to close sources, made his disappointment at her lack of support abundantly clear. There was undoubtedly a crisis. Of course protecting the family was vital, but was he not an important part of the family who needed support in his demanding new job? Friends' wives talked Norma through her panic and withdrawal, advised her, admonished her, sketched in the possibilities of her new role. She may have begun to see the magnificent opportunities available to her. Things are subtly altering. Now Norma, who has always served diligently in the constituency where she is immensely popular, has Barbara Wallis, John's longtime friend and now constituency secretary, also keeping her engagements diary at Number 10. By May her workload as the PM's wife had grown so much that she had her own secretary based at the House of Commons. She is in demand as a patron of good causes, Mencap being her pet charity, and she receives endless mail. If she can be persuaded, the potential for her to do good work is enormous. Her excuse for staying away from London and Number 10 is that she has a working daughter living at home and a school-age son coming home nightly. Her mother stands in whenever possible but with a real will, arrangements that would free her further could be made. James has already offered to board at school. Norma says, 'We can't afford it.' But, as friends point out, this is one solution. Elizabeth, working now as a veterinary nurse for racehorses, is already leading her own life and could easily find a flat.

Norma has already acknowledged that family life is changing as the children grow up. 'I think domestic bliss is now just an ideal because the children have reached a point in life where they are doing their own thing.'

It is also time for Norma to do her own thing, to use her intelligence, artistic knowledge and interests to carve out a role for herself. She is now being offered more book projects but so far says she is too busy to do them – but later demand for books by Norma Major may not be as great as demands for books by the Prime Minister's wife. Unless John is to be Prime Minister for a substantial period, these opportunities may not last.

Her loathing of public appearances is the biggest barrier to Norma's branching out in her own right. If she can overcome this, more openings for a new and fulfilling life must surely follow from her star role as the Prime Minister's consort. Like John she lacks confidence. 'I just hate people looking at me. When I go to functions and all the press and the photographers are outside, I do dread it. I have the feeling of not being able to cope with it.'

Her confidence was as shaky when John was first elected MP for Huntingdon. Paddy, Lady Renton, the previous incumbent's wife, had been the toast of the constituency. Petite, blonde and dynamic, social and sociable, a terrific organiser, speaker and participant in fund raisers and other party events, she was the perfect constituency wife. Agent Andrew Thomson remembers that Lady Renton was very helpful to Norma, introducing her to the routine of the MP's wife. But Norma feared she would never be able to fill Paddy's shoes. Norma, for instance, loathes speaking in public. However, Thompson says, 'I told her, "You're not Paddy Renton Two, you're Norma Major One." ' People persuaded her that she would be just as effective in her own style and gradually this has proved to be the case. Like John, she gains confidence with time.

Inside Number 10, the settling down process seems to be well underway. Norma was poised and in control, being interviewed at a time she had chosen, and confident enough of herself to speak quite openly about those first impressions.

'I can remember to this day what I was wearing. It was a sleeveless check jacket, brown and cream, and short skirt and blouse – quite pretty.' (She had made the outfit herself.) 'And I had tall leather boots that were just fantastic. White boots. It was the boots that did it.' She laughs at the memory of the reaction she received from the young councillor and continues, 'He was wearing – I know this sounds grotty, but – a brown suit.'

Norma is someone for whom clothes reveal the inside story about the person. She dismisses John's sartorial past with the explanation that, 'When you're young, you're feeling your way all the time, aren't you? But as you get older you say, "Oh, brown suit and Ben Sherman shirt." '

She clearly still dismisses such clothing but John is no male fashion plate, and notably unfussy about his

clothes even today. Reporters have commented that
the new Prime Minister could do with a couple of
new suits that fit properly. Friends laugh about his
six grey ties. Jeffrey Archer says, 'He doesn't care
about his clothes. I gave him a tie once and wrote
across the bottom: "To go with your other one."
He said, "I have another one. I've got three now."
He was teasing me.'

Norma remembers that, 'We were pretty hard up
when we were first married and I made him shirts
for a while. I made him a bow tie. In fact, he's only
just abandoned (it). He sometimes wears the rosette
I made him quite early on. He does things like that.'
As she talks, there is a strong sense of proprietorial
pride.

Aine Kennedy remembers Norma asked John two
key questions during the dinner party. 'She asked
him: "Do you wear braces?" and "Do you carry a
purse?" '

These were key questions, Norma explains, because, 'I think it really was love at first sight, but
if I had discovered he used a purse or wore braces,
I couldn't have gone further with him . . . well, I
had a boyfriend who wore braces and a hand-knitted
V-necked tank top and the braces used to show and
he used a purse as well – not a handbag but a purse
– and I think it does go with a total image, doesn't
it?'

Norma asked these questions after some initial
pursuit of John. She says that, at first, 'I made
most of the running.' Was John shy or simply
not very interested? That first day the couple were
introduced by Peter Golds, Norma took John home
after the count to Primrose Court.

She says. 'I had a car. It was a pretty late night. I remember taking him home and thinking there might be some future here. I think I worked slightly harder at it than he did.'

She doesn't remember whether they got talking about what their interests were or whether he had discovered in another way that she was interested in op era, probably from Peter Golds. She says, 'I thought I had better get this going so I organised a party.'

At the time Norma lived in Beckenham with her mother. She says, 'I've never really been a party lover then or since, but I did throw this party and invited him, and he said he was going to a performance of 'Elijah' and couldn't come. I still had the party and it was a nice evening but a bit pointless really as he didn't come. But I realised he was interested in music. I then got tickets for 'Aida' and he had some excuse for not going to that either, so I must have been rather persistent. I think it was genuine. He was quite busy politically and most evenings were tied up.'

This pursuit of John by Norma reveals something about both of them. First that Norma is an enormously determined woman who, when she wants something, is clearly as tenacious about achieving it as John can be. But, it seems, much less subtle.

Why didn't John pursue Norma, having reacted with such interest at first sight? Perhaps the answer lies in his fear of not being able to have something he has set his heart on? He wouldn't be the first man to go into reverse on seeing the woman he really wants. He says firmly, 'She phoned me late one afternoon, two or three days after we had met, inviting me to go to the opera. Although I have never told her this, I had put down the phone half an hour earlier after trying to see if there were some theatre tickets so I could phone her the next day and invite her. I never told her that. I thought it was a good idea not to.' This reveals much of his instinctive caginess; what he revealed next was that even in 1970 he was a clever tactician.

There was a reason behind his search for theatre tickets. 'You see, I'd made a muck of something. She'd organised a party and invited me, and she's always said, "Well, I organised this party and you didn't come." There was a reason I didn't come. I didn't think it was a great idea to get to know Norma at a party with loads of other people around. I just thought it would be the wrong setting, so that was the reason I didn't go. It wasn't lack of interest.'

He adds, 'I didn't have any doubt about Norma at all. It was only about three weeks, maybe a little longer, after we'd met that we were engaged. If I'm perfectly clear about something, I do it very quickly.'

So while Norma planned and schemed to get to know John, he coolly reeled her in. Before they were engaged there were some romantic evenings. John says, 'We'd been to the opera together – I'd fallen asleep – and we'd done a couple of other things as well. I think we'd been out for the meal at which she'd bankrupted me. We went somewhere rather swish, and they served up this huge bowl with large prawns on the outside. Norma has a very healthy appetite. Don't be misled by the fact that she's slender. She'll eat most of us under the table. Anyhow, at this rather smart restaurant Norma sat there munching her way through the prawns, which it turned out were about 75p each! It was a huge bill.

'The other time we bankrupted ourselves was just after we were married. We had £80 in the world and we went and bought a wicker chair that cost us £65 out of that £80. We brought it home in a Mini with all the windows open. It was an amazing enterprise.'

Before all this, when the courtship entered its first tentative days, Norma was not fazed by the thought there might already be a girl or girls in John Major's life. There were a couple, she admits. She says, 'One was older than me and older than John, and the other was younger and more dolly. Other than that, I never particularly bothered, to be honest.'

Her tone is that of someone who is the rightful heir to an inheritance. There were no real competitors. If there were other girlfriends, she says with a victor's satisfaction, 'Maybe they didn't have tall white leather boots.' She conveys the air of having known with some intuitive certainty that John was her destined mate, she set about her efforts to begin the relationship.

She cannot remember quite when they got engaged. 'He went off on a housing trip to Finland and we had got engaged before then because we had discussed the fact that we couldn't afford to get married.'

This rather quaint, old-fashioned view is typical of John and Norma. Even in the swinging Sixties when the catchphrase 'Live Now, Pay Later' was coined, they lived, with the exception of the wicker chair purchase, responsibly and frugally. John, of course, had a mortgaged flat at Primrose Court and a salary from Standard Chartered Bank. Norma had trained as a domestic science teacher but did not like teaching. Not surprisingly for such a gentle person, London's schools were much too rough for her, so she was dressmaking for a living. They had to budget carefully. Norma says, 'There was no question of buying an engagement ring. Anyway, I had a ring which I wore as the engagement ring.'

When John went off to Finland, Norma decided to have her jaw-length hair trimmed and restyled. 'My hair had reached a point where it was dreadful and needed to be sorted out. I had a cousin who had opened a hair dressing salon. It was out of London so I couldn't afford to go often but I did go whilst John was away. My cousin had just come back from a course at Vidal Sassoon and she said she could update my image and take ten years off my age. I should have been warned! I sat there and let her do it. I must have been mad – half an inch all over and a long tail down the back. I drove home through a mist, I was so horrified. I had just met this gorgeous guy and had my head shaved. It was quite traumatic.

'My mother cut the tail off. There was nothing else I could do about it. It wasn't so much that it looked dreadful, it just wasn't me at all. For the next few months I wore a wig. John came back from Finland and probably didn't see me as I actually was for some weeks after that. Once it had begun to grow it wasn't so bad.'

Fortunately there were a few months to go to the wedding which had to be fitted into a gap between John's political engagements, either before or after the Conservative Party Conference in October 1970. Norma says, 'And we had to decide where we could afford to go for a honeymoon.' So they were married on October 3 at St Matthew's Church, Brixton.

Norma's hair was by this time just level with her earlobes and worn with a deep fringe. The local *South London Press* reported that her dress, which she designed and made herself together with those of her bridesmaids, had 'a bodice of guipure lace sewn with crystal drops merging into a velvet skirt and train. During the service a solo of "Ave Maria" was sung by soprano June Bronhill, a friend of the bride.'

Clive Jones was best man, and the reception across the street was, according to Aine Kennedy, the biggest she had ever seen. 'The receiving lines were so long. Then there was a buffet table all around the hall and the crowds in there were just amazing. There must have been hundreds of people there. John was so popular and he knew so many people.'

The groom had to sit down at the reception because his leg had given way the night before. Clive Jones remembers, 'He'd had his stag night the night prior to that, and the evening before the wedding we just got together with two others. We had a quiet evening, a few drinks, and then his leg started playing up. So I rushed back home and got all my gear for the next day and slept on the settee at John's. We weren't at all sure that he'd be able to get out of bed and I might have to end up lifting him in and out of the bath. I didn't, fortunately.'

Before the ceremony Clive and John dressed in their wedding clothes and went with some other councillors to a local housing estate for a prearranged meeting. Clive says, 'When we got there he spent the bulk of his time sitting on a bollard. He didn't actually do the walkabout we normally would do. He talked to some of the tenants. Again at the wedding he just about managed to walk down

the aisle, and coming out he was leaning on
Norma.'

After the honeymoon in Ibiza, John and Norma
returned to domestic life at Primrose Court. John
went back to the bank and his council work and
Norma continued dressmaking. They were so short
of money that their kitchen was fitted with tallboys
covered with formica. But the room was not to be
used much. Norma says her first big disappointment
was that John never came home to dinner. 'The
most trying part of it was getting a meal on the
table and gauging when he would come home to
eat it. I remember one night I had gone to a lot
of trouble with candlesticks and everything and he
rang and said he would be delayed, then he rang
again and said he would be delayed further.' In the
end that particular dinner was ruined. Norma quickly
became used to the situation and no longer bothered
to prepare special dinners, or even any dinners at all.
After a while you get quite casual about meals. We've
stayed that way which is a shame for the children.
We don't often sit together in a disciplined way. I'm
sorry about that. Maybe we should have made more
effort.'

She admits she does not like cooking anyway. It
doesn't go with being a homemaker, perhaps, but
then she has never had an admiring audience for her
dishes. 'The children aren't interested in food.' John,
of course, has a taste for terrible takeaways. Which is
just as well since the life of politics makes for snatched
snacks and late leftovers rather than leisurely meals.
Political people are hungrier for ideas, action, results,
the process of winning elections, than they are for
gourmet cooking.

The SDP, an organisation of people largely new to street campaigning, brought the concept of wining and dining into political life. Even that was mainly a media joke based on the then leader Roy Jenkins' well-known love of claret. Dining, of course, plays a stronger part in the life of successful politicians than beginners. Little closet dinners and dining clubs are the way in which factions pursue their ends, and like-minded politicians develop their policy ideas and strategies.

Still, someone should have warned the new bride about life with an up and coming politician. Aspiring and campaigning politicians in opposition strongholds, which is what Brixton was for the aggressive young Tory group, seldom sit down to dinner. They snatch fish and chips after meetings that end just before the pubs close. Evenings spent canvassing usually end at 9 p.m. out of consideration for the householders, but there is always something to talk about afterwards with cronies. Politics is an unending and tireless game with advance gameplanning and strategy, gossip and policy discussions all part of the entertainment. For the young politician, especially, this is all part of the excitement of the life. In the early days of his marriage John was also still a councillor and completely committed to his work as Chairman of the Housing Committee. During their short courtship Norma may not have had the opportunity to realise how much time he did spend on his grass roots activities or how seriously he took them.

Norma tries to put a brave face on it, but her dissatisfaction is still evident despite her words. 'I don't think I really minded actually. I think you get over trying to adjust your life to fit in with what he wants to do. I wasn't in the business of obstructing him in any way. If that was what he wanted to do, that was fine with me as long as I knew where I fitted into that. I suppose it's been like that ever since. Once you accept that you can't put a meal on the table and expect he is going to come home on time. I suppose in a way if he worked in a nine to five job it would be a real pain. You need to establish some sort of guidelines. I honestly don't think I did mind once the fact was established. Once we had a freezer that helped. It was the days before microwaves. That would have helped.' Now Norma uses the freezer extensively. Before general elections she cooks a three week supply of meals and pops them in the freezer all labelled: General Election.

Norma's acceptance of this limitation on her domestic creativity reeks of resignation. Her disappointment is palpable. She had so much to offer as a homemaker: it was her vocation and she had even trained for it. She has said it so often, 'I am a homemaker.' But it is said with a shrug, as if implying, 'But no one appreciates what it might have been.' Is this why there are no flowers or personal bric-a-brac in the flat at Number 10? Has Norma lost heart at trying to create something for John to pass through with his red boxes? Does it perhaps imply a disillusionment with married life, perhaps her marriage?

To admit it would be to lose face. At a time of life when, like many women, Norma faces the fact that her children are leaving the nest, it may be too much also to consider that her marriage is not what she has always dreamed it could be.

There are perhaps problems in the great divergence between John and Norma's private aspirations during their twenty-year marriage. Political wives do get left behind at every stage of their husband's career. Once he is elected, the MP's wife, like Norma, will often live with the children in a constituency-based main home and become her husband's substitute there. Not all MPs' spouses accept the role, but both husbands and wives of politicians have to learn to accept that they don't often get their spouse to themselves. So, unless she is a fully participating partner in the political life, a new wife who is constantly looking forward to quiet evenings with her man is going to be disappointed. Some enjoy or make good use of the long spaces between the more private moments. Norma did not and still does not like being so separated from John. She has said that she has 'often felt wistful for the ordinary life we might have led together'.

One day she confided, 'Even when I go to functions with him, we sit at opposite ends of the dinner table, or if it's a hospital or something I get taken around one wing and he gets shown another, so even though we're doing these things together, I'm still not bloody well with him.'

Ordinary life is out of the question for political animals. Norma is not one of those. Her interests lie in the arts and literature. One political correspondent relates the story of how John and Norma attended a private dinner with a senior academic at a recent Conservative Party Conference in Blackpool. While the group talked politics Norma was silent, but when the conversation turned to the arts and academic subjects she blossomed.

It's not fair perhaps that politics demands so much of marriage partners: more often than not women. While intensely political partnerships do exist, most are marriages where love has brought the wife to sacrifice her own interests, prevented by the sheer weight of constituency duties from pursuing a life of her own. Norma is one such. Domestic circumstances have also played their part. She says that even when she was writing her biography of Joan Sutherland, a labour of love that took twelve years and much 5 am rising, the domestic situation intruded. 'I think the family obstructed me in a number of ways which they need not have done when I was writing my book; but it was partly me, other things have to come first. I could never have said to John, "You've had too many meetings this week." ' Norma's own sense of duty prevented her from putting her work before the family even in minor ways. It is typical of her selflessness that, however unhappy she felt, she would not try to restrict John in order to make her own life easier.

The same applies to his cricket. 'He has seen more cricket in the last few years than in all the time we have been married, and I've never stopped him from going to anything like that.' Fortunately, John has never tried to get her to attend cricket matches with him. He does go to the opera with her sometimes. But, then, she says, 'Opera doesn't go on all day.' There remains the problem for Norma, however, that whatever else she would like to do with her life, John's career constrains her. Through her great sense of duty and loyalty, she remains reluctant yet loyal. Frustrations, she says, build up inside her. 'I don't explode, I just sulk.' She also cries. There are times, she has told reporters, 'when I have cried into my pillow and none too quietly.' But John, she says, 'Is very good when I cry, very sympathetic.' Unlike many men who are helpless when confronted with a woman's tears.

The domestic trap closed in very early after their exhilarating courtship and spectacular wedding. Four or five months after the Ibiza honeymoon, Norma realised she was pregnant. She was supply teaching at the time. She says that after they were married, she was dressmaking still and working for Simplicity Patterns. Then, 'I took a job supply teaching because we were really desperate. I did try to get evening class work but they were paying such a pittance for it that I just didn't think that was on. So I did a stint as a supply teacher at Norwood School and it was a hell of a job. Norwood School was pretty rough at the time. I was ill at the time and started to get gruesome backache and stomach ache and sickness. I went to the doctor and found I was pregnant. He said, "I shouldn't carry on working if I were you or you will lose this baby." But I didn't need much encouragement to stop.'

Elizabeth was born just over a year after the Majors were married, in November 1971. Norma says, 'I didn't go back to teaching, I carried on sewing. I did a lot of sewing all the time when Elizabeth was quite small. I had a workbench in the bedroom.'

Meanwhile, Jean Lucas had grown anxious. 'I was afraid he would get sucked into domesticity.' Norma remembers that, 'Jean told John she thought I was too young for him. I'm a year older than him as it happens.' Could Jean have been jealous of her protégé's defection into marriage? Norma says, 'No, no, that never entered my mind.' Jean says, 'I was rather known for Jean Lucas's young men, but that was only because I needed helpers and the young men were willing, enthusiastic workers.' She thought John very promising and was afraid he might be distracted from what she thought would be 'a brilliant political future'. Some observers think that Norma may have felt Jean was luring John into politics and away from his family. Others say Norma was always completely supportive of his political ambition. It seems unlikely he would have got so far had she not been.

Yet, as a number of friends say, and as she has admitted herself, Norma would have preferred John to be more of a family man. When asked if he likes domestic life, she says, 'He likes the idea of it.' Robert Atkins, however, says, 'Family is the key consideration and there was one point before he got Huntingdon at which he said to me, "I'm going to jack it in and become Chairman of the bank and watch cricket for the rest of my life." He's very much family-oriented.'

Politics is such an all-consuming life that families of politicians can and have often suffered as a result. John is not a man who would treat his family as mere accessories. He sees them as people in their own right, with lives of their own. He values them greatly. But, naturally, the higher he has flown, the harder it has become to spend time with them.

The politician who returns to a loving home is far more likely to succeed and to remain balanced and happy than one who goes home to an empty house. Politics is about endless negotiation, infighting, struggling, pushing and battling to achieve objectives. It's a world of convenient friendships, alignments, enmities, small and large betrayals, jealousies, insidious opposition, out and out fights. Pity the man or woman who does all this without a pair of loving arms to return to at the end of a long hard week in the rough world of Westminster. This loving, well-run home Norma has provided for John. Like so many other things provided by loving women, it would be more noticeable by its absence. John is not a man to take anything for granted, but in Norma's heart there may be a feeling similar to that experienced by many wives that her love and the myriad details of her devotion, expressed in anything from fresh clean shirts and packed suitcases for trips abroad to household accounts kept and a list of constituency jobs done, are not fully appreciated. A woman's work may never be done but a Parliamentary wife's work is endless.

Does this then explain the slight atmosphere of resentment that sometimes develops between John and Norma, little different indeed from the kind of tension that exists in many marriages? Norma's admission that she sulks, letting her annoyance and upsets build up until they overflow into tears, is revealing in this context. Norma, after all, doesn't want to fight with her husband, but like so many other women she may not be able to suppress the feeling that her and her family's interests are being contiually subordinated to the demands of his career.

He is no angel at home either. Friends report outbursts of temper, shouting matches and moods. Norma once complained to a local friend that John was making a terrible fuss about the way his suitcase was packed for a trip abroad whilst he was Foreign

Secretary. There are fights with Elizabeth. Robert Atkins says, 'He's a man who's got a low boiling point. He gets very angry with his daughter and I've heard them have ranting, shouting matches.' He adds, 'That's true of me too. I get very angry with my family. You have to discipline yourself so much in public life not to be angry any more than you can avoid, in case someone is watching.'

Baroness Blatch says that John's relationship with his daughter is stormy. 'Elizabeth just keeps going on at him. It usually ends with her bursting into tears and running from the room.' Despite tensions and moods, Atkins says, 'John's greatest love is spending time with his family.' Before a photo session, they were at ease with each other, Elizabeth teasing her father affectionately as he in turn levelled accusations at her: 'And he steals my bacon sandwiches.' He wanted the sweater she was wearing with her riding clothes for the photographic session that afternoon. Naturally, John has only two sweaters, a navy blue one being worn by Elizabeth with her jodhpurs, and a charcoal grey one which he was wearing himself.

There were jokes about Elizabeth wearing his sweaters to muck out the stables. John finally seemed to be forcing good humour, on the edge of irritability, as if he really wanted to order his daughter to hand over the sweater. He managed to contain himself, turning to Norma instead and complaining vigorously about the fact that she had somehow managed to get his shirt collar outside the sweater. 'It looks awful like that. Did you do that? You must have done it. How did you manage to do that?' Norma stood helplessly by, just looking at him, while he wound himself up. Elizabeth giggled at his fussing while the photographer looked on. Moments later, John was sitting on the sofa with Norma, playfully rubbing noses with her as they got ready to pose.

This was in September 1989 and John was Britain's new Foreign Secretary. He was then, as always, keenly aware of getting the right image across in photographs.

Before Elizabeth was born in 1971, the Tory group lost their seats on Lambeth Council. Did that mean that Norma would at last have him to herself? Alas, no. By this time John had already decided it was time to stand for Westminster. He was selected for St Pancras North, a Labour stronghold in inner London, considered good only for experience for a young Tory initiate and a long way from Beckenham, where they had now moved. This did however bring them near Norma's mother who would babysit Elizabeth and keep Norma company while John went straight from the City to the constituency at least two evenings a week.

His Agent in St Pancras North, Margaret Elliott, now Jay, the practical North countrywoman who later became Douglas Hurd's Agent, says, 'He would come at least two nights a week, straight from work, and I would make him sandwiches. He didn't drive at the time although he was 29, so he had to go home on the train.' He travelled up to St Pancras again on Saturdays. This went on for two and a half years until the first of the two elections in February 1974, and again for the six months to the second election that year, in October. Norma's recollection is that, 'Nearly every evening he was over there for several years, from 1971 to 1974, and he hung on to it even after losing that election in October 1974.'

By 1974 Norma was pregnant again, this time with
James. But she valiantly helped John by canvassing
and appearing with him at meetings.

John had by now passed his driving test. 'I didn't
learn to drive until I was 30 because I couldn't afford a
car. Norma actually taught me.' Laughing at himself,
he continues, 'We discovered, on the way to the
driving test, that I'd never done a reverse turn.
So we did two, both of which I made a complete
pig's breakfast of. Norma groaned and went off for
a coffee. I took the test and passed.'

After October 1974, John still hung on for a while
at St Pancras North. As the winter of 1974/5 with
its high inflation and depressingly dark weather
brought economic as well as actual chill on to the
depressed nation, his political enthusiasm seems
to have faltered. The presence of a new Labour
Government under Harold Wilson may have affected
him. But part of the problem was his uncertainty as
to what to do next. Margaret Jay remembers he was
very loyal and hardworking and didn't want to let
St Pancras North down after working with them for
three years and two elections. But really it was time
to move on.

Norma was supportive. She says, 'We began to
realise he would have to start looking for something
else. He toyed with the idea of becoming a councillor
in Beckenham and I said, "If you want to win a
Parliamentary seat you will actually want to keep
yourself free now." ' So John began applying for a
more winnable seat. For him this was the beginning
of a two-year period of uncertainty, even self-doubt,
when he held no political office and seemed to get
nowhere in his applications for a seat. He was, says

Norma, 'Pretty clear about where he was going and how he was going to get there. I remember he and Margaret Marshall were looking for Parliamentary seats and worked out a list of all the seats who had members who were about to retire. Central Office used to circulate a list and he would apply for anything that was convenient as well as winnable. There was a feeling of getting a bit desperate because he was getting interviews and then not getting any further. Eventually he didn't even tell me what he was applying for.'

This was the period when John's applications were being confused with the other, less qualified and experienced John Major. It was the period of despondency in his political career, the period when he told Robert Atkins he might 'jack it in'. However, for Norma there began a season of domestic bliss. She had her husband at home in the evenings at last.

He was good with the children. In the earlier days when Elizabeth was a baby, Norma says, 'He was wonderful. He would get up in the morning and change the first nappy, and he would bring Elizabeth into bed with us and I would feed her and probably put her back to sleep for a while. It was all quite civilised. He was very good.'

She cannot remember so clearly how John behaved when James was born in 1974 except that he was restless. This is also the time when Ian Cameron Black says, 'He was going nowhere at the bank.' It was the doldrums in the deep sea of his ambitions. But at home he played the good father and husband, taking Elizabeth to her ballet classes, ferrying James to football matches, watching cricket. David Rogers recalls Saturday mornings when the two families

would lie in except for John who would get up and
cook beans and fried eggs for the kids. Norma says,
'He was good. My mother remembers he would come
in and say, "Do you want to cook the dinner or bathe
the children?" and we would take turns.' It was never
likely to be that way again.

After Jean Lucas had spotted the mix up of the two
John Majors at Central Office, things improved and
there were lots of shortlists. Both John and Norma
had to travel to meetings of constituency executives.
By the time Huntingdon came up, she was as excited
as he was. It fulfilled a number of requirements,
being a safe seat and still close enough to London
for John to be able to continue at the bank at least
until the election. Norma says, 'We were keen on
finding something near London. The morning he
was invited for the interview for Huntingdon, I can
remember sitting up in bed and saying to him that I
didn't even know he had applied for that area. But
I was thrilled because I knew (it) quite well and had
spent a lot of my childhood not far from there.'

John had begun the habit of keeping some of
his political plans to himself. This was to develop
further. Norma's anxieties about the children and
their schooling would have been a factor at this
time. If he were selected for a winnable seat
such as Huntingdon he would want to live in
the constituency. So Norma had to be sure that
it was a place where she would like to live and
where the children would be happy and able to
go to suitable schools. It was perhaps easier to tell
her once he was shortlisted than put her through
the process of worrying about these things for
every constituency that came up. It was a great

relief to him that she was so happy when he got Huntingdon.

He says, 'Norma thinks it was fate. She was convinced I would get Huntingdon as soon as the invitation to interview plopped through the door. As a child she'd been evacuated nearby. Her mother was a widow. Her father died two days after the war when Norma's mother was 22 and had two babies, Norma and the younger brother Colin. He died a few weeks later, leaving her mother with just Norma. So her mother had two or three jobs all the time and Norma, of course, had to go to boarding school. In the holidays (she) had to be looked after and went down to see some friends just outside Huntingdon. So Norma knew the area and she was always confident that I'd get the seat.

'On the way to the final selection, when everybody said I hadn't got a hope, because everyone else was known and it had gone down from four hundred to four, Norma said as we reached the Buckden roundabout about three miles away from the Commemoration Hall, "You realise what today is, don't you?" I said I hadn't the faintest idea. I had my mind on the speech. She said, "It's the anniversary of the day you were selected for St Pancras North." She was quite certain I would get it.'

It's hard to do your best if you feel your spouse is against you. To know your nearest and dearest is completely on your side allows you to go on with so much more confidence. Norma's enthusiasm for Huntingdon was therefore a great boost as well as a relief to John. She confesses though that, 'I wore a red dress to the selection meeting.' Unconscious opposition to his becoming a Tory MP?

Norma, whatever her fears of disruption of domestic bliss and dreams of a more ordinary life, has worked devotedly for John and is immensely popular in the constituency. And for the first few years while he was an MP, and even when he began his rise first through the Whips' Office and then through Health and Social Security to his first Cabinet post as Chief Secretary, she still saw him every weekend, and there were few trips abroad to unsettle the busy but predictable domestic rhythm.

But, more recently, as John began reaching the higher Cabinet posts, her attitude was visibly less helpful. Robert Atkins says, 'When we talked about the possibilities of becoming Prime Minister, there was a question mark over Norma because of him being a family man. He was very worried, as I would be, about the effects upon (the) family. That was the key consideration.

'I remember Norma was very worried about the change to Foreign Secretary. The Chief Secretary is a fairly low profile job. Becoming Foreign Secretary meant that he wheeled around and about a lot at a key time for their daughter, taking 'A' levels. It upset (Norma) and I remember she talked a lot to my wife Dulcie at about this time. But as soon as he became Chancellor, which put him back in the Treasury again and he was familiar with things, she became much happier. I know that he talked everything through with her and she became much easier. She's not a weakling. She's a very determined lady, knows her own mind and is determined the family will not suffer. Practically, I think that's the right attitude.'

So what are Norma's problems with John's career? The story he tells about her childhood is revealing in this context. Her father served in the Army in World War II and Norma, who was born in February 1942, would have been very close to her mother during those first few years of her life, and aware of her loneliness and anxiety.

This may explain Norma's otherwise inexplicable fears when John became Foreign Secretary. Because, of course, Foreign Secretaries travel a great deal. The absent husband response learned from her mother is now present in Norma's life. And, of course, although she never knew him, she experienced her mother's reflected grief after her father's death. At Great Stukeley, there is a large framed photographic portrait of a man in World War II military uniform on the drawing room windowsill. Norma says, 'It's my father, but I never knew him,' and she explains that he had been killed at the end of the war. Her father's importance to her is reflected in this picture so prominently displayed in a room where there are otherwise no family or other photographs to be seen.

Added to this is the fact that, as the only child of a single parent prevented from spending much time with her, Norma has a deep, unsatisfied and lifelong yearning for closeness with a loved one. So perhaps it was her dream to have the kind of family life with John that she never had in her youth. How tragic then that she should have been trapped unwittingly into repeating the pattern of being so much apart from the person she most loves.

For John, though, Norma mirrors the strengths and affection he received from his own mother. It may be significant that Gwen Major died three weeks before his wedding to Norma. Such events are not uncommon when a spouse replaces a parent in a man or woman's affections.

Norma's attitude to John's rapid rise must therefore be seen in a different light. Jeffrey Archer says she is puzzled about what has happened to John and herself and to their life together. Perhaps she is puzzled with herself. On the one hand, she clearly rejoices in John's success. The pictures of her standing outside Number 10 with him on the morning of November 28 1990 showed nothing of the grudging attitudes that were later attributed to her. Norma smiled and dimpled shyly, flashing a special grin over John's shoulder at some friend in the crowd, completely unconscious that the gesture was picked up on the cameras. In her low key, casually cut and full skirted blazer suit, barely made up, she looked and seemed like a delighted schoolgirl at a prize day as John waved and answered reporters' questions. Before they went inside, he pulled her close, one arm around her waist, his other hand raised in a bold wave. They looked the closest, the cosiest couple, more like honeymooners than partners of twenty years.

Yet the image quickly soured. Norma spoke of not changing her lifestyle. The Sunday papers on December 2 ran features with headlines like 'The Reluctant Handmaiden'. Norma was said to be very shy, uninterested in public life. She did her best, but even when she opened a special charity occasion in Huntingdon, John came to make the speech for her. In these early interviews, she said she did not want to live at Number 10 or Chequers. Since then she has said that what she really said was, 'I would love to spend time at Chequers but the family must come first.' In an interview with Jean Rook she indicated she had been unaware of his ambition to be Prime Minister. What was really going on?

One of John's close friends told me that he did not like to discuss his ambitions to be PM in front of Norma. 'Oh, you can't talk about that in front of Norma,' he would say. Her reaction to his promotion to Foreign Secretary and Chancellor was clearly enough to deter her husband from revealing that Number 10 was also a twinkle in his eye. Robert Atkins thinks Norma was not very well during 1989 when John got the Foreign Office. She was, he reports, feeling very low and tired. She is said to have lost fourteen pounds in weight from worry during the three months when he was Foreign Secretary. He says, 'There was a little unhappiness there but that's all passing.' He adds, 'Norma can be very moody sometimes and it upsets him very much when she gets moody.'

The first time John's chances for the premiership came out in the open with his family was the day he decided to stand for the leadership after Mrs Thatcher had resigned from the contest. Several days after he had been to Buckingham Palace to sign on constitutionally as Prime Minister, Norma told Jean Rook that, 'We haven't had a moment properly alone to say anything really. All John's had time to mutter to me is, "The timing's right and when the ball comes your way, you have to grab it and get on with the job." '

Norma told Jean Rook that she never dreamed of owning the key to Number 10. 'Never, never in my wildest moments, and I don't think he did either.' She went on, 'When John's career started, I was quite excited to be the wife of an MP, but I don't think that I've got used to the idea that he's in the Cabinet, let alone this. Later, I knew his dream was to be Chancellor, but he honestly never lay in bed thinking what the next job was going to be. I don't even know if it ever struck him he could be PM. If it did, I assure you he never mentioned it, and he tells me most things.'

Atkins says, 'I think that she knew all along but she didn't want to admit it to herself . . . He hadn't talked to her about it until it happened. But certainly he'd decided, and it was quite important once it happened that Norma was brought alongside. My wife played a tiny part in that, by talking to her a lot. Norma doesn't like picking up the phone and ringing people so Dulcie will phone her, and once she's on the phone she's chatting away like nobody's business. She's very normal but she's quite shy in some respects, a little timid in her approaches to other people, and yet really one of the most super girls I know.'

Her first response in those immediate days was to say that she would keep a very low profile. She told Rook, 'Of course he's thrilled and I think he's confident. I think he's more confident than I am about my job. I'm not quite sure what that is yet, but I've always taken things one step at a time, and I keep telling myself this is just another huge step.

'Of course as the wife, I don't have to follow Mrs Thatcher, thank goodness. I only have to follow Denis and from my point of view that's marvellous because he hasn't created any precedent, except keeping out of the way, and that suits me very well.'

Does it suit John? After being Prime Minister for a few months, he gives the impression, talking about his wife, that perhaps it does not. But even if Norma was at Number 10 more often, would there be much chance they could enjoy each other's company? Norma has complained John is not as much fun as he used to be. She says he slumps when he has a chance to stop. But under the same circumstances, who wouldn't?

Former Prime Ministers wives' behaviour was compared to Norma's. Audrey Callaghan had said that there was really no point in being at Number 10 all the time because one had so little chance to see one's husband except when he popped in for a half hour chat and cup of tea. Writers recalled wistful Mary Wilson writing poetry while Harold caroused into the small hours with union leaders. If there is a role for the Prime Minister's spouse it seems that of lady- or gentleman-in-waiting. Denis Thatcher dodged media attempts to lure him into indiscretions by never giving an interview. He spent his time on his own affairs and kept out of his wife's way. Prime Minister's spouse is a role without a job description, but the sky's the limit for a candidate with an idea of its full potential.

Wives of foreign leaders occasionally show what can be done. The very political Madame Mitterrand has made excellent use of her opportunities. Raisa Gorbachev has not been slow to capitalise on her position. Nancy Reagan was a force, but only interested in what she could do to support her husband in his role. Rosalind Carter, however, was classified as a Steel Magnolia, taking up causes of her own, and Betty Ford in her brief time used her own experience of alcoholism and breast cancer to help millions of similarly afflicted American women. But a First Lady with big ideas can be dangerous. The British way is to stay in the background and avoid embarrassing one's mate. After all, remember what kind of a press Glenys Kinnock, First Lady in Opposition, received for her CND affiliations and Greenham Common visits. Back seat driving accusations and endless media jokes against his wife made the Labour Party leader look hen-pecked and foolish.

Still, even if the PM's wife were to confine herself to sponsoring charities and work within the national party, and to other non-controversial forms of participation in literature, the arts and music, she could achieve much that would not otherwise be open to the wife of even the most senior Cabinet Minister. Norma Major is not a woman to want to exploit that potential. She is no Madame Mitterrand. She is not even a political woman. But she is community-conscious and is beginning to develop new strengths. As her children leave home, whether John remains Prime Minister or not, Norma may yet blossom; may even, one day, achieve her dream of domestic bliss in retirement.

Whether that is a long way distant or around another of those surprising sharp bends in the course of John Major's life, will depend much on the way he handles this, his most brilliant opportunity of all.

After the first edition of this book was completed at Easter 1991, Norma Major gave me a further interview about herself for *Woman's Journal*. Subsequently she agreed for the interview's first use to be in the *Mail on Sunday*'s 'You' Magazine. I had volunteered to show her the copy and she saw it and said, 'It's fine.' Uproar followed its publication. Norma had given no interview since the one given to Jean Rook of the *Daily Express* in December 1990 and it had taken me months to coax her into giving this one. Very little was known therefore about Norma Major and now this interview revealed new facets of the Prime Minister's retiring wife: her character and many of her feelings about her role, her marriage and her aspirations. It was intended to be so, for Norma's earlier assistance in the preparation of the book about her husband had concentrated on her relationship with him. Now, Norma's own life was the focus.

Undoubtedly, it was her distance from public exposure so far which brought such a clamour of excitement at the otherwise unsensational revelation that Mrs Major's way of regaining control of her life on returning from Prime Ministerial engagements with the Queen and other dignitaries was to Hoover the kitchen or clean the hob. Norma's complete preoccupation with domesticity fascinated the press. It was a fair indication that the more one tries to remain a private figure, the more exciting every tiny peep into one's life becomes for the onlooker. No wonder journalists were stimulated into a flood of comment by Mrs Major's revelation that the Prime Minister brings his red boxes of government paperwork to bed. The quote that she thought he was 'bloody selfish' to do this even brought a leader about the long hours worked by British executives. But the papers were a-twitter for another week over Mrs Major's admission that, yes, red boxes or not, matters were satisfactory in the Prime Minister's bedroom.

Does the reader of a life of a new Prime Minister need to know anything about his marriage? There were some who asked this and similar questions, seeking to dismiss such details as irrelevant while clearly gloating over the chance to comment on them. Hypocrisy was rife. The answer in any case is, yes, the reader does need to know. There is no demarcation line in the politician's life which separates his work from his family life or his sexuality. We need to know what emotional pressures may bring stresses to a leader's decision-making process. We need to know whether the mind that determines our futures with sometimes snap decisions is likely to be clouded or clarified through his relationships.

So, the pressures brought to bear on John Major's life through the qualities and needs of his wife are directly relevant to our understanding of the man who is shaping our national future and becoming internationally respected. Norma Major may be an insignificant political force in herself, but she has been John Major's partner in his twenty-year rise from Lambeth Councillor to Prime Minister. Many questions remain, however. Has Norma been the reluctant partner described in this book and in many newspaper articles? Has she been a domestic shadow, often unaware of her husband's high ambitions, as described by two of her husband's closest friends, Robert Atkins and Jeffrey Archer? Did John Major indeed keep his ambitions for Number 10 secret from Norma, as Robert Atkins described? There can be no mistake that Atkins and Archer said what is quoted in the foregoing pages about Norma's attitudes to John's successive promotions from Foreign Secretary onwards. Their comments were recorded on tape and transcribed to a high degree of accuracy, kept within context when quoted and treated meticulously.

Between January when I first talked to Norma about her view of her life with John, and April when we talked further about Norma herself, there were several telephone conversations in which we both talked quite freely about our lives and expectations and exchanged confidences. I have since kept the content of these conversations largely to myself. Through them, however, I began to understand Norma and to sympathise enormously with her situation. The most interesting aspect of our conversations in retrospect is the development both of the relationship between Norma and myself and of Norma's own view of herself.

First, the relationship. When we met in April we found an easy camaraderie that had been missing on the chill, dark January day when I arrived, still suffering from the effects of a bout of flu, for my first visit to the flat at Number 10. In April, I commented upon this and Norma said, 'I'm always difficult with strangers. It doesn't matter if the acquaintance is quite brief, the second one is always better.' She added, 'I lack confidence. I'm not exactly wary of people. I don't like strangers. It's nothing to do with not liking people. I've never been happy going into a situation where I have to meet a lot of strangers all in one go. It gets a little easier, I suppose. It has got to get easier, because it's part of the job now.'

Her view of herself came over strongly both during this conversation of some two to three hours and in a subsequent phone call about this chapter. That phone call was the subject of much misreporting.

The *Sunday Times* sent a reporter to see me without an appointment while I was at a health farm taking a three-day break from promoting my book. As I was checking out, I agreed to see the reporter and we sat down over some tea. I asked him to use his tape recorder as I wanted to be sure of the accuracy of his report. Alas, he chose to write a story based on a distortion which I had several times corrected, that Norma Major had demanded changes to the book. She had not done so. There had been no angry exchange as described by the *Times*' reporter, but simply a long chat, much of which was devoted to making arrangements for the 'You' magazine team to style and photograph her. In the end the photo session was cancelled because it could not be held soon enough for the copy date. During the conversation, Norma raised points of factual error and of difference of opinion. She had no basis for making demands. Number 10 approved the book but there was no agreement on content. The Prime Minister did not wish biographies of himself to be written and would not authorise any, including this one. However, he had given his approval and both he and Norma had been very helpful. I offered them the chance to read the manuscript in time to offer factual corrections, especially of the Majors' own contributions, or discuss any controversial areas which might cause hurt. The contributions of others could not be changed even if Norma had disagreed with them and possibly she did. The Prime Minister's corrections came in good time but Norma's were too late to be included in the final amendments.

The *Sunday Times* has since printed an apology for libellous allegation, but I am still widely assumed to have 'had a row with Norma Major'. While a reticence has grown up from Norma's side after the *Sunday Times* report, there was before the report no row, nor any basis for one. Norma simply corrected one or two facts. For instance, she told me that John moved out of the big room in the Foreign Office only because it was being redecorated. The Prime Minister had told me that he had moved rooms and that the Foreign Office staff were not used to someone who chose to work in a small room (Chapter 2). Norma said he moved into a different room than the alternative proffered because there was a larger desk. It was a trivial point and most of the others she raised were similarly small details. For instance, Norma insisted with some firmness, 'John does not like junk food. He likes plain food.'

The most significant disagreement lay between Norma's view of her husband's story and the views of John's close friends. Norma told me, 'It is not true that John doesn't talk to me. He does talk to me.' This was a reference to Robert Atkins' comment that John had said, 'Oh, you can't talk about that in front of Norma' with reference to plans for becoming Prime Minister. She had also been quite agitated in her insistence that she had never been reluctant to help John. I told her I believed I had made that abundantly clear. I also gently reminded her that the comments which she had made during the period after John became Prime Minister and the reports of friends about her attitudes to John's last three promotions were prominently on the record and that I did not feel I was being unfair in reporting them. If she wished, I would insert her comments on those reports. She seemed happy with this. The only problem was that, unknown to me, the book had that day gone back to the printers for final corrections and binding before I had seen the proofs myself, due to the extreme pressure of time on publication.

On reflection I realised from her comments that night and during the April interview that Norma's view of herself differed from that which her earlier interviews projected. She had been depicted by the comments of her husband's close friends as fearful of the prominent role she might now have to play and reluctant to play it. Now, embarrased by these perceptions, she seemed to be seeking to amend them.

Norma had also been portrayed as frumpish and mousey. I recalled my first meeting with her when she had indeed seemed so to me too. Earlier in this chapter I drew attention to the way in which she had, even in January 1991, struck me as more stylish and self-confident than on that other occasion in her house near Huntingdon. By April the impression was even stronger. Norma is no fashion plate, but she has her own style. She told me she resented the fact that writers who had described her as frumpy were now claiming her transformation to be due to their own observations. Referring to the outfit she had worn daily during the week of John's election as leader, and which had drawn criticism, she said, 'Damn that blue suit. But probably whatever I'd been wearing on that occasion they would have criticised. But they perceived, they set me up as being dowdy and frumpy and all the rest of it. And they discovered I'd been out and spent £5,000 on clothes, which wasn't true, and they are actually giving me a fairly good press about my clothes now. But they didn't know me well enough beforehand to know whether I'd changed or not. But they liked the idea that I was terribly dowdy and because of what they've said I've changed. I don't actually think I have. I've had to go out and buy clothes because I didn't have enough clothes in the wardrobe to do the job that I'm required to do.'

She reflected on the clothes she once wore and went on, 'I used to make my own clothes. It was actually cheap to make clothes then. A paper pattern didn't cost much. Material didn't cost much. You made a mistake, it didn't matter'. She indicated the pale green suit she was wearing. 'There was a time when I wouldn't have hesitated to have made something like this. But I couldn't possibly do it now.' She clearly regrets that she has not got the time. But the Norma who would have occupied herself with sewing now fills her time with answering letters and buzzing back and forth between Huntingdon and Downing Street. Her tasks are menial and her feeling is one of inadequacy. She says she feels 'manoeuvered' and 'nibbled to death'.

Norma has not yet seized the wider opportunities available to a Prime Minister's wife. She always seems to find herself ensnared in minutiae. She confesses that she is no good at delegating and that she feels she is not really doing anything when she merely graces an occasion. She told me she would rather make the teas for a Mencap function than turn up to present a big cheque. Can she change herself enough to keep up with the way her husband's life has changed in the two years since he became Foreign Secretary? Perhaps, looking back at all the other Prime Ministerial spouses, she may legitimately ask, Can any ordinary wife keep up with a husband whose career has gone supersonic?

She is trying harder now. In August she and the children accompanied John to Kennebunkport. It seemed a carefree time. US papers carried a picture of Norma waving from the transom of George Bush's infamous cigarette boat to John on shore. A day later she was with John in Moscow and thereafter in China and Hong Kong. There Norma, given a bouquet of paper flowers by a child at a camp for Vietnamese refugees, touchingly expressed her compassion. It was the first time she had ever been on record in a remotely political context, but she told reporters how she felt. It was ironic that the symbol which moved her was a bunch of paper flowers, for Norma is unmoved by real blooms. She told me she does not like to have them in the house. Yet the paper bouquet made by people whose imprisonment denies them access to real flowers was a message of yearning to which Norma could not fail to respond. Her reaction was no different from that of any ordinary woman. Yet, as Prime Minister's wife, her response spoke volumes.

Norma is not especially ordinary. Not many housewives write biographies of opera stars while performing constituency back-up for a political husband. But she sees herself so. However, even Norma knows that ordinary wifeliness and ordinary life are not now possible. Indeed, this awareness goes back some time. She told me that when John became an MP, her mother's sister said, 'Why couldn't we be ordinary like everybody else?' Norma added, 'I thought it was quite an interesting remark. I didn't realise quite how far it was going to go.'

Now that it has gone so far, Norma may be forgiven for wanting the self she appears to have been a year and two years ago to be perceived differently. If hindsight could change reality, Norma would turn that seemingly resentful, recalcitrant figure into the woman she sees herself to be today. Of course there are many Normas, kaleidoscopically merged into the present. Norma, the attractive 28-year-old with the biggest brown eyes John Major had ever seen, and the long white boots that saw off the competition for this 'gorgeous man'. She was also the girl whose predominantly domestic aspirations prompted her to seek a husband. Many a girl of her generation found her Mr Right among the promising ranks of the younger Conservatives. Norma makes no secret of the fact that, once smitten, she determined to prove John suitable and to net him. Her approach shows her characteristic practicality and perseverance.

Norma is an extraordinarily determined woman. Stubborn, some friends have said. Not as stubborn as John, who she says is not easy to sway, 'just like his mother'. But when she needs to, she can defeat him with her own brand of heels-dug-in refusal to cooperate. Norma's way of fighting for what she wants is to go mute and wait until her angry silence wins. But she can also push aggressively for what she wants and now, with hindsight, I believe that she gave me a private example of her techniques.

I think that when she told me she thought her husband was 'bloody selfish' to go through his red boxes in bed, she was getting at him. Since she okayed the copy in which I reported the anecdote, she also had a chance for second thoughts, and

still used the opportunity to put her views across.
I also now believe that when the notorious telephone
conversation took place she was subtly pressuring
me to change what I had written. Her friendly but
forceful manner implied a right beyond that offered
to correct error of fact and to indicate any areas which
might cause distress. I believe, also with hindsight,
that when reporters and commentators wrote that she
was angry about passages in this book, they were
correct, although they were extrapolating rather than
reporting, for Norma would never publicly admit
her anger. But her anger was not simply over
anything with which she happened to disagree or
wished to disavow. This was anger inherent in her
personality.

Norma's anger needs understanding in the context
of the Prime Minister's life. In this light, many of
the tensions in the marriage observed and reported
by others are explained. That anger is manifested in
her admission that at times her sense of frustration is
so great that she throws things. For instance, she told
me that when Elizabeth was a baby and they lived in
the small flat in Primrose Court, she once threw the
baby's bottle at the wall with such force that it burst.
Much later, in the house at Huntingdon, she threw
the entire manuscript of her Joan Sutherland book
across the kitchen. These acts of pent-up frustration
show that Norma is not the demure figure she seems.
Camouflaged by middle-class, middle-aged clothes,
she is still the mouse that roars.

As I looked more deeply into Norma Major's
character and at the transcripts of our many conversations, I realised that she has probably been angry
from childhood. Angry in a way that is akin to the

anger of children abandoned by their parents. Like
the orphans and fostered children I have encountered
in journalistic research, Norma Major was separated
from her parents at an early age. For purposes of
psychological comparison Norma was, in a sense,
abandoned by a father who died and a mother who
placed her in boarding school from the age of four so
that she could work. Norma the adult has nothing
but praise for the mother whose independence and
hard work are so typical of modern Tory heroism.
But Norma the child may have felt, as such children
do, an irrational anger that still lives within her,
unexpressed. Her mother, she says, 'did three jobs.
She had a rather difficult childhood, far more difficult
than John's childhood. She was determined things
were going to improve. That was why she did actually
do three jobs, one in the daytime, one in the evening
and one that she was able to do at home. She didn't
do the jobs to send me to boarding school. I went to
boarding school to make it easier for her to work. But
she was determined that she was going to improve
things.'

Norma stresses that her mother did not mean to
dump her at school. Yet, having tried retirement,
her mother still prefers to work and it would seem
that this may also have been the case when Norma
was a small girl, since the school she attended catered
for theatre children and stayed open throughout the
holidays. Norma experienced fear of the dark at
her next school and had to be put to sleep in
a room apart from the dormitory, and with the
light left on. She still experiences claustrophobia
occasionally. On a canal barge holiday a few years
ago with John and the children, she told me, she

woke to find herself clawing at the window, trying
to get out.

At the time she was away at school Norma was
developing the determination to be a nanny. She
says, 'I wanted to be a nanny from the time I could
speak.' She played with a doll that was realistically
'squishy' textured, telling me that she would feed it
with a bottle and change its nappies and wash them
and dry them on the clothes line. Perhaps Norma
was living out her own unfulfilled needs to be babied
and cared for by her own mother. And perhaps too,
the obsession with that 'ordinary life' she wishes she
might have led with John and the children starts
there. Seen in the light of her childhood experience,
Norma's extraordinarily tenacious drive to hang on to
normality and domesticity are more understandable.
Yet in that attempt she has intensified the frustrations of her childhood, marrying a man who repeats
the pattern of the absent male established by her
soldier father. No wonder her descriptions of her
need for homemaking as an alternative to the high
life of Prime Ministerial social engagements sound
almost like therapy.

But Norma's homemaking ambitions are not only
frustrated by John's career demands. They are also
conditioned by his own homemaking aspirations.
The dream house in Great Stukeley which is John's
passion is not Norma's preference. When I asked
her about the house, she told me she finds it gloomy
and she likes light. She said, 'He was always more
enthusiastic about it than I was.' Norma saw the
house first and went back to tell John. She says,
'I must have given a very good description of it
because he'd obviously fallen in love with it.' She

says she knew they couldn't afford it, so she was not concerned at the time. But her reservations were that 'James was walking to school and Elizabeth was taking the bus. She was going to Guides and he was going to Cubs and to the village football matches. It was all very cosy. It was lovely to sit, not to have to disturb your day all the time thinking the kids are coming in a minute or you're going to have to go out and meet them. Clock watching, it's such a relief when you suddenly realise you've got that little bit of independence. I could see, moving to Stukeley, that all that freedom I had suddenly gained was going to be gone. They couldn't go out on their bikes on that dreadful road. We'd lose the babysitter, it was a longer journey. Sometimes I was on the road driving for three hours. It's not unique. Mothers do it, but suddenly that was what the problem was for me, because I suddenly thought, golly I'm just beginning to see the light at the end of the tunnel. This is going to create lots of problems. But he did love the house and although we couldn't afford it, we somehow managed it.'

Norma's unselfishness has been John's benefit. But can Norma's dissatisfactions also be John's disadvantage? Can these preoccupations of the Prime Minister's wife influence his performance, or affairs of state? Perhaps not directly. Yet many stories of marital tensions may owe some of their origin to Norma's greatly frustrated need for a more conventional rhythm. She told me in April that peace of mind and rhythm of life were most important to her. Now, she said, 'I am beginning to feel life taking on a rhythm. I think stability. I mean, however chaotic it is, or however difficult the job is, sooner or later it

will level off. It becomes a habit. I suppose you get
used to the rather odd way of living.'

At that time, April 1991, Norma exuded more
contentment than I remembered from our previous
meeting. The conversation when it turned to John
seemed more relaxed, the body language suggested
current intimacy. Yet one cannot exclude the
extremely widespread stories that suggested there had
been a serious rift between John and Norma. Some
of these stories concerned divorce. In the original
manuscript there was a paragraph about rumours
which circulated about the marriage difficulties of
the Majors. Norma read the paragraph and told
me, 'John has never spoken to me about divorce.'
I had written that I thought it unlikely that the
couple would divorce for practical reasons and that
their relationship was fundamentally sound. The
paragraph did not appear in the final version of
the book. I had conceded it to my publisher who
thought it best to leave out mention of marital discord
as a matter of taste. The matter of this missing
paragraph became a cause célèbre in the newspapers
after the *Sunday Times*' inaccurate report of the
conversation between myself and Norma Major.
Meanwhile, amusingly it seems, the publishers of
a rival biography had asked its author to try to
find some personal anecdote to liven up his book.
He chose the very topic which had made my book
infamous. And no one seemed to care.

But to that paragraph there is a footnote. I was
later told a story that it was Norma who had
asked for the divorce. That made more sense in
the context of the story of a supposed love affair
between John Major and a named woman who is

the subject of approaches by tabloid newspapers to
tell her story. One is reminded of the story that
Jacqueline Kennedy, weary of supposed infidelities
by Jack, threatened divorce before her husband ran
for President and was placated. But such a woman
would understandably remain angry.

Would revelations of this order, had they substance, shake the Prime Minister out of Number 10?
It seems unlikely, since other Cabinet Ministers have
survived divorce and remarriage. British morality is,
however, oddly two-faced. That which is secret is far
more damaging when revealed than something which
is open and free of guilt.

8

PERFECT TIMING

'The question is, does the whole strand of policy go in a coherent direction? If it goes in a coherent direction, then you have a politician who knows where he's going and why.'

TO MANY IT SEEMED AS if John Major became Prime Minister by happenstance, that luck or convenience or opportunism were the prime forces at work in his rise. To many, he seems ill equipped by background, education and length of Cabinet service to have been elevated so young and so soon. But this is not true: John Major's life to date has provided ideal training for the job he now holds. By gift and experience, he is exceptionally well qualified to be Prime Minister. Time in office has nothing to do with it. Timing, of which offices held and when, is all. John Major's timing is perfect. The more because he is, in all that he represents, perfectly timed in his arrival in office at this point in history. Britain today, Europe today, the world today, are ready for the particular gifts and skills John Major has to offer both as Prime Minister of a leading nation and, when he has found his feet, world leader.

If this sounds overly ambitious, it is because in the general perception the man himself seems still a shadowy outline, a sketch in which so many details are either lightly pencilled in or not even vaguely suggested. He has followed a Prime Minister who had eleven years in that office and four years in opposition in which to make herself, her purposes and methods manifest. Who Major is and what he is about cannot become visible in a few minutes as though he were a soap opera character. Even JR took time to develop and ripen in viewers' perceptions. How much longer then a real life leader, someone who has been keeping his head down for two decades? As John Major says, 'It's not a judgment that people can make until you've been there for some years, and even then it's not immediately apparent you can make the judgement.'

But we live in instant times. As soon as John Major was elected, TV ran snapshot documentaries of his life and rise, newspapers cobbled together impressionistic features in which accurate and imaginary quotes and images combined to give immediate shape to the new leader. The circus angle was big, dominating and perhaps distorting the reality, obscuring the man in a tangle of bosky tales. There were anecdotes about the reversals of fortune which had brought John's family to live in a two-room rental with shared facilities in Brixton, about his poor school record, first jobs and breakfast habits. There was the story of his failed bus conductor exams. One source said it was his arithmetic that failed him. He himself said it was his height, and embellished the story with his account of the little West Indian woman who pipped him for the position dancing around joyfully shouting, 'I got the job, I got the job.'

It is not that this has nothing to do with John's life, simply that it distorts the picture to pay so much attention to the colour and miss the shade. That is why people write books – newspaper and magazine articles are frustratingly limited in scope and size, for writers, readers and subject; canapés rather than seven-course meals in all their variety, complexity and balance. But why write at all so early in John Major's career? In a TV interview in February 1991, Jeffrey Archer said, 'I don't know why people are writing books about John now. They should wait until he has been in the job for years.' But the need now is to understand how the man arrived, who he is, so that we know him better and see his future actions in a more understanding light.

So much collective energy is wasted in misunderstanding. Even before John Major had been in office a few days, political figures and columnists were second guessing and arguing against what they postulated would be his administration's aims. But in his past is his future. What he has done has a bearing on what he does next. The experience he brings to the job of Prime Minister is acknowledged by his colleagues to be absolutely ideal. The time as a Brixton councillor gave him a perfect grass roots grounding. The steely qualities he veils so well were also developed there in the rough ground of a Labour-dominated working-class neighbourhood. The techniques of creating an electoral fighting force out of a demotivated and embattled minority party; the determination exercised and developed in fighting to win when opportunity came in the shape of a national swing; the basic knowhow of these elements of grass roots politics are an excellent foundation for any politician.

A Prime Minister who has this grounding is in excellent shape to pick and choose election timing, for he, much more than one who has had an easier passage to Parliament, can read the runes of electoral swings and mood swaps. He consults his old friends like Jean Lucas who are still plugged into grass roots networks. He is less dependent on his professional advisors and more keenly instinctive in his own timing. And this particular piece of timing must be perfect to the second: to get it wrong now would be to lose all at the eleventh hour. After coming so far and preparing himself for so long, failure would be astonishing. Yet he is nervous now in a way he has never been before. This is the job he was born to do. If indeed his timing is perfect, and he is now the right man with the right experience to move the Thatcher era reforms to the next phase, then he cannot fail.

So what has made the man from nowhere the man for our time? His agenda, still secret in detail but known in outline, is to extend the opportunities and the choices made available through the Eighties to yet more people, so that no one feels, or is, left out. His own experience has enabled him to see how to extend opportunities to people who might otherwise miss out. As a councillor, his work in Brixton, especially his responsibilities in housing and social services, gave him a special insight into urban poverty. This is why he can say, 'I don't believe everyone can pull themselves up by their bootstraps and make it.' This is why he knows that a meritocracy must also take into account the needs of those who cannot compete with the more vigorous or succeed with the best.

Does this mean the poor are always with us? Not in John Major's plans: for he believes that able or less able, each one must receive enough, whether housing, food, health or other care, to meet their needs. Unto each according to his needs, was the Marxist version. The ends may be common but the means of achievement are diametrically opposed. For Marxism believed first in the creation of the state, which was afterwards intended to wither away, its objective achieved. But states never do wither away unless smashed to pieces by determined reform as in Britain, or by revolution as in Eastern Europe. John Major and his Tory cohort believe in the creed of individual human endeavour: the state is only needed to contain the expression of individual motivation for the attainment of the greater good.

Until he came to Parliament, John Major was on the outside. He knew it but never made issue of it. He will not admit he regrets having travelled such a hard road, only that he would wish the changes that have been made in the past decade, and the ones to come under his own stewardship, will make it easier for the able to put their gifts to work for their own benefit and that of the less able. It is from his time as the maverick outsider that his whole political ethos springs: that time, some thirty-five years of it, is the source and the fount of his coming programme.

John Major is not only a remarkably exact product of his unusual background, of the past that has led him to this point, he is also a product of the British people's evolving aspirations, and an exact fit with their immediate future.

His aptness for the times is reflected in his popularity with voters. Despite a falling off in the Conservative lead following the Gulf War's ending, the Prime Minister's personal popularity remained extraordinarily high. In March 1991, his personal rating was 58% while the Conservative Party's rating was down to 40%. John Major's personal presence and characteristic of being perceived as a regular bloke are a factor in this. These qualities combine with his comparative youth, the fact that he is a member of that most populous generation, the baby boomers of the Forties, now in their forties, and the undeniable appeal of his much vaunted classlessness, that misnomer for class mobility. In this, however, the journalistic sketching drew accurately the fundamental lines of his character, his motivation and life. John Major's upward rise through the layers of status is his personal hallmark but also that of his generation.

Among the many who, like him, appear to belong to no class are many self-made businessmen and highly successful professionals. The former have risen through determination and wit; the latter often through educational achievement – doctors, lawyers, MPs and others, who stand above their origins and their peers yet lack social definition apart from their attained status. And there are the artistic meritocrats – singers, writers, actors, dancers, designers, directors, musicians – many of whom, like John, came from nowhere. This diverse band of achievers from many different social origins is united in the social mobility which has culminated in their class-free status.

The mood favouring such success was growing for years, but came to fruition during the Eighties. Whatever aspirations had been frustrated under socialism could now bear fruit, especially among the generation which had learned its politics during the Fifties and Sixties. The appeal of the classless society is enormous to a group which has come to realise that class was allowed to get in their parents' way. Generations born since 1939/40 have a different view of their place in society from that of generations born before. Labour MP Jeff Rooker once put it succinctly: 'They're gaffers' men,' he said, talking about the pre-war generations. He meant there was once a deference to superiors and social betters that is now gone.

For better or worse, the majority among the younger age groups are concerned to get on without the hindrance of class, the paraphernalia of accents, old school ties and name dropping. Resistance comes only from those with something to lose. Typical was a sneering article in one British newspaper by the daughter of a former Cabinet Minister. Knocking the Prime Minister for what she claimed was his 'sneering and ridiculing' of education (a misinterpretation of his remarks: he said he was not impressed by qualifications), she also damned meritocracy with reference to accents and the inverted snobbery which now prevails over these. True, inverted snobbery is as much of a hindrance to progress as snobbery, and as discriminatory. But while the caste system of class hierarchy remains, snobbery will be parodied by its inversion among those who now find it more fashionable to rise by their own efforts rather than by those of their parents, grandparents or earlier ancestors. And even they really have nothing to lose but their stultified second-rate pretensions of superiority.

Class barriers, as John Major keeps saying, are a hindrance to the nation's progress. By demonstrating in his own life that it is possible to rise regardless, given certain gifts and persistence, and to do so in the Tory Party, he has made merit and its reward an approved and believable cause. John Major's arrival at Number 10 is thus probably the most emotive event since the making of a Princess from the kindergarten teacher Lady Diana Spencer, who, though titled, was not royal. Di became a lodestar for an age that believes in its heart in upward mobility, but which also still upholds the dream of high places which are remote yet still attainable to those not born into their privileged enclave.

John Major is not a leveller. He does not deride, despise or disclaim the existence of established social echelons such as the aristocracy. But perhaps a meritocracy is not fully realisable where some people still achieve position through inheritance of titles or wealth, in unfair competition with meritorious individuals with no such connections? 'It doesn't bother me,' he replies, and continues: 'I forget who said it, but there is no threat to privilege from the people on the fringes of it. And that is the point. You don't want to tear down what other people have got. You want to build up what other people have got.' He was criticised within days of becoming Prime Minister, and after the fanfare of his classless society remarks, for awarding a hereditary title to Denis Thatcher. He said: 'I don't find myself offended by hereditary systems at all. I really don't mind at all.'

What is important, he argues, is creating in people's minds the sense of their freedom to move from class to class. He says, 'The people who are aristocracy today weren't always. If you go back far enough, a lot of them come from peasant stock. Some passing king probably made them Earl of this or that for some passing service.' John Major views the handing out of titles as part of reward for merit. He seems unfazed by the implications of patronage and of inherited privilege for a merit-based culture, believing perhaps that people will strive more strongly to rise where there are glittering prizes.

His parents' life though should be a warning that it is as easy to fall as to rise. If things go wrong, as many house purchasers have discovered, one can lose rather than gain from enterprise and investment. But as John Major's life shows, it is often true that he who dares wins. The lines Sir Walter Raleigh wrote to Queen Elizabeth I, his patron, and her riposte, should be the meritocrat's motto:

> *Sir Walter*:
> Fain would
> I climb
> Yet fear I to
> fall.
>
> *Queen Elizabeth*:
> If thy heart fails thee,
> Climb not at all.

For the men and women who have made their fortune, the hope of earning royal patronage is an encouragement to donate large sums to charity. And there's nothing like a title to show you have arrived. Even proudly republican Americans crave and sometimes receive knighthoods. Royalty is also fashionable in republics. Americans rose early en masse to watch the royal weddings of the past decade. There is value in fairy tale heights of title and privilege, and there must always be the excitement of gaining honour or losing wealth to make the game enthralling enough for the real high fliers. John Major's aim is not to demolish the edifice, but to open the doors and windows of the fusty House of Class and blow fresh life into its ossifying notions. On the subject of getting rid of entrenched and limiting, often self-limiting, ideas, he comments, 'Oh, it takes time and I think a lot of them are going. I think there has been dramatic change in the last twenty years and there will be more in the future.'

This cause of class liberation, for which his own life has made him advocate, is the foundation of John Major's future deeds. The house that will rise from this foundation is one whose doors will be unlocked and in which all are welcome. The theme of his life is to become the theme of his administration. But this is not an egalitarian theme, though that interpretation has been placed upon his sentiments. Despite scaremongering by members of groups such as No Turning Back that compassion means more public spending, John Major's aims do not diverge much from those of his predecessors. There is more verbal and emotional emphasis on fairness and kindness, but the theme is still libertarian rather than egalitarian.

Slowly, bit by bit, in speeches and interviews, he is revealing the structure of his intentions. His methods are as those of the Thatcher years: to create wealth and discipline public spending in order to enable the enhancement of both public and private services to their consumers. He says, 'I want to see more privatisation, competition, more choice. The aim is still to reduce personal taxation, to bring choice and consumer responsiveness into public services such as schools and education, to increase home ownership, to encourage new businesses. If there are to be changes of emphasis now and then, this will not be a loss of direction.

'The question is, does the whole strand of policy go in a coherent direction. If it goes in a coherent direction, then you have a politician who knows where he is going and why. That doesn't mean there won't be tacking and trimming. Politics is like that. Life is like that. Politicians aren't dictators. They can't drive everything in the direction they want to go, but they need to put things in the general trend. It takes a while for the public to form a picture, but I think they will increasingly see the direction that I want them to see.'

The stress point within the Tory Party is, however, still the issue of public spending. There have been fears that David Mellor, now Chief Secretary, is likely to be less strict with departmental budgets than was deemed correct in a Thatcher administration.

Norman Lamont's increase of 2.5% on Value Added Tax to pay for an across the board reduction in poll tax provoked further fears. However, this is not a bad move. Taxes on purchases may look inflationary but they help to keep consumer demand down and reduce the danger of increasing the trade deficit. They preserve individual choice, whereas income tax hikes limit personal spending discretion, as indeed do mortgage rises based on interest rate rises which act like a form of tax. If the government also wants to increase thrift, which can cost the Exchequer billions in tax breaks, this is one way of financing it. If saving looks attractive and goods are expensive, people will save more rather than incur debt to buy goods. When there is less spending, the inflation rate does not take off, the trade balance looks healthier and the unions remain docile for fear of unemployment rises. Of course there is a limit to how much revenue can be raised from one source but differential VAT rates may yet be used, helping the Chancellor control the direction of spending.

But there is still fat to be cut from public spending. John Major's surgical skills with the budgetary knife during his days as Chief Secretary to the Treasury have not disappeared. The desire to improve public services does not imply an intention to spend more: where more activity is needed, it can be done more creatively, at less cost, with enhanced efficiency. Insiders say John Major's own skills while Chief Secretary were that he could not only limit the size of a department's budget in his haggling sessions with its Secretary of State, but could also propose more cost efficient ways of achieving the same end. This innate skill for problem solving was an asset in a Chief Secretary and is a distinct advantage to a Prime Minister.

However, the greatest advantage to this Prime Minister of having also been Chief Secretary for two years is that he is familiar with the costs and priorities of each department of state. Since he became Prime Minister less than a year and a half after ceasing to be Chief Secretary, he will not be much out of date.

While Chief Secretary he made the position clear in his first lecture to the Audit Commission on changes within the public service which 'amount to nothing less than a revolution in progress'. The

Audit Commission is Parliament's watchdog over government expenditure.

The Downing Street press office has recently reprinted extracts from the speech, no doubt with the intention of validating, which the extracts do, the Prime Minister's long standing position on public service issues. For instance, one of the several objectives extracted states, 'The public will get better services for the same or less cost.' And another, 'We are determined to provide high quality services whilst maintaining our objective of continuing to reduce the share of national income taken by the public sector. These twin objectives can only be achieved if we are successful in implementing policies for improving value for money.' These remarks are entirely in harmony with John Major's aim, restated since he became Prime Minister, of making public services deliver the goods to the public.

At the time the lecture to the Audit Commissioners was delivered in June 1987, John Major was fresh from the job of Minister of State for Social Security. He said, 'Shoddy public services should not be an option. Nor should they be tolerated.'

After that time, the profile of electoral opinion on public services showed increasing concern with the health service. MORI's voting trends summaries showed that between January 1987 and January 1988, the number of people who felt the National Health was the most important issue rose from 17% to 64%.

Doing anything, of course, provokes a backlash from one quarter or another. Whatever the Prime Minister wants to do will bring opposition. And there is much he has hinted he would like to do. Education is one area where there must be changes.

He is passionate about this. His own experiences have provided him with the impetus to pursue an improved state education system in which good teachers are valued and rewarded; children are properly evaluated, disciplined and prevented from truanting; in which parents have more power in the running of schools; in which schools are enabled to opt out from council control. He is anxious that his own pattern of missed opportunities does not recur, generation after generation. Following the Gulf War's ending in late February 1991, a clamour rose from the right demanding to hear what the Prime Minister really intended to do. The poll tax was the initial focus of dissent, and the government's failure to find a quick solution to that problem caused John Major much discomfort. The problem with the poll tax was that it was radical but not radical enough. What was needed was not just a new tax based more realistically on individual voters rather than their houses, but a total revamp of local government finance. No one seemed to have focussed sufficiently on this before. What emerged now suggested Heseltine was unable to come up with anything original and John Major, while taking in a jumble sale of ideas from all around, could only articulate the principle that the tax would be a hybrid which still supported the principle of some link between the voter and council expenditure.

The poll tax farrago illustrates the problems which occur when radical proposals are not thought through all the way.

This and other issues bothered the Tory right. The No Turning Back Group and the newly formed Conservative Way Forward, and others who adamantly want to preserve the direction of Thatcherite reforms, were on the attack. Using the *Daily* and *Sunday Telegraph* as vehicles to parade their opposition to the Prime Minister's as yet unstated detailed aims, they kept up a continual assault; so much so that he began to feel hurt at what he deemed disloyalty. Whispers and rumours abounded that he was going to renege on the Thatcher achievements and turn into a public spender to make the Labour Party blush. The Prime Minister began carefully to outline his aims in speeches and interviews.

Alas, the speeches with their detailed statements were not printed in full, but the main points turned into headlines proved further fuel with which to light torches of dissent. Quotes from interviews were chewed over and it was alleged the Prime Minister was attacking and devaluing education.

He attempted to dispel the idea that he would improve public services only by increasing spending. In his speech to the Central Council Meeting in Southport in March 1991, he outlined, 'Five great principles that will guide us. 1. That we are a national party. (That was to counter the idea that the Conservatives are so weakened in Wales and Scotland that they are now mainly an English Party.) 2. That we give opportunity and power to the people. (This rhetoric embraces the Thatcherite themes of increasing competition and ownership.) 3. That we need a strong, stable economy in which the wealth that is created is owned more widely. (More Thatcherism.)

'4. That we want a citizens' charter to deliver quality in every part of the public service. (John Major's Magna Carta: this idea was the headline grabber though it also grabbed much criticism.

It embraced improved democracy and standards
in education, more work for ombudsmen and
auditors, inspectorates and published inspection
results, performance-related pay, contracts of service
with NHS patients, and so forth.) 5. To work, not
for short-term gain but for the long-term good of
the nation. (A Gladstonian sense of responsibility to
future generations' sentiments.)'

He ended his speech with a paean to idealism.
'Idealism, yes. But practical idealism. Democracy.
Plain common or garden decency. It is those values
I believe in . . . Commonsense values. Conservative
values. The values which I and all of us in our party
will fight to uphold.'

The speech reads better than it came over when
delivered. Most of his big speeches do. Their
content, their fluency and exactness of meaning,
the occasional patch of pure open-hearted sincerity
amid the inevitable rhetoric, diplomatic sentiments
and cross party fire, stands out on the page. But style
of delivery affects the way his thoughts are received,
and John Major's failure as an orator is a weakness.
Jean Lucas mentioned this: 'We will have to think
about having a different sort of party conference
because John is not good at making the big speech
to the big audience.'

How about a spot of training? The Prime Minister
has refused to be made over and trained. Yet, people
from his past often refer to the gradual improvement
in his public speaking skills. Andy Thomson claims
to have helped his delivery. 'He used to drop down
at the end of a sentence. I cured him of that.'

But attempts to restyle the Prime Minister as a
speech maker, unless they are very professional, may

only result in the destruction of his simple homebody touch in favour of a ham's facility. His off the cuff speeches, delivered without much tone, colour or expression, and with little sense of timing, are still attractive for their content and sincerity. When he tries to inject emotional colour to his prepared scripts, he fails dismally. He says he hates to deliver prepared speeches, preferring to speak off the cuff from a few jottings on the back of an envelope. Can anything be done about this? He is excellent in one to one interviews on TV, and best of all direct to camera in short messages such as his Gulf War message to the nation. Previous work on the impact of TV in elections has shown that a good direct to camera delivery is worth any number of speeches delivered to audiences and filmed over their heads.

However, not even the best techniques in the world will avoid the tendency of democratic nations to divide on any one issue. Governments who cause the fewest waves are those who do least to change situations but who keep the economy strong. The latter is John Major's prime aim. After that objective, he may not turn out to head quite such an obviously radical government as that of Mrs Thatcher but there is an intention to be radical. Change is still in the wind that blows out of Downing Street. John Major has a way of creeping up on things and bringing about alterations without confrontation, or even anyone noticing what he is doing. However, one problem to be faced by the man who got where he is by dint of his skill at keeping out of the spotlight is the inevitable response to any changes which he instigates by those watching his every move.

If John Major means to change anything at all, he

only has to think it and he will be attacked by one group or another. This is a new experience for which he is ill prepared. An advantage of being Mr Nice Guy is that everyone is always in favour. Start really doing something, saying something, and some of the people will be against.

But isn't this the same John Major who can go into a room where the majority are against him and walk out with a majority in favour? It is. But the skill that works with small roomfuls of people does not extend to those outside the room. The Tory Party, whose internal trauma helped to rock Mrs Thatcher out of the boat, is still passing through its own upheaval. John Major inherited a situation which did not change because he became leader. The situation is that the party is not at one with itself. Nor should it be. For perhaps it is now more than one party. No more so than Labour, whose uneasy coalition determines that its leader has to be all things to all factions and capable before anything else of unifying the party. To a lesser degree, the Conservative Party is in a comparable situation.

Mrs Thatcher's leadership brought ideology and passion into the Conservative political debate. But ideology and passion divide rather than unite. They separate sheep from goats and radicals from conservatives. They demand direction and leadership and challenge to the forces of inertia and restraint. Ah, for those bygone days when the Conservative Party was a united front of pragmatic common sense. Will John Major also lead with passion and ideology?

This question may never be fully answered. Major keeps his passion under wraps and his beliefs, be they ideological or not, are used like lace stocking tops to maintain interest without actually revealing the goods. Nevertheless he has inherited a divided party and so far there has not been much evidence that he can perform the task for which he was claimed to be ideal: that is, to heal the rifts.

In November 1990, Heseltine the challenger was discredited by his betrayal of Mrs Thatcher, the leader still overwhelmingly supported by the constituencies. Could there have been forgiveness for Heseltine? Would he, with inspired rhetoric and nationwide tours of the constituencies, have restored himself as their darling? Probably not, for there is still much unreconstructed anger at the loss of Mrs Thatcher. But at least the restlessness still evident in this party, with its divergent wet and dry streams, its libertarians and its centrists, would have been vented on him. John Major would have lived on to stand for the leadership later. The danger at present is that the party is fundamentally divided, that it will take time to settle down, possibly time in opposition, and that Major's techniques for sorting out individual rooms will not work from party platforms.

The best devices for creating party unity are external pressures. So a war, an election, some big international issue, can do what speeches cannot. Deeds are more powerful than words in swaying public opinion. The Gulf War gave John Major a prolonged honeymoon. Instead of being confronted with an opposition attack on interest rates and the economy, he had instead the chance to use his skills as a unifier and bring all the parties together behind British participation in the war.

Former Chief Whip John Wakeham says, 'He made a positive decision that we would seek to get all party support for what we were doing. This was achieved by briefing the official people in the opposition privately about what was happening, so that they could be involved and could go along with it. John started from a position of saying, "Look, it is in the best interest in dealing with this conflict that our forces in the Gulf believe or are convinced that they are fighting a battle with the united support of the House of Commons behind them." The Labour Party decided it was in their interest. But at no time did you prickle people into doing things despite themselves.'

Paddy Ashdown, the Liberal Democrat leader whose gracious response to the Tory leadership crisis paved the way for good relations with the new leader, also acted constructively during the war. John Major naturally had kept him in the picture and dealt with him personally to secure the Democrats' support. Ashdown was rewarded by the opportunity to appear statesmanlike and informed, thanks to his military and foreign office experience, which a month after the war ended was reflected in a 50% public satisfaction rating for his performance as Democrat leader as against 58% for John Major and a lowish 39% for Kinnock. As the Labour leader was not willing to talk to the author, it was not possible to discover his feelings about John Major's approach to national unity during the war's seven weeks. Major was however criticised by Tory right-wingers for having given Kinnock an opportunity to appear statesmanlike and responsible.

Kinnock emerged from the war far behind Major in public esteem. But these criticisms reflected the fear among a substantial group, whose views were voiced almost daily at this point in the *Telegraph* newspapers, that John Major would prove a softy, that consensus rather than clarity would be his stance, that there would be fudging and smudging on all the issues Margaret Thatcher had indelibly defined; in short, that the party had let in a Trojan Horse for social democracy. Matters were not helped by praise from Dr David Owen for Major's Bonn speech of March 11 1991, or by known Tory wet and Conservative Party chairman Chris Patten's approbation for the social market concept awakened by remarks in the Prime Minister's Bonn speech.

This was not two weeks after the Gulf War ceasefire. Relief at a successful campaign, topped by the boy PM waving a captured Kalashnikov or leaping on a captured tank and addressing his troops like some latter-day Henry V, gave way to grumbles and unease that Major was making unnecessary haste to embrace the Germans. Unlike other international issues, Europe is still a powerfully divisive factor, the issue whose handling was the cause of Margaret Thatcher's removal. A majority of the British people may feel that Mrs Thatcher's instincts, if not her approach, were right. Yet others also believe her approach brought more results than would a less combative posture in cutting through the multilingual flannel of bureaucratic proposals.

John Major can handle the Europeans more smoothly and diplomatically than his predecessor, and perhaps with the use of his celebrated velvet steamroller techniques, achieve his objectives in discussion and negotiation with other EEC leaders.

These techniques depend upon surprise, his strategy remaining unrevealed until the meeting. Giving away one's standpoint ahead of a meeting alerts the opposition and allows adversarial positions to become entrenched. This is not John Major's style. Stealth is his weapon. But it could also be a handicap. Whatever he does in the smoked-filled conference chamber will be second guessed and criticised even before he has done it, by either wing of his own party. Conservative party divisions on Europe reflect those elsewhere in the nation's body politic and in the nation at large, although not proportionately. They are simply between those who accept the drift if not the rush towards single currency and political union and those who want to retain full national sovereignty, come what may.

Major's instincts are always to keep doors open while preparing and persuading for change. If his premiership has a particular hallmark it may be that of applying his special skills for negotiation and persuasion in Europe. His brief time as Foreign Secretary served its purpose by allowing him a personal foretaste of European protocols and positions, of which he then developed further experience as Chancellor where he grappled directly with the Euromonetary policy issues, coming up with his own proposal of a Hard Ecu to be used alongside national currencies.

His own view on the immediate issues of monetary union are that, 'It's reordering and changing. We can't go on as we were in terms of Europe. We should be at the centre of Europe if we're going to properly protect our interest.

'And being in the centre of Europe doesn't mean we've sold out, doesn't mean we've suddenly become Europhiles and adopt every fetish that emerges from the European Commission. Of course not. What it does mean is that we are in a better position to influence the way in which the whole of Europe goes. It's about time we lifted our eyes and looked beyond our own shores. There's a lot happening.'

He agrees that we are far from advanced enough along the lines of European collective decision-making to consider political union of any kind. 'We're a long way short. But we have to conduct those arguments. I mean, the one thing that is absolutely instinctive about the British, always, has been that in terms of politics they are very practical. If it can be done, okay. If it can't be done, why waste your time on it? Deal with something else that can be done.'

In the Bonn speech he referred to this again. He quoted from Konrad Adenauer's memoirs: 'It was clear to me that a united Europe could only arise if a community of European peoples could be reconstructed, a community in which each people made its own irreplaceable contribution to European economy and culture, to Western thought, imagination and creativity.' And John Major went on, 'There are many things we can and must do in common with our European partners. At the same time, Europe is made up of nation states – their vitality and diversity are sources of strength. The important thing is to strike the right balance between closer cooperation and a proper respect for national institutions and traditions.'

He then states the British agenda for the debate that is to come on Economic and Monetary Union. In summary, he listed, first, price stability as a prime objective of monetary policy. Loathing of inflation is the key to his economic views on both domestic and European monetary policy, and his reason for favouring British entry into the Exchange

Rate Mechanism. Second, he said, 'Economic and Monetary Union must be based on free and open markets. Stage 1 has a long way to go before we can proclaim that Europe is truly open for finance.' And, 'Third: the development of monetary cooperation must depend on much greater progress towards economic convergence between member states. The gaps at present are still too wide . . .'

In his Southport speech of March 1991, he said, 'No one should fear we will lose our national identity. We will fight for Britain's interest as hard as any government that has gone before.' But surely the fight must be from a different point of view to that waged by Mrs Thatcher? She was always, and remained, despite her latterly acquired world statesmanship, a Little Englander. She was, and is, absolutely committed to England, and to England over and above Scotland, Wales and Ulster. England is at the heart of Mrs Thatcher's political passion; its defence, its revival, its survival and its power. This may not have been a fully conscious admission on her part, but it was for England's sake especially that Mrs Thatcher would never let Britain lose one micron of its sovereignty. Tragically, this is why her premiership had to be consigned to history. In the long view, the one thousand year view, the forces of history are moving unstoppably towards global government, towards the One World of which the One Europe is but a stepping stone.

John Major is right. It is better to shape the new Europe from within than to fight its negative aspects – its homogenising and totalitarian tendencies – from without. He does not speak of a long view but he realises where the path leads.

He has also made himself clear on the Great Britain question that he emphasised in his Southport speech. He said, 'We are rightly proud of our national traditions, all of them: English, Scottish, Welsh and Irish.' And, with a phrase that evoked Abraham Lincoln's 'We will stand four-square for the union', he went on, 'There is something unique about the United Kingdom, a country which draws together in partnership the rich tradition of four great nations. We have much to learn from each other and much to give. We must cherish the diversity that gives each of them character. But above all we must stand together.'

This is a microcosm of his view on Europe. His clearly stated position shows John Major to be in favour of ultimate Economic and Monetary Union and of a form of political union which nevertheless preserves the heritage, autonomy and diversity of the nations. The breadth and depths of his views, while Margaret Thatcher was Prime Minister, were hidden behind a smoke screen created by his choice of a very anti-European PPS, Tony Favell. When Favell resigned in protest after Goeffrey Howe's speech which led to Mrs Thatcher's being challenged and defeated as leader, John chose Graham Bright, an old friend and a more moderate figure, thus dropping his screen. Clearly, the European issue which was at the heart of Mrs Thatcher's demise could not be used as an obstacle to John Major's election. Favell's resignation, as John's friend Robert Atkins points out, was more an opportunity than a disaster.

John Major emerged as the Great Negotiator who would carry Britain's cause in Europe. But, word had it, the objectives had not changed: the alteration was one of style not content.

He is an honest man, as politicians go exceptionally so. But he has a deft way of dodging confrontation by concealing himself and his viewpoint behind a veil of diplomatic phraseology. He would be angry at any suggestion that this is in any way dishonest. But compared to Mrs Thatcher, no less honest and who, we all know, attacks, confronts, criticises, goes for the weak point and exposes flaws without mercy, he can be tangential. He can be subtle to the point of obfuscation. He has the instinctive calculation, ingenuity and persistence of the music hall joke wife who wants her husband to buy her a new fur coat. Perhaps his method of persuading Mrs Thatcher to join the ERM had been of the same order?

How else could he have worked in six months a feat Nigel Lawson had failed to accomplish in four years, using his own characteristically confrontational techniques? Was it that the fruit was ready to fall, or were John Major's methods and timing combined more effective? He says, 'We talked about it for a long time to decide what was right. We just talked about it, and if you look at what has happened since then it was undoubtedly the right decision. Since then we've lost the Prime Minister in dramatic political circumstances, we've had a Gulf War, we've had a recession, we've had a narrowing of three points between Sterling and the Deutschmark and Sterling has kept its exchange rate, interest rates have fallen by 2% and both will fall more soon. I think that's a success.'

When it was suggested that his timing on ERM entry was faulty because the business cycles were on a downturn and ERM entry only added to problems caused by these and an interest rate squeeze, he argued, 'If we hadn't gone in then, what would have happened with those political events over the last four months? (December 1990 to March 1991) Sterling would have fallen. What happens when Sterling falls, interest rates go up. We'd have had higher interest rates, not lower.'

He explained how he had arrived at the conclusion that ERM entry was both necessary and timely. He said, 'A matter of logic. Every day I sat at the Treasury (as Chancellor) and I saw Sterling being kicked around by rumour. And when Sterling is being kicked around, the economy is being kicked around because it affects monetary policy, and monetary policy ripples through and affects everything else.

'The more I realised, day after day, was that the most priceless gift you could offer British business over the medium term was a stable exchange rate and a stable inflation rate. And what was the best mechanism to achieve this, or the best and most proven mechanism to achieve it over the years would be an Exchange Rate Mechanism.'

It was a discipline on British industry? 'Oh it is,' he said. 'It was intended to be. Nothing soft about it and neither did I say it was. I actually made it perfectly clear at the time that it wasn't a soft option. It wasn't a pre-election boomlet, it was a serious discipline that would have painful side effects and I set that out publicly at the time.

'Everybody, because they were being very smart and clever, said "Ho, ho" behind their hand because they thought this was a very clever little political trick. They now know it wasn't. It wasn't a political trick at all. It was a very considerable discipline of British industry that was absolutely necessary and we will get the benefit of that in the 1990s. If we hadn't done it, if we'd hung around until the other side of the election or whatever, firstly we would have had huge turbulence over the last few months in the economy and secondly, in the Nineties, when we were actually going to need an inflation rate the same as the French and Germans, we would have been a good deal higher. We would have lost several more years. I may be wrong, but I was quite clear in my mind that it was the right thing to do and that we had to do it.'

In January 1991 with David Frost on TV AM, he said again that the enormous credit boom of 1987–8 was unforeseen and unprecedented but, he added, welcome, because it was an investment-led boom that 'Was what we had been looking for for a long time. But equally, as companies felt confident and secure, they invested a lot, a good deal of it in overseas equipment, widening the trade gap. And just as they felt confident so did millions of individuals in the country, and they went in for their bit of expenditure: a new car, a new house, a new fridge. It was the aggregate of those two that caused this credit growth (£40 billion) and has led to the subsequent inflationary problem.' He insists that the statistics simply did not reveal what was happening and that was why he had them changed. 'That was a combination of circumstances that is unlikely to repeat itself, particularly I may say now we have attached ourselves to the discipline of the Exchange Rate Mechanism.'

Sir Alan Walters, Mrs Thatcher's former economic advisor and the man whose stoic opposition to ERM brought Nigel Lawson to resign, began in March

1991 to voice his condemnation of ERM entry and of the continuation of high interest rate policy. He wrote a letter to *The Times*, co-signed with several other leading economists, demanding immediate devaluation of the pound. In his well-argued book *Sterling in Danger* he sets out a strong case against the ERM. He admits that exchange rate variability between members of the EMS has been attained but cites statistics which show that there has not been any gain in stability of effective exchange rates with other OECD countries. Gains in exchange rate stability between EMS countries, he claims, are offset by increased exchange rate variability between the EMS countries and non-ERM currencies such as the dollar. Another of his claims is that the statistics also reveal that the EMS, of which the ERM is a part, is not a discipline on inflation.

The question raised, since Sir Alan has declared his opposition to the exchange rate policies being pursued by John Major, is who is right? History will provide the answer. As to who is most qualified to be right, surely Sir Alan is the trained economist? But economics is a life science and too many variables are involved to make the game of prediction safe. Hands on experience of economic management such as John Major gained in banking and the Treasury should give him a chance of holding his own with the trained economists.

As for ERM, the truth about Britain's entry is that Major persuaded Mrs Thatcher to agree to the pre-party conference entrance in 1990 because he convinced her it was the only way in which interest rates could be reduced. The immediate increase in exchange rate stability guaranteed through the

support of the other participants in the ERM allowed
a one-point interest rate reduction then. This came
after, as Chancellor, he had been 'hassled and harried'
first to put up interest rates in 1989 and then to bring
them down from 15% during 1990, but had refused
because of the impact that would have had on sterling.
He said, 'I refused and I took a great deal of nonsense
in the press about not being able to do anything. The
point was that it wasn't right to do anything. I'm not
as easy to hassle and harry as people may think.'

He is convinced he is right about ERM membership's value to sterling. In terms of a future within
a progressively unified European Economic and
Monetary system, he has to be right. But he made
it clear in his speech to the conference on October
11 1990 that ERM entry 'does not mean that we
are now on a road leading inexorably to a single
currency. It does demonstrate yet again that we
take our commitment to Europe seriously and that
we mean what we say'.

He says, 'It had been the government's policy
for a long time to join the ERM when the time
was right. The question was, when was the time
right? There were a series of compelling arguments
to advance, I advanced them and Mrs Thatcher
listens to arguments. As early as June we reached
an agreement that we would go in in October.'

Although Sir Alan Walters formulated the basis
of what became the Madrid agreement in which
Mrs Thatcher set out Britain's terms for joining the
ERM, his true position is one of non-joiner. He has
more recently attacked it as the slippery slope to credit
controls and the end of a free market in money for
Britain. In an article in the London *Evening Standard*

on April 5 1991, he struck out at recent proposals by the Bank of England's Governor, Robin Leigh-Pemberton, to limit mortgage borrowing. This, to all free marketeers, shocking proposal, was he believed known to the Chancellor before it was made. He said, 'It would be foolish to conclude that the Chancellor was unaware of what the Governor was about to say . . . The Treasury clearly could not say a word, but the Bank with its quasi-autonomous status could clearly send up a trial balloon to see where it floated.' This balloon, Sir Alan suggested, was part of an orchestrated plan to float the idea of credit controls seriously. 'Indeed, support for credit controls – carefully considered and targeted, of course – appeared in all sorts of establishment quarters such as the *Financial Times*, March 30–1. There it is said that there is a good case "against exclusive reliance on interest rates to control exaggerated swings in the credit cycle". There is a suffusing air of "something must be done." I believe that this spells the end of free financial markets in Britain.'

Sir Alan wrote that he had been expecting credit controls to rear their heads ever since 1985–7 'when so many Tories joined the European bandwagon'. He explained: 'The reason was simple, all the participants of the ERM employ credit controls and none of them relies, like Britain, on the price of credit, the interest rate, reflecting the free play of market forces. Government directives and "influence" over-ride the market. Clearly a free Britain will be the butt of all the excess credit demands or supplies from our ERM partners.'

If Britain were to remain in the ERM, Sir Alan continued, 'it would be obliged to play the game and bring back the corset and other credit limitations which Mrs Thatcher abolished in 1979/80.'

ERM entrance was one small step for Britain and one large step for European union. It was certainly a step closer to Europe than Sir Alan Walters or Margaret Thatcher would in principle care to accept because they were both fundamentally opposed to any loss of sovereignty. But from 1989, Walters was no longer formally advising Mrs Thatcher, thanks to John Major's refusal to take the job of Chancellor if Walters remained. ERM entry was the first small loss for Britain of independent management of its exchange rate and interest policies; perhaps a larger step towards abolition of the free market in finance, and therefore of economic sovereignty.

Yet, John Major, with his velvet steamroller techniques, convinced Margaret Thatcher that it had become necessary as the only alternative to continuing with a punitively high interest rate in autumn 1990, a rate needed to dampen the inflationary fire lit by that same investment-led credit boom of 1987 and 1988 that Treasury statistics appear not to have revealed until it was too late. It seems extraordinary that even the hot house isolation of senior political figures should prevent the perception of what was afoot, when everyone at high street level seemed to know exactly what was happening and even the banks were issuing leaflets offering customers the chance to release cash by remortgaging their properties.

It is ironic that it was the inflationary consequence of that latter period of Nigel Lawson's economic stewardship of the United Kingdom, coincident with John Major's two years as Chief Secretary, which made it eventually a desperate necessity to enter the

ERM in order to stem the massive tide of recession which had developed under 15% interest rates. Ironic because Lawson's resignation over that very issue paved the way for John Major becoming Chancellor and therefore being a credible leadership candidate. One thing this extraordinary piece of timing achieved was to give John Major direct insight into both causes and cures of the current economic crisis, which gives him enormous authority in the economic sector as Prime Minister.

Sir Alan raises another question of vital importance to the future. He wrote, 'We are in for a party rapprochement towards a caring, regulative, redistributing society – a sort of Majockism (Major Kinnock hybrid).' He meant the description to imply that the all too brief season, the decade and a few months of Mrs Thatcher's liberal economic thinking, is finished. Is it? John Major constantly reassures critics that there is continuity on the need for competition, to break up monopolies, to improve state services by introducing private sector standards of cost saving and efficiency, citizens' charters and so on, to extend opportunity and choice. He has stated his intentions quite clearly. His critics and the alarmists among them especially are concerned that the means may not fit these laudable Thatcherite ends, that there has been a sharp swerve away from free market principles and that interventionism is creeping back. This, all free marketeers know, wrings the dynamism out of the business sector, substitutes dodges for direct dealing, slows growth.

Perhaps John Major intends intervention to wither away in time? But that in the meantime, while it lasts, he can offer British industry a modicum of

discipline and protection. Or perhaps he has a more
ingenious way of using fiscal carrots to bring about a
transformation of Britain's industrial capacity so that
when boom comes, British companies and individuals
can choose from an array of home-produced goods
instead of sucking in imports. This, not ERM
membership, is the basis of German prosperity and
the Deutschmark's dominance.

He may not have gone that far yet, concerned
mainly as he is with destroying medium-term
inflation, mainly through stabilising the currency. His
experience at the Treasury as Chancellor, following
within months of his two years as Chief Secretary,
have given him an enormously comprehensive
understanding of the British economy. The year
as Chancellor also enabled him to build an image
and a reputation as someone who could handle the
economy deftly. One of his Cabinet colleagues told
me, 'I thought when John became Chancellor it would
be harder for him to become leader than it was when he
was Foreign Secretary, because everyone blames the
Chancellor when things go wrong with the economy.'
Things certainly were wrong when he took over. But
he demonstrated resoluteness and toughness and,
after the first weeks of reading himself in and adjusting
to being in yet another new job, a degree of assurance.
He made good in the job and was well regarded by the
public. He was and is at ease with economic matters.

When interviewed by David Frost, one of his
earliest face to face TV encounters after becoming
Prime Minister, he only really came to life while
answering questions on the economy. His answers
on foreign affairs and other topics were more
limited and revealed a lack of confidence. Once

the economic questions began, his body language changed, his linguistic fluency improved, he relaxed and responded with perfectly choreographed answers like a prima ballerina to music.

There is no doubt that John Major was very much at home as Chancellor. His two years as Chief Secretary to the Treasury had been preceded by other Treasury jobs. From 1983, while a whip, he specialised in Treasury legislation and in 1984 was made Lord Commissioner of the Treasury. His period in banking has given him an image acceptable to the City of London. He was soon well regarded there after becoming Chancellor. However, his banking experience may not have been as strong a foundation for his job as Chancellor as has been believed. His connections have undoubtedly helped. According to his friend Ian Cameron Black, John has often consulted another friend and his Durand Gardens landlord, Stan Hurn, about financial terms which he did not understand. Hurn, a merchant banker, is an expert in Eurocurrency Syndicated Lending. Eurocurrency is the pool of money which is outside individual government controls. It exists not just in Europe but flows mainly through European banks to international borrowers. 'He told me, "I'm a strong currency man," and I used to say to John, "Look around the world, there isn't a country with a strong currency that doesn't have a strong economy." Clearly influenced in his four years of tutorials while Hurn's tenant, John Major is an absolute believer in strong currency. Hurn says he has the ability to grasp subjects and before you know it he's picked up what you're talking about and is asking very penetrating questions.

To John Major, the ERM is the route to a strong
currency and thereby, it follows, a strong economy,
without which a nation is powerless. He outlines
his views, describing what he would have said in a
keynote speech had he remained as Foreign Secretary
until the spring of 1990, the thirty-year anniversary
of Harold Macmillan's 'Winds of Change' speech at
Cape Town. 'I was going to point out the extent to
which the world is changing and our role in it and
that there were different themes that we had to pick
up. We had to realise on the economic front that unless
we were competetive we weren't going to remain with
the political power and influence because of what we
are, because of our history as well as our economic
power. Over the years, that will not survive unless
we are an economic power as well. And that has to
be fully understood.

'The other point that I would have made, on the
diplomatic front, (is) the point I've made on the
European Community – that we had to be in it.
And externally I would have made the point that
I don't believe we use the historical influence we
have within the Commonwealth to the fullest effect,
and I think we should. When I went to Trinidad as
Chancellor and introduced the Trinidad Terms, it
was quite astonishing how warm the feeling was in the
Commonwealth, not because I'd produced something
they liked, but here was Britain taking a lead in a
matter of concern to the whole Commonwealth.

'And I think there's a great deal we can do. If you
actually look at the standards that this country sets in
many ways, they are as good as any in the world. Now
we should capitalise on this. If you talk to the people in
the Gulf states, for example, when we weren't talking

about the confict while I was out there, they actually
referred to the sort of lead that Britain had given over
the years in that sort of area. And I thought there
was a rich range of things to cherry pick from and
talk about. I think we have a lot to offer and I think
we should offer it.'

His brief experience of the Foreign Office has
given him a crash course in its methods. When
he answers questions on foreign issues it is with a
mandarin-like pedantry that suggests someone who
is not thinking originally. He can leave foreign affairs
safely in Douglas Hurd's capable hands, but he needs
to develop some flair himself. He seems flat-footed on
many issues. While the Kurds were being massacred
by Saddam Hussein, he appeared outside Number
10 and said, 'I don't recall that we ever asked the
Kurds to rise up against Saddam.' His tone was
faintly indignant and his blank facial expression
evoked shades of Neville Chamberlain. There was a
reason for the Prime Minister's response; he explains,
'The question was edited out of the telecast which
asked me why I wasn't doing anything for the Kurds
although I had urged them to overthrow Saddam.'
Next day £20 million of aid for Kurdish refugees in
food and blankets was announced. It was all the more
unfortunate for his image that his aid announcement
came within hours of Mrs Thatcher's impassioned
plea on the Kurds' behalf.

However, he saved his face and made a radical
contribution to resolving the tragic situation with his
speedy proposal to the EEC summit at Luxembourg.
The concept of enclaves for the Kurds in Northern
Iraq supervised by the UN was the kind of strong
and creative initiative with which John Major can

carve for himself an image of concerned and practical leadership.

It was tragic that the Western nations had needed, for the sake of politics, to wait until world and their own public opinion pushed them into action on the Kurds. The politics of the Iraq uprisings were of course difficult. It was not politically possible for the Allies who had liberated Kuwait to intervene in the internal politics of Iraq until it became acceptable to do so.

Prior to that there were difficulties on the Western side. It was seen as desirable that the Iraqi people would remove Saddam Hussein themselves. But, among the rebels were the Shi'ite Fundamentalists of the south. This posed a political problem, for no one would welcome a Fundamentalist regime in Iraq, which would tend to unbalance the Middle East yet further when combined with the Imams' power in Iran. The Kurds have long been a separate and neglected issue. Until that was tackled, it seemed, the new order in the Middle East was being allowed to take care of itself. Moral leadership was needed and eventually it came from John Major, not a moment too soon after his earlier lapse.

Looking, however, at his scanty diplomatic record on foreign issues other than in Europe, he cannot be criticised too much. On Hong Kong he followed Geoffrey Howe, but soon began putting in his own initiatives. In August 1989 he instructed British diplomats to press for changes to the draft deal for handing over the colony in 1997. Just over a month later, at the Commonwealth Heads of Government Conference in Kuala Lumpur, he promised he was drawing up a package to offer Hong Kong citizens wider rights of abode in Britain, and during his three months as Foreign Secretary it was announced that British passport holders would be allowed into Britain after the handover. More recently Douglas Hurd has announced British dissatisfaction at negotiations with China over Hong Kong's new airport.

John Major's method is to move quietly, discreetly and behind the scenes, rather than give advance warning to adversaries of his plans. This close to the chest style runs through his entire life and all areas of policy. When asked in September 1989 what he would do about the Vietnamese boat people who were to be repatriated at that stage, it was thought forcibly, from their Hong Kong camps, he threw the question back.

I suggested that as Hong Kong could not be expected to house such a large number of refugees and no one else would accept them, America might be asked to share political responsibility for them; then the Vietnamese government might be offered investment credits for specific developments to create jobs for the returnees, provide direct aid for resettlement, in return for guarantees and an inspectorate to ensure individual refugees were not mistreated on their return. 'Yes,' he said, 'that's the sort of thing.'

True to form he did not want to discuss something which was sensitive. Two weeks after the discussion, it was reported that a deal had been struck with the Vietnamese government which included paying reintegration assistance for each returnee and assurances from Hanoi that those deported from Hong Kong would not be persecuted.

There are some areas in which he has more feel, aptitude and response. Africa is one. He

was popular with Commonwealth leaders in Kuala
Lumpur, having already made clear his strong views
against apartheid. He did however fall foul of the
meeting over the controversial sanctions issue. Sir
Sonny Ramphal, veteran Commonwealth Secretary
General, since retired, comments, 'The backdrop to
John Major's appointment was one in which we had
had many quarrels with the Prime Minister but very
good relations with the Foreign Secretaries, many of
whom had come out of an international diplomacy
background, kindred people who understood the
world.

'We didn't know John Major. We knew that his
work at the Treasury would have brought him
into contact with some international issues, mostly
industrial countries cooperation, not North–South
issues. So my own instinct was: 'We are having
a new Foreign Secretary who is going to be quite
green on the issues before the Commonwealth.' On
the other hand, all my experience had taught me
that it was very important not to make judgments
about leaders in advance of their performance. So I
welcomed the fact that there was a newcomer who
could advise the Prime Minister in a new way. That
was what we wanted most of all because, after all,
Mrs Thatcher was alone on sanctions in relation to
South Africa. We had hoped that Kuala Lumpur
would provide a situation in which we could move
forward.

'This meant sanctions would remain and South
Africa would be brought into negotiations. It was
important that the Commonwealth should appear
united on this and that anything implying support
for the South African government, such as British

disavowal of sanctions, would prevent the situation from moving forward. The Foreign Secretary plays a limited role in the Heads of Government meeting which is a personal interchange between the (leaders). At Kuala Lumpur it was thought the foreign ministers could usefully deal with the more bruising stages of sanctions negotiations so a committee was set up. The previous conference two years earlier had had a similar committee of foreign ministers, but Mrs Thatcher had refused to allow Sir Geoffrey Howe to participate. However, she was willing to allow John Major to do so.'

This is how he came to be involved in what Stan Hurn says was a 'baptism of fire' as Foreign Secretary, 'a very bruising experience'.

'I negotiated for seventeen hours or so and it was the Commonwealth against me,' John Major remembers. 'We negotiated a text that was satisfactory except in four areas and it was very tough going. In four areas it said "Commonwealth with the exception of Britain." The Prime Minister was then absolutely satisfied with the text, didn't change a dot or a comma, indeed was very gracious about how difficult it had been to negotiate. We discussed it and the Commonwealth set out their position in a communiqué. We had in four places "the Commonwealth with the exception of Britain", and nobody knew why it was accepted because it (the reason) wasn't in the communiqué.'

The Foreign Secretary and Mrs Thatcher were in different parts of Kuala Lumpur but they discussed this problem on the phone. 'And one of us, I can't honestly remember who now, said, "Why don't we put out a statement explaining our position on those four points?" And we did. And because it offended the

amour propre of one or two distinguished diplomatic
journalists, they began running this huge story that
the Prime Minister was doing what she had done
to Geoffrey Howe, that is, overruling the Foreign
Secretary. And it was wholly untrue. I told the press
out there that it was untrue and when I got home
there were these great banner headlines in the paper
saying there had been this huge row, and it wasn't the
case.'

Sir Sonny's view was slightly different: 'Instead
of forming the committee and asking John Major
to join it, because Mrs Thatcher would have vetoed
that anyway, we just asked the foreign ministers to
meet as a group and function as a committee of the
conference. And that was how we brought John Major
into active participation in the work of the conference
on Southern Africa.' The committee included foreign
ministers of Canada, Zimbabwe, Australia and Tan-
zania. As Sir Sonny had hoped, the row which would
otherwise have erupted between Mrs Thatcher and
leaders such as Kenneth Kaunda of Zambia and
Robert Mugabe of Zimbabwe, was kept to foreign
minister level. Sir Sonny told me, 'That was how it
turned out. They did have a row at foreign ministers'
level. John Major had quite a blooding, but he held
his own and came out of it respected. People didn't
regard him as speaking solely for Mrs Thatcher, but
as making a genuine attempt to bridge differences,
and to the extent that the differences couldn't be
bridged to find a way forward by maximising what
was positive and minimising what was negative.'

This blooding of John Major, the quiet man who
would always rather do things nicely, proved both
his mettle and his abilities in the art of the possible.

352 JOHN MAJOR

Sir Sonny says, 'He might have had quite a bruising encounter, for example, with Gareth Evans, the Australian foreign minister, who is very outspoken. But the crucial point is that he found it possible to get agreement, and it was a worthy and honourable agreement in language which recognised the extent to which Britain did not agree and emphasised areas in which Britain could agree.

'It sent to South Africa a signal that the Commonwealth was united in its opposition to apartheid, in the sanctions that had already been imposed, including by Britain, and calling for change. The agreement was sent to the Heads of Government at their retreat and they all agreed that it represented a very good effort on the part of the foreign ministers, and actually it was Mrs Thatcher who said, "Let us agree it and let us invite the Chairman to announce it as our collective statement."

'This would have been the first time in about five years at the Heads of Government meeting that on the issue of South Africa, the Commonwealth would have come out with an agreed statement. The Prime Minister (Mrs Thatcher) and I went down from Lankawe, which is an island off Penang, to the press centre on the Sunday afternoon to tell the press: and this was very good news, this was the height of achievement of the conference. The Prime Minister was very pleased.'

Meanwhile, the statement was produced, released, and the way it had been achieved explained to the press. Sir Sonny continues, 'To our absolute amazement, we found the press centre in an uproar because Bernard Ingham (the Prime Minister's press secretary) had briefed the press in advance of our coming down and in a manner which did the very opposite of the statement, emphasised what was negative and minimised what was positive and the basis of agreement. In other words, he had briefed the press in a way which continued the image of Mrs Thatcher as rejecting everything the Commonwealth stood for on this issue, and which had already been achieved and agreed. And then, within about half an hour, (he) actually circulated this statement representing the British position, a statement which was utterly inconsistent with the statement which had just been agreed by the Prime Minister and which had been approved by the foreign ministers, including John Major. This really was disastrous.

'Prime Ministers like Brian Mulroney (Canada) and Bob Hawke (Australia) used much stronger language than that because they regarded themselves as having been deceived. They had come to a consensus agreement with Mrs Thatcher and they saw it repudiated unilaterally within half an hour. They spoke out the following morning very, very strongly. That must have been a devastating blow for John Major. He couldn't come forward and repudiate his Prime Minister and he said very little. He stuck by the agreement he and his fellow foreign ministers had reached and which had been accepted by the Heads of Government. He kept his head down and I think people felt very sorry that this Foreign Secretary who had made such a very good start with his colleagues really had had the rug pulled from under him.

'Bernard Ingham must take a very major part of the responsibility. I think he would have advised after she had agreed that this was wrong and that they had to counter it, notwithstanding the agreement. Bernard Ingham has not been a friend of the Commonwealth or of the Heads of Government meetings and has been responsible for a good deal that was contentious and counter-productive, but this was far and away the most scandalous interference.'

John Major, the brilliant negotiator who always seemed to get his own way, who had kept his head down throughout his Parliamentary career, avoided or merely been courted by journalists, now learned that the hardest part of politics is not what you do but how you are interpreted. Or, more cruelly, how even the most precise, exact and accurate statement of your views, intentions and actions on any particular subject are misinterpreted by speed readers and speedwriters of the media. This is a lesson he has found hard to assimilate at times, but it is an area where his experience of being a public relations officer for Standard Chartered Bank should come in handy. Brian Haynes, the PR consultant with whom he worked during this phase of his banking career, says he found John one of the best managers he was given to work with, that he learned much and had an evident aptitude for public relations. John Major has used this experience on the way to becoming Prime Minister. He has used it to conceal rather than reveal, to present himself diplomatically rather than affront anyone, to draw veils and screens around any contentious viewpoint he might hold within his own party so as to be all things to all men, and a few women. His experience at Kuala Lumpur, while nasty, should have been salutary. This blooding was the sign that however carefully a document or statement is worded, it can still be misinterpreted.

So far, there are indications that John does not take kindly to being misinterpreted, or to being advised in newspapers how to run the country. He is actually advised by his many friends and colleagues and, being an eclectic, picks good people, listens keenly to a wide variety of views and facts, mulling them over a long time before arriving at the decision.

This is the best way to make decisions. But he has been accused, because of this tortoise-like process, of being indecisive. But in fact the opposite is true. David Rogers told me, 'John has always been very good at taking decisions, at working his way through a pile of paper work and telling the civil servants what to do.' Bigger decisions, as he himself maintains, are often taken in a flash, but others are taken after a sometimes lengthy period of digesting the facts. So, the perception that he is indecisive is untrue.

David Mellor says John Major is a good chairman of committees. He is expected to bring these skills to Cabinet. He listens, allows arguments to be aired, brings discussion to fruit, and weighs the balance of opinion. His colleagues find this a relief after Mrs Thatcher's critical knockabout. But is John no more than a chief executive? Signs are that he can and does offer fresh thinking on stale issues, that he can offer political initiatives. He is said to pick up ideas quickly and repeat them; he will pick up a phrase or a concept and develop it into his own. Thus he absorbs the best from those around him and acts as a channel for the expression of new and useful ideas, finding the best way to bring innovations to practical resolution.

Following his initiative over the Kurds, John Major proposed a new protocol for arms sales, saying the United Nations should keep a register of all nations'

arms sales so that there would at least be some record
of which countries had bought which weapons. The
idea may not have been his own, but he saw its
merits and was able to add practical thoughts for its
development into a workable plan. This is the essence
of John Major's effectiveness as Prime Minister. He
gathers together the people and the ideas that can
move the world forward and he determines the most
rational and practical method of making things work.

But there has to be a period of adjustment for the
observers. Journalists and political figures alike had
become accustomed to Mrs Thatcher's apparently
clear and strongly put viewpoints rather because
they were always assertively and often adversarially
delivered, so they are accustomed to dividing into pro
and anti ranks immediately. Getting new ideas across
takes repetition and time.

The problem is that with an election looming John
Major may not have that much time to present
who and what he is. In the late twentieth century,
where day to day affairs are media-dominated, the
long patient march of progress is not seen as
having a particular direction. Instant judgments
occur at every point, every day, on every issue.
Headlines, news bulletins, columns, discussions,
divide and segregate opinions all swiftly gathered
and recycled and therefore open to misjudgments and
misinterpretations. It is the nature of journalism to ask
the question, uproot the lie, challenge the obtusity,
unmask the imposter, rehearse the arguments for and
against an issue. This is the proper function of the
Fourth Estate.

Politicians resist for they would like newspapers
to consist of their own unedited press handouts.

Journalists attack because they want to penetrate politicians' subterfuges and because it is their duty to do so. The free press is not *Pravda*.

John Major seems uncomfortable in this atmosphere of instant opinion and of constant critiques and attacks on what he feels are his honest efforts to run the country for everyone's benefit. He would have been more at home in the nineteenth century, despite the fact that he is no orator, simply because then people paid attention only to the bigger issues. Now, the news factory cannibalises every statement and speech as quickly as it is received and turns it into a form of instant entertainment. A Prime Minister who does not understand this aspect of the competitive free market in news is one who is likely to be at its mercy.

After four months in office, in which the first three were occupied by the approach and conduct of the Gulf War, only one month had exposed the new Prime Minister to normal day to day news coverage. He showed inordinate sensitivity, was said to read the first editions every night before turning in – the worst time, surely, to read anything critical about oneself. At Easter, an exhausted PM was being advised by friends and colleagues to avoid reading all but a selection of cuttings, thus following his predecessor's example.

If there is another solution it may be that the Prime Minister's own approach to the media is mistaken. If journalists get the wrong idea it could be because the idea's originator needs to anticipate their misinterpretation. John Major has said he does not intend to fence himself into a corner on any issue by revealing his intentions before all the relevant aspects have been explored. But

the Downing Street Press Office has also to take
into account the opinions of groups who may not
want to support the Prime Minister and who will
delight in sketching an unflattering interpretation of
whatever he has said, those within his own party and in
opposition. The situation can therefore be helped by
very adroit handling of the Prime Minister's viewpoint
by his press office, and perhaps by a more cynical
anticipation of how it will be received. But the real
problem at the heart of his sensitive relationship with
the press is his strong desire to seek approval. This
is a weakness, almost a fatal flaw, and in its light the
Prime Minister needs to be protected and managed in
relation to the media.

Veteran Press Secretary Bernard Ingham was
among the first to be sacked when John Major
took over at Number 10. This may not have been
related to any particular incident, but the new PM has
a long memory. He would certainly have remembered
the business at Kuala Lumpur. Besides, he would
hardly want his mouthpiece to the world to be the
wily old courtier of his predecessor. The new Prime
Minister instigated an almost immediate clean out at
Number 10 of Mrs Thatcher's old coterie of advisors
and appointed his own people: younger, less public
school and Oxbridge, more from the class-mobile
groups of his own generation. He wanted a fresh
start with fresh faces. He wanted to run things his
way.

The Prime Minister's first appointment was his new
Press Secretary, Gus O'Donnell, the tall, soft-spoken
and very canny civil servant who had served him well
as Treasury Press Secretary. He constantly refers
to Gus for advice and uses him as his general in

his war against the newspapers. More recently the Prime Minister has gently moved a few other of Mrs Thatcher's closest advisors out of the kitchen Cabinet, including Charles Powell, the former foreign affairs advisor. He has brought in Judith Chaplin, his advisor from the Treasury, to be his political advisor; his secretaries are long standing allies and friends; in his Cabinet, many are from that group of Cambridge graduates of the Sixties whose views, like John's, were forged by Iain Macleod's philosophy. They include Norman Lamont, Kenneth Clarke, John Selwyn Gummer and David Mellor.

So now, surrounded by friends both among his advisors and Cabinet, John Major should feel he can move forward along the lines which he has long planned. For he has always known what he wants to do, and now his only problem is whether the electorate will permit him a mandate to do it. Naturally his every statement is leaped upon as a clue to his direction. Baffled, his audience accuses him of being directionless. People simply cannot get used to the fact that he is not Mrs Thatcher.

The poll tax issue was an immense distraction from the real path of his administration. This path has been stated many times: it is to follow in the 'dry' economic footsteps of the Thatcher years, to expand choice and opportunity yet further, indeed to do what the electorate want in safeguarding the Health Service, but improving it and other public services by a variety of methods, not necessarily increased spending.

The path on Europe is not visibly changed from before, for the views John Major advocates now are the same ones he pronounced while Foreign Secretary under Mrs Thatcher. It is mainly the rhetoric that is different, though he has also made an effort to establish rapport with Mitterrand and Kohl and talks to them on the phone regularly. In other foreign affairs, he has a good relationship with Bush, has established some sort of accord with Gorbachev, is watching the Soviet situation carefully, has declared that there must be no hasty disarmament, is interested in North–South issues and more knowledgeable and sympathetic on these than many a previous Prime Minister.

His biggest worry in 1991 is the general election he must hold before June 1992. He is on a time limit, and on one at a time in which the business cycles and the world economy are still bottoming out. Getting the economy shipshape is a balancing act fit for an acrobat's son. In his career to date he has used to great advantage the talents of intense concentration, awareness, balance and timing.

Timing is now the key to his success – the timing of that election. To win it with a sufficient majority to carry out the programme he still keeps up his sleeve, unwilling to let people at it before the right moment for fear of what they would do in terms of misinterpretation and misjudgement. Mrs Thatcher learned that she was castigated and opposed constantly, for her first two years especially, before what is now the accepted wisdom on libertarian economics had been received by people conditioned under two decades of socialist and centrist government to think the stateist way.

The answer is to say it, to say it again, and to go on saying it, until the idea is received and dissent is then reduced to manageable proportions. The British hate anything new, so much so that they attack it even before they know what it is. And they do not yet know, despite being told quite clearly but not yet often enough, what will be the nature of John Major's new order.

The world under John Major is both a kind world and a practical one. It seeks to extend the fruits of the Thatcher revolution to everyone, to remove the limitations of class, creed, race, and hopefully of gender, so that the Prime Minister's 'society at ease with itself' can move forward purposefully to its destiny in a wider and would-be wiser world. But whatever it implies in terms of supranational groupings, this vision does not relinquish that cricketer's pastoral dream of 'an English heaven'. Most keenly of all, it does not give way under the weight of opposition. In fact, the more opposition the better. It simply strengthens John Major's resolve. As he insists, 'Nothing makes me more determined to do something than someone telling me I can't.'

POSTSCRIPT

October 1991

Since the first edition of this book was completed, John Major has had six more months in office: four tumultuous months in which the still new Prime Minister has begun, ever cautiously, to reveal his plans for Britain. But due partly to his own reluctance to show his cards in advance, a quality explained in earlier chapters, and partly to poor presentation, few yet comprehend those plans. The question must still be asked: is John Major a man of real substance, with a clear plan for the future political agenda? Or is he merely a charming and competent manager of people and events, who will be found out to have no clear direction? John Major has a still largely hidden agenda and, as he has himself said, 'people will be surprised' when they find out what he really wants to do.

The next most urgent question is: does he have the time to deliver his programme, to convince the British electors that he is not merely Mr Nice but also a man with a real idea to shape the future? The first setback is that despite clear statements, speeches and even action backing up his views, he and his intentions are, to the majority, still a mystery. One reader wrote to the author, 'Thank you for explaining this enigma who is our Prime Minister.' And indeed this is what he still is to many people: an enigma. He is still underrated, still an uncertain figure whose skills and plans remain unseen and unassessed; still grey and boring to those who have not heard, read or perceived in him the steely strength, toughness, anger and stubborn rebelliousness against the status quo.

These qualities are, of course, still difficult to discern, for newspapers concentrate on day-to-day headline news and focus for entertainment on details which are comparatively trivial. Among journalists and other critics, the view that time will only find John Major out is popular. These cynics assume that there is nothing behind the bland administrator's front: the ravenous consumer of red box contents is just a civil servant's dream who decides swiftly on the day-to-day minutiae of governance but who has no clear direction, no dominating vision. If he has a vision, these critics say, he has not the conviction nor the passion to carry it through.

Criticism also focuses on the way government under Major appears more reactive than creative. The poll tax compromise was forced by public rage, the Kurdish initiative was provoked, or seemed to be, by Mrs Thatcher's impassioned appeal. There is a fear that Major governs by compromise and defensive parry more than by goal-oriented planning, initiative or attack.

But these critics do not come from the majority who elected Major as Tory leader or the public who still favour him, perhaps for no coherent reason, over his Labour rival. They are perhaps still content to enjoy the comparative quiet of John Major's leadership. The storms of conflict precipitated daily by Mrs Thatcher's goal-oriented, creative and adversarial leadership and by her impassioned belief in the policies her government pursued, had seemed, after a decade, exhausting. Change rampaging through British society and intitutions had brought prosperity unknown since before World War II and extended it to a greater number of people than ever before in Britain.

Yet, once the economy turned sour, beliefs in the ethos of the decade – enterprise – also curdled. Would the epitaph of the Eighties, once the Nineties began to assert their depressing flavour, be 'Look back with Longing' and if so, how far back would the British public look? Did they long for the spoon-fed days of the Socialist Seventies? Or did they simply want to pause and get their breath back before opening their minds to a new vision?

I believe they are waiting for the new vision. For the moment this is seeking to be born from reflection and doubt. The Eighties ended while the Western world was exhilarated by a new birth of freedom. Yet now, Britain seems to need a pause for thought as well as rest: a pause from the hard climb up the mountain to admire the view. If they look back and exclaim, 'Oh brave old world that had such creatures in it', then are their creatures heroes or monsters? Are they heroic entrepreneurs, innovators and job creators sparked to life by the rebirth of the enterprise culture? Are they leaders like Gorbachev and Thatcher, who perceived history's turning point and have led the East's forgotten Europe, even the Soviet Union, towards self-realising liberty? Free enterprise and the creatures in it have come a long way. But the enterprise of greed and crime has also flourished and the monsters, many since held to account for their greed and crookery, many yet to be unmasked, have multiplied. Like every good movie director, history has cut to a contrasting scene. John Major's appearance on the set seems to offer sanity and sobriety, a down-to-earth realism after the high-flown dreams. But many, hooked on adrenalin, find him boring both in person and in purpose. So there is doubt: will he ever be the leader for our time?

There are signposts. As has been explored at length in this book, John Major's political motivation is inspired by his own life experience. Contrary to those shallow and politically illiterate reviewers who suggested this book eschews politics, the author has shown how John Major's political themes originated in his life's experiences, and how that experience motivates his entire political philosophy and the programme that will emerge if he survives to enact it. Politics is about ideas that change history and not about inconsequential infighting between overblown egos.

John Major is not an egoist. His themes have the ring of history in formation but, like the man, they are often overlooked or dismissed by his self-appointed intellectual superiors. The theme of the class-mobile society drives his hidden agenda. Such as has been revealed so far bears this out. Important strands of policy which have emerged during the past months are linked to the same aim, that of removing the barriers to individual advance. As ever, they are understated and underrated. But they are pointers to the plan he has long held in his mind.

Firstly, Major believes absolutely in a strong economy founded on a strong currency. Without strong sterling, he believes, a strong economy is not possible. His economic policies are intended to achieve both a strong currency and a strong economy and then to bear the fruit of social reforms which will develop the class-mobile democracy of which he dreams. Thus the EMS and any currency links with Europe will be guided by that objective: to keep the pound strong and allow British exporters to compete successfully among the world's traders.

Defeating inflation is a passion for John Major and is the second strand of his economic policy. Major knows from his own youth that inflation erodes the wealth of those least able to compete. It also erodes the currency, and affects export and import prices and the trade balance. The painful economic policies since November 1990 under his chancellorship and his premiership are evidence of a tenacious and stubborn commitment to bringing down inflation. This also rewards and encourages private savings, another Major value.

His economic policy revolves around social reform. Major has made speeches about two important social themes. The first is the need for far-reaching educational reform. To the Centre for Policy Studies he said, 'The origins of our nation's insufficient regard for education, and particularly education for work, lie deep in our nation's culture.' He referred to the traditional British 'suspicion of brainpower' because 'it made the squirarchy uncomfortable', a mistrust which he says was 'reinforced by the Left with its mania for equality. Equality not of opportunity but of outcome. This was a mania that condemned children to fall short of their potential; that treated them as if they were identical, or must be made so . . . a canker in our education system which spread from the Sixties on and deprived great cohorts of our children of the opportunities they deserved.'

He went on to speak of the 'disdain for industry' and 'the superior attitude to vocational training'. He wants, he says, to 'infuse education with greater awareness of the needs of the economy. We are therefore tackling not one problem but two. It is not merely a matter of adjusting the curriculum, or restructuring institutions – important though those changes may be. We are changing a culture – and cultural changes take time.'

The second social reform he has offered is the Citizen's Charter, which he launched during July. It initially appeared as a proposal during the first weeks after the Gulf War. John Major has long been impressed with the Magna Carta and has sought through the initiative he calls his 'big idea' to revive its principles. If democracy can be said to have originated in the contract between King John and his barons, will democracy be similarly propelled into a new era by PM John's Charter? He is certainly attached to the idea. However, though it was dutifully reported, it was not received with much enthusiasm and indeed seemed to fall flat.

The Charter is based on experience that John Major has gathered while a councillor and an MP. He is more aware than most of the obfuscating techniques of state-employed officials and the frustration of consumers of state and local authority services in trying to get redress. Theoretically, the job of obtaining that redress should fall to Members of Parliament and local councillors, but only a relative handful of voters ever make use of the existing channels to complain. The Citizen's Charter proposes more than seventy measures to ensure high quality public services, including the right to sue unions for wildcat strikes; reimbursement of fares for delayed rail passengers; an ending of the Post Office monopoly; maximum waiting times for NHS treatment; and performance-related pay for public sector employees. The Prime Minister wants the Charter to be 'one of the central themes of public life in the Nineties' and said it was only the beginning of a series of initiatives to improve public services. With public spending amounting to £5,000 per head, his intention, he said, was to be 'about finding better ways of converting the money that can be afforded into even better services'.

The real challenge for the government will be to make the Charter work. It is enormously ambitious but would seem to be the right step for a government that has taken privatisation most of the way but which has also to guard the consumer's interest when vital services such as water and power are controlled by private monopolies. It is also the right step for a government that acknowledges that state services such as the NHS and education are with us to stay, but that their performance can be improved by greater public pressure for efficiency and standards of performance. Behind the Charter lies the intention of inspiring greater public awareness of the channels for redress, thus improving bad services through individual action. This is indeed a fine democratic idea, and a landmark in the progress of the free enterprise culture. It is an idea as powerful as Mrs Thatcher's 'popular capitalism' and another phase of the same historic drive to create a society in which individual liberty is balanced by an awareness of and an opportunity to exercise individual responsibility.

However, the Charter's announcement failed to generate significant debate. It could have been better presented and should be followed up, restated, persuasively sold. The failure to present initiatives effectively and to excite public interest in his ideas seems to be a characteristic John Major problem. Whereas his predecessor excited division and debate with every utterance, Major's announcements are inevitably non-controversial, even when their content is worthy of discussion. Even opponents failed to argue against the Charter but dismissed it derisorily. Was that because no one could possibly disagree with either its sentiments or its proposals? Or was it because there was insufficient conviction behind its presentation from those involved?

Spokesmen questioned on current affairs pro-grammes seemed defensive and unconvincing. Francis Maude, Financial Secretary to the Treasury and a key figure in drawing up the Charter, is a relatively junior minister, though tipped to go far. His lack of experience as a frontline salesman of government policies revealed a poor grasp, perhaps by the Prime Minister himself, of the techniques needed to sell his ideas to the public.

The lack of debate is also partly due to John

Major's own personality and temperament. He seeks to be unobtrusive and to accomplish his ends without exciting opposition. If he is doing anything momentous, we will find out afterwards and not before, because Major, as assessed earlier in this book, is a secretive man who keeps his cards out of sight. His roughly acquired street wisdom has emphasised the value of surprise as a weapon both in the negotiating chamber and in political initiatives. His dislike of adopting a high profile is an innate, as well as learned, characteristic. Had he already held a five-year mandate, this might be useful in that the government might achieve much without inciting the kind of opposition which greeted the Thatcher administration's every proposal. However, in an election year when the government and the Prime Minister need to sell themselves to the voters, such discretion seems a liability.

John Major is popular, however. Also, he is believed competent by a majority and his rating has been improving, after a spring sag, almost to the 61 per cent satisfaction with his leadership attained at the end of the Gulf War. After his successful chairing of the G7 summit in July's final week, 53 per cent of those polled were satisfied with his performance as Prime Minister while 33 per cent were not.

By early September 59 per cent were satisfied with his performance as Prime Minister. His performance during the Soviet coup of late August, his confident performance at the joint press conference with the US President and the praise awarded him by George Bush during his visit to the US on August 28–30, and his handling of his visits to China and Moscow raised him in the public's esteem. He displayed statesmanship, steadiness in the face of dramatic international events, and initiative and authority in his approach to other world leaders.

His steadiness electorally is an advantageous quality. The low-key responses, the commonsense statements, have evidently left an impression that, however unexciting he may appear, the country is safe in his hands. This was also the impression during and after the Gulf War. There are many who with hindsight believe he should have called an election then, letting the war, with its high level of public support, carry him tidally into a new term. But few spoke of such an action at the time. The war dominated and preoccupied media and public alike. The political leaders were focused intensely on the daily tasks of governing the British forces in their alliance with the US and twenty-seven other nations against a dictator whose presence seemed the most dangerous manifestation of political evil since Hitler.

At the time of writing, the outcome of John Major's electoral fortunes remains uncertain. The spring, still overwhelmingly popular with Tory MPs anxious over the pace of economic recovery, is fraught with dangers ranging from a possible economic downturn, still worsening white-collar unemployment, continuing high rates of bankruptcies and house repossessions, and more shock local taxes, all affecting the predominantly Tory South-East where Liberal Democrat candidates could win surprises and reduce a narrow Tory majority over Labour. An unpredictable international situation (the USSR, Yugoslavia), further BCCI revelations, and possible pressures on the pound all contribute to the dangers of waiting until May 1992. In addition, the Prime Minister would have his hand strengthened at the European summit in Maastricht in December if he had renewed his party's mandate by then.

The problem of Major not having attained his mandate yet is twofold. One is that he cannot act internationally or domestically with the certain authority of one who has won an election. Coupled with his low self-confidence, this created for much of 1991 a lame duck image, and this could only become accentuated in the long dark months before May. The other effect of limping on through the final days of a difficult term is that by the time Major took over in late 1990, the government's legislative programme for the Parliament was virtually complete. There has therefore been little for the government to do that might create an impression of boldness or decisiveness, since there was not yet a programme to enact. There are still a few loose ends to tie up from previous legislation, such as hospital opt-outs. But the announcement of intended legislation has largely been kept a surprise for the election manifesto. This has also contributed to the impression of reactivity as opposed to creativity.

The news emphasis during 1991 has thus tended to be on government response to external events. Many of them, such as the uncovering of Department of Trade and Industry knowledge of uranium sales to Iraq, are embarrassing. Because there is little that is positive to counterbalance them, they seem disproportionately negative. The government appears not only to have outlived its legislative programme and its will to govern, but also to have outlasted its competence.

With the war over by March, John Major faced the

first of these reactive dilemmas. The poll tax, that inherited mess, dominated the agenda. As the first test of his competence as Prime Minister, it reveals both flaws and skills. Of course, the Prime Minister was far from alone in facing the problem of what to do with a concept that had been so badly explained in principle and which in terms of practice had been far from properly thought through. Environment Secretary Michael Heseltine's genius for finding creative solutions evidently deserted him at this time. There were two distinct Tory lobbies: one for retaining the principle of a tax on heads, the other for a return to a tax on property. Both had to be accommodated. Unless something wholly new could be thought up, compromise was inevitable. The Prime Minister was desperate for ideas, received many and was reported to be dithering between various courses of action.

Was the PM dithering? John Major has told me he likes at least twenty-four hours to think before arriving at a decision. The question of how to deal with the poll tax was not likely to be resolved overnight by anyone. The PM went into his particular decision-making process, which is to listen to several viewpoints with an open mind and then mull them over. He was said to be reaching a decision only to change his mind and go off in another direction.

Perhaps this was a misreading of the fact that John Major has an exceptionally open mind. His early misfortunes and his upwardly mobile life have conditioned him to be adaptable. He also strives to reach the best possible solution to any problem. So, if he had arrived at a decision that R was the best of the

available choices, he would still enter the decision-
making process all over again if a new and hitherto
unconsidered solution S were offered. Nevertheless,
the solution eventually selected revealed compromise
qualities which disappointed the more ideological
Tories. The new leader showed himself to be more
pragmatist than idealist. The poll tax had been
intended to create a link between taxation and
representation. The concept was tenable, typically
Thatcherite. It sought to place responsibility and
accountability for local authority spending equally on
individual electors' shoulders. But the main problem
was that local authorities determined the amount of
poll tax paid in their communities according to their
spending requirements. The poll tax could not really
succeed without a complete reorganisation of local
government finance. Those opposed to the poll tax
ignored the vital democratic principle upon which it
was based. No taxation without representation has
been the cry of electoral reformers throughout the
centuries. But now the voters were to be forced to
pay up for their rights. And unequally.

The poll tax was launched at a time when rates
would have risen anyway. But the idea had never
been properly sold and was clearly a leaden albatross
around the new Prime Minister's neck. It had to be
removed before anything else could be accomplished.
But John Major's eventual solution was an enormous
climbdown for the government. By paying a once-
and-for-all £140 per resident, the Exchequer brought
the very high poll tax figures down and mollified
public anger. But the decision to replace the pay-as-
you-poll connection with a mainly property-linked
tax was a significant reversal of principle.

The new local tax has the tidy look of a practical solution. But it is expected to prove a further embarrassment to the government by spring 1993 when it comes into force and voters in the more populous and higher property-valued, Tory-voting South-East begin to feel its bite. The poll tax may be dead but the problem of local taxation has not yet been resolved. Major's government, distracted for the time being by other pressing problems, has popped it onto the back burner where, if untended, it will undoubtedly ignite and may well burn down the house.

Long term, the economy is still the dominant issue affecting government popularity. The Prime Minister, having brought with him Treasury experience, is still unable to deliver the right figures for inflation or trade, though there is a steady improvement. The gradual reduction of interest rates during the summer had a mild influence on consumer spending. But the recession's sharp teeth refuse to let go of their prey, consumer confidence. Interest rates could go lower yet, but growing unemployment, especially among car-workers, the white-collar workers of London and the home counties, and the high-tech regions of East Anglia and the Thames Valley, shows that different forces are at work to those of the ebullient Eighties. If spending is not taking off as it did in recent years when the borrowing rate dropped, it is because a different psychology is operating and also a different sense of reality.

The use of interest rates as the sole means of controlling spending has hit an inevitable iceberg. The dream of the home-owning democracy is going down fast and taking consumer spending with it. Mortgages account for the single highest monthly payment in most houshold accounts. High interest rates affect disposable income by acting as a tax on the mortgage. Whereas governments of the past used the corset on bank lending and hikes in purchase tax to cool down spending, monetarist ones lean on the interest rate.

Either way, it is a tax on disposable income. The only arguments in favour of the interest rate hike over other forms of taxation and credit control are that theoretical consumer choice is preserved and that the money raised via the banks' profits can find its way by less blatant means through tax on bank profits into the Exchequer.

The unfortunate economic reality is that confidence is badly dented, but worse, reduced resources are stretched by high interest debt repayment. Formerly confident businessfolk who incurred big, expensive debts during the Eighties are now struggling to pay large amounts of interest with diminished cash flows. Confident consumers, who likewise saddled themselves with second mortgages and credit card debt, are paying too much of today's income for yesterday's goods. Only a further increase in credit would ease the pressure, and neither the creditors nor the consumers want more of that at the moment. No wonder there is now little money around to buy goods, hence the businesses' diminished cash flows.

The only solution available to the government if it wants to win an election is to loosen interest rates more drastically, thus releasing consumers from their credit caution. But this would undoubtedly encourage inflation to start creeping up again. The trade balance is always the first to be affected, as it is easier to buy goods from overseas than to wait for British manufacturers to climb back up to pre-recession production levels. Unemployment would therefore probably drop sufficiently slowly to prevent the government from having to face wage inflation as part of the spiral. The only hope would be that the pound sterling, now harnessed to the EMS, would remain at a level which would still allow exporters to sell enough abroad to balance imports and stave off bad trade figures at least until after an election.

Such is the nature of the cycles which dominate the British economy and which are exacerbated now that it cannot produce enough competitively priced goods domestically to permit a sustained boom without a negative trade balance and price inflation. The stimulation of a flowering of new young businesses to enable Britain to compete effectively as a producer and seller of goods and services abroad as well as at home was a key theme of the Thatcher enterprise culture. The young growth has been severely scythed by the present long recession, and the rhetoric of that lost era has died with business confidence. No longer does the cry of encouragement to enterprise echo along Whitehall from Downing Street. Instead the Prime Minister is concerned with themes and areas of reform untouched by the Thatcher years. The Citizen's Charter and the stress on education – more far-reaching in concept than the Thatcher government's educational reforms – are among these.

The economy remains on the sick list and the emphasis in the Prime Minister's speeches is on recovery through bringing down inflation rather than on a resurgence of business growth. The Prime Minister and his Chancellor say they believe the economy is at last turning the corner. But it's a long corner this time and their belief may be confounded. John Major is wise not to play the miracle-worker, but perhaps unwise not to engender a little inspiration. A little rhetoric would enliven the bread and water diet of British business now – a canapé of confident prediction about the economy he wants to build, the striving, thriving, yet caring community of Britain heading for a new century. How the devotees of Mrs T mourn the excitement her ideas and conviction generated! Divide she did, but she at least cared nothing for the fact that some would always be against her. John Major, alas, cares too much to have everyone with him; too much, that is, for those who would like to see a higher ideological profile for the government; for those who still hanker after the confident cut and thrust of Mrs Thatcher's era and for her inspired if controversial direction.

There were signs of change in Hong Kong early in September 1991 when Major thumped the table, Thatcher-style. But generally, he does not come out and fight publicly when controversy arises. Much to his colleagues' surprise, he encourages discussion, even argument in Cabinet. It may also be said that his style of government, more of shared responsibility than his predecessor's, encourages him to allow his cabinet colleagues to defend their own corners when issues arise affecting their departments. Mrs Thatcher, in the spirit of 'the buck stops here', gave her government's view to the news cameras on a range of departmental concerns. Perhaps it seems so only in comparison, but Major's silence while Secretaries of State handle awkward issues gives an impression that he is ducking. When Peter Lilley lamely described the matter of possible sales of mustard gas ingredients to Iraq as 'a lot of fuss about nothing', the Prime Minister stayed out of the firing line and let Lilley handle the problem. Accustomed to Mrs Thatcher's hands-on approach to every issue, observers were disappointed that there was no Prime Ministerial statement, perhaps along the lines of, 'We will investigate and if we have reason to believe the Kurds have been affected by such a sale we will make recompense.' This might have been an appropriate sentiment from a Prime Minister who had already declared his wish to see an enforceable UN ban on arms sales.

Was his silence one of deference to his colleague's responsibility or the result of an instinct to stay out of hot water? Does the Prime Minister lack courage? Is he merely, as a devotee of traditional Cabinet government, letting his colleagues assume responsibility for departmental matters? Or is his deep-rooted desire for approval, formed by his earliest childhood experiences, responsible?

The fact that he does not get into the thick of every fight may have helped him maintain a high approval rating even while that of the government was still trailing Labour. But it might be better in the long run if he intervened. Prime Ministerial silence on central issues can look like gutlessness. There are signs of change. When juvenile car thieves rampaged through Newcastle in September, the Prime Minister's voice was heard ahead of the Home Secretary's condemning the youths' behaviour. Perhaps his confidence is beginning to emerge after the summer break in the same way and after almost the same length of time as it emerged when he was Chancellor. Perhaps he is also becoming aware of the fact that his desire for approval is now often a source of comment.

John Major's compulsion to win approval was first highlighted in the character analysis in the earlier chapters of this book. Now, other writers refer to it. John Major hates criticism. But he is often reluctant to reply to critics. Again, this may be due to fear of reaping more negative comment. His instinct seems to be to duck out of sight rather than to riposte. An example arose when he was criticised by some inadequately informed newspaper columnists as having had bad judgement for granting interviews to this author. A press storm based on an inaccurate report carrying libellous comment in the *Sunday Times* engulfed the author. Parliamentary correspondents asked questions at Downing Street briefings, but received only the ambiguous reply that all three biographers had been treated equally. This seemed like double speak. The Prime Minister had read the manuscript and, while noting one or two factual errors, one of his own contribution, otherwise found nothing offensive in it. His office made it clear that his approval of the book's contents would permit him to have his picture taken with the author. And on that occasion he even said, 'There are a number of perceptions in this book which are absolutely true and which no one else has thought of.' His chief press secretary told the author, 'I love the book.'

So why, instead of ducking out of sight behind his press officers, did he not greet the ridiculous storm with humour and aplomb? A brief witty remark on the lines of Macmillan's 'a little local difficulty' would have quelled the mob. He might even have had the panache to say, 'Will any other prospective biographers please send in their vital statistics and photographs to the Downing Street press office.' People close to the author thought the PM's lack of courage and candour discredited him.

The Prime Minister's reticence seemed all the more illogical when, after a month of widespread daily publicity given to the author's comments that the PM is 'sexy', among her less sensational analysis of her subject's high intelligence and competence, the Tory Party suddenly came from behind to a 1 per cent lead and the Prime Minister also gained in poll popularity. This sudden upsurge of enthusiasm for the government and its leader could not be explained by such negative trends as increased unemployment, business failures and house repossessions, a worsening trade balance, static inflation and still penal interest rates. John Major confessed to the author his fears that the press might use the book as an opportunity to comment negatively about his past, as he said he had not been able to understand journalists' behaviour during the preceding months. When his fears materialised, however, his reluctance to comment on the matter of his controversial biographer only encouraged the press in their pursuit of a story. The more he blushed, the more journalists revelled in the opportunity to embarrass him. His deep-rooted desire for approval was again proving an Achilles' heel.

Desire for approval may also prevent John Major from developing the degree of attack he needs to demolish the Opposition in the pre-election period.

Perhaps his anger will save him. For several weeks in July, correspondents had noted an increased virulence in Major's dealings with the Opposition during PM's Question Time. Then, late in July, the BCCI débâcle brought continuous attack from Neil Kinnock. At one point the Prime Minister rose to reply, clearly incensed. He said, 'If the Honourable Gentleman is calling me a liar, then I suggest he does so openly rather than continue to insinuate it.' When Kinnock attacked him further, the Prime Minister rose again and for some fifteen seconds before replying, gripped the table separating the government and Opposition front benches and looked down at it in tense silence. He was evidently quelling the rage he felt at being depicted as a liar.

This anger, an old enemy, may become a friend. Major's lack of passion is often noted as a fault. If he fails to achieve recognition for his initiatives abroad as well as at home, it may be because of his lack of emotional energy when addressing the issues. It is not that he lacks emotion, only that he contains it too successfully, perhaps because it has at times been uncontrollable. Yet each time he has expressed himself with anger he has made world headlines. The first was the celebrated instance during the Gulf War, when in the House of Commons he tersely said of Saddam Hussein that, 'whatever his fate, I for one will not weep for him.' The next was on the above-mentioned occasion with Neil Kinnock.

It is perhaps sad that a man who is able and committed should be judged negatively because his rational faculties dominate his emotional expression. But it is a fact that emotion reaches more parts of the body politic than rational argument ever did. Emotion excites response where rational statements induce coma. And this is a consideration that should be of serious importance to those whose task it is to sell the Prime Minister new policy initiatives as an electoral asset.

John Major's great fear of criticism combines with his endemic lack of self-confidence and extraordinarily cautious nature to castrate his image as a leader of strength and ability. He appears fearful. Unlike Mrs Thatcher, he does not appear to relish his power or thrill to his task. After eleven months in office he is still widely perceived as boring. Would he rather be watching cricket, one wonders?

How can he capitalise on his strengths and overcome his weaknessess? If John Major is consistently underestimated, his own lack of self-confidence may be the cause. Now, however, having launched his Citizen's Charter and made important speeches on education and the need radically to improve educational opportunities, he is obliged to direct much of his energy into the foreign rather than the domestic sphere. This may be an area in which the Prime Minister can still develop a more confident profile and role which will enhance his image as a leader. Mrs Thatcher certainly benefited at home from the great stature she gained as a world leader. This, achieved through her forthright and determined expression of her beliefs, won world-wide respect for her and her country and enabled her to capture the popular imagination in many countries, from the Soviet Union to the United States.

Can John Major do the same? Right from the start of his premiership, he was hurled into the foreign

arena. First the EEC Rome summit, then a trip to
the US, followed swiftly by the Gulf War and more
foreign visits to Germany, Moscow, the Middle East
and Bermuda in March. His recent and much praised
chairmanship of the July G7 meeting in London was
the start of a new cycle of foreign meetings which,
while distracting the PM from domestic issues in a
possible election period, offer him the opportunity
he so desperately needs to develop an authoritative
image. And indeed this appears to be the case.

Yet until this time Major has failed to attract
interest among foreigners. Americans have referred
to him as a cipher and a non-event. Will Major
astound them by developing as a world leader whose
initiatives achieve the recognition they deserve? At
the time of writing it seems likely, though, that he
will not astound the world with words of idealistic
fervour but will plod on characteristically, rationally,
ever the hard-working, rather anxious-looking figure
who nevertheless impresses all whom he meets with
his sincerity and integrity. Eventually, though, he may
have as much, perhaps more effect on the world's
shape and functioning than a more impassioned
leader, with his tenacity and strong will.

John Major is the kind of leader whose work is
valued after time has passed. His unobtrusiveness is
too deeply ingrained for him to make a great impact
in the present. His continuity is vital to there ever
being a fair record of his achievement. If he lasts
as Prime Minister, history may well commend him
for his achievements in the future development of
the EEC, in the movement towards a more effective
United Nations, in a new view of arms control and,
in Britain, in the progress towards greater class

mobility, increased democratic empowerment and a further advance of free enterprise in a competetive yet responsible economy.

If the Nineties have a distinctive code, it is undoubtedly one in which on an individual, national and global level, in business, politics and private citizenship, selfish liberty becomes balanced by responsibility, and separate greed becomes balanced by a vision of cooperative and shared prosperity. This is John Major's creed. Much depends on his ability to convey it and bring it to material reality.

Earlier in 1991 Major seemed frustrated by the fact that his message seemed to be failing to get through. Perhaps he has at last admitted to himself that techniques are important. During the summer, a subtle change seems to have taken place in Major's style and presentation, so subtle it was barely noticeable. Yet it became noticeable for its effect. When he shared the podium with George Bush at the Kennebunkport press conference, he both looked and sounded more assured. There were changes in his style: the impression of greater confidence was in part due to a slower pace of verbal delivery and a more relaxed pose. He seemed easier before the cameras and the defensive tension with which he has often answered press questions had been replaced by calm authority. His voice had also lost some of its higher notes. Had John Major undergone some training? He needed it but would never wish to admit it. He told me once, 'If I do that, then people will say I did it because they said I should, and I'm very stubborn. I don't like to do things because people say I should do them.' The training, if it took place, paid off at once. From about August, John Major began getting a better press. His new commanding style was no less modest, no less rational, but it had more impact. Of course, he was also rested, a little fatter and sported a much shorter haircut. He had new double- and single-breasted tailored suits, some blue toned as a change from the clichéd grey. They gave him more shoulder breadth and a more authoritative look. But it was the lower-pitched, slower-spoken speeches and responses to questions which conveyed the greater degree of assurance which at once began to make him look like a real Prime Minister instead of someone training for the part. At the Party conference in Blackpool in October, Major's speech reiterated his commitments to a non-federal Europe, to low inflation, an enterprise-rich, property-owning democracy, free of class barriers and the other key points of his programme for education and social change which were pinpointed earlier in this chapter and in this book. But it was the delivery that showed designer polish. Heralded by the press the previous day as more likely to be a fireside chat than an oration, the speech was far better delivered than earlier ones to large audiences. Skilled advisers had evidently been heeded. Major's own personal style and warmth were enhanced by measured pace; his relaxed manner, his characteristic little jokes and his lethal grin were a welcome alternative to any Heseltine-style imitation.

Afterwards, the PM moved amidst the throng, shaking hands, smiling, joking, totally at home among his Party's faithful, working the crowd in the way those close to him have learned is John Major at his devastating best. The many who have ignored his attributes may now begin to find it easier to value what he has to offer. Meanwhile there are others who have been watching and weighing from afar. On hearing the Prime Minister's name, the Washington representative of an African nation exclaimed, 'Ah, the man of the century!' John Major may not have made it yet as the intellectual's darling but, as his popularity rating at home reveals, he is impressing the greater number whose well-being his Gladstonian motives seek to benefit. Africans are among those who watch keenly for changes among Western leaders which may benefit their interests. Word travelled fast that the new British Prime Minister was a social and racial liberal with sympathetic understanding for and much interest in Third World issues. His performance and reception at the October 1991 Commonwealth Heads of Government meeting in Harare is expected to cement that view.

He has already shown his hand on human rights. As Foreign Secretary he spoke bluntly about apartheid's unacceptability. More recently, his moral position was evident in China. His visit there was criticised in the context of Hong Kong's future and there were many who thought it was wrong for a British Prime Minister to meet with the Tiananmen Square murderers. Major deftly deflected critics by taking the opportunity to challenge the Chinese leaders on human rights. He may even have relished a canapé of chilled revenge on the mandarins of the Foreign Office while confronting those red mandarins of Peking. He displayed his formidable negotiating skills when he read them a list of names of political detainees and with relentless quiet insistence pursued his arguments for their release. One, a Hong Kong citizen, was released almost immediately, while officials continued to discuss the status of others. Downing Street regards this as triumph enough in the face of Foreign Office disapproval of the Prime Minister's tough stance.

John Major believes change in China is more likely to be achieved through maintaining dialogue with the disgraced regime than by isolating it. Among the arguments he used to persuade them to improve human rights was the recommendation that this was the way they could win the Western nations' approval and return gradually to more beneficial international relations. His position on the Vietnamese boat people is less robustly righteous and his evident compassion for their plight less easy to translate into correct action. The Vietnamese tragedy remains as it was when John Major was Foreign Secretary.

John Major's foreign trips seem to be enhancing his image as a world leader of integrity. This is not a fabricated image but one based on the man's own character. The autumn of 1991 will be a period of intensive international activity culminating in the European summit at Maastricht in December. Already the European leaders are experiencing a tougher John Major than the man they welcomed in November 1990 as Mrs Thatcher's thornless successor. Through his remarks on Eastern European participation in the EEC, he has left them in no doubt that he favours the wider European economic union of his predecessor's in preference to the federal union of the few.

John Major's autumn of international statesmanship is to take place against a backdrop of steadily improving domestic economic indicators, falling inflation and interest rates and the long-awaited return of consumer confidence, and perhaps an election victory. If he is to be the man of the century he needs a decisive majority so that he may devote more energy to international statesmanship. In the history books, that is where he may make his greatest contribution, and for one much underestimated as Foreign Secretary and Prime Minister, that would be a fine vindication.

INDEX

Futura now offers an exciting range of quality titles by both established and new authors. All of the books in this series are available from:
Futura Books,
Cash Sales Department,
P.O. Box 11,
Falmouth,
Cornwall TR10 9EN.

Alternatively you may fax your order to the above address. Fax No. 0326 376423.

Payments can be made as follows: Cheque, postal order (payable to Macdonald & Co (Publishers) Ltd) or by credit cards, Visa/Access. Do not send cash or currency. UK customers and B.F.P.O.: please send a cheque or postal order (no currency) and allow £1.00 for postage and packing for the first book, plus 50p for the second book, plus 30p for each additional book up to a maximum charge of £3.00 (7 books plus).

Overseas customers including Ireland, please allow £2.00 for postage and packing for the first book, plus £1.00 for the second book, plus 50p for each additional book.

NAME (Block Letters) ....

ADDRESS ....

....

☐ I enclose my remittance for _____

☐ I wish to pay by Access/Visa Card

Number | | | | | | | | | | | | | | | | | | |

Card Expiry Date | | | | |